Acclaim for the original edition of *Nudge*

"*Nudge* has changed the world. You may not realize it, but as a result of its findings you're likely to live longer, retire richer, and maybe even save other people's lives."
—*The Times* (London)

"Probably the most influential popular science book ever written."
—BBC Radio 4

"This gem of a book . . . is a must read."
—Daniel Kahneman, Nobel Prize–winning author of *Thinking, Fast and Slow*

"Engaging and insightful . . . The conceptual argument is powerful, and most of the authors' suggestions are common sense at its best. . . . For that we should all applaud loudly."
—*The New York Times Book Review*

"This book is terrific. It will change the way you think, not only about the world around you and some of its bigger problems, but also about yourself."
—Michael Lewis, author of *Moneyball* and *Liar's Poker*

"One of the few books . . . that fundamentally changed the way I think about the world."
—Steven D. Levitt, coauthor of *Freakonomics*

"Utterly brilliant . . . *Nudge* won't nudge you—it will knock you off your feet."
—Daniel Gilbert, author of *Stumbling on Happiness*

"*Nudge* is as important a book as any I've read in perhaps twenty years. It is a book that people interested in any aspect of public policy should read. It is a book that people interested in politics should read. It is a book that people interested in ideas about human freedom should read. It is a book that people interested in promoting human welfare should read. If you're not interested in any of these topics, you can read something else."
—Barry Schwartz, *The American Prospect*

NUDGE
The Final Edition

RICHARD H. THALER
and **CASS R. SUNSTEIN**

PENGUIN BOOKS

PENGUIN BOOKS

UK | USA | Canada | Ireland | Australia
India | New Zealand | South Africa

Allen Lane is part of the Penguin Random House group of companies
whose addresses can be found at global.penguinrandomhouse.com.

First published in the United States of America by Yale University Press 2008
First published in Penguin Books 2009
This updated edition published in Allen Lane 2021
Published in Penguin Books 2022

005

Printed and bound in Great Britain by Clays Ltd, Elcograf S.p.A.

A CIP catalogue record for this book is available from the British Library

The authorized representative in the EEA is Penguin Random House Ireland,
Morrison Chambers, 32 Nassau Street, Dublin, D02 YH68

ISBN: 978-0-141-99993-7

www.greenpenguin.co.uk

MIX
Paper from
responsible sources
FSC® C018179

Penguin Random House is committed to a
sustainable future for our business, our readers
and our planet. This book is made from Forest
Stewardship Council® certified paper.

For France,
who (still) makes everything in life better
—RHT

For Samantha,
who knows what matters
—CRS

Contents

PART IV: Society

PART V: The Complaints Department

Preface to the Final Edition

The original version of *Nudge* was published in the spring of 2008. While we were writing it, Thaler got his first iPhone and Sunstein his first BlackBerry. In his first term as a United States senator, our former University of Chicago colleague Barack Obama had decided to challenge Hillary Clinton for the Democratic nomination for president. Senator Joe Biden was also doing that, without a whole lot of success. Real estate developer and reality television star Donald Trump was proclaiming that Clinton was "fantastic" and would "make a great president."[1] A financial crisis was emerging. Taylor Swift was nineteen years old (and had not yet won a Grammy), and Greta Thunberg was just five.

To say the least, a few things have happened in the intervening years. But *Nudge* continues to attract interest, and we have not been much inclined to tinker with it. Why a revision now? As we discuss in the book, status quo bias is a strong force.

Very much in keeping with the book's spirit, we were induced to emerge from our slumber by a seemingly small matter. The contracts for the American and British paperback editions had expired, and new ones had to be agreed upon. Editors asked whether we might want to add a new chapter or possibly make other changes. Our immediate reaction was to say no. After all, Thaler is famously lazy and Sunstein could have written an entirely new book in the time it would take to get the slow-fingered Thaler to agree to anything. Besides, we were proud of the book, and why mess with a good thing?

But then we started thumbing through copies we managed to find in our home offices, where we found ourselves during the year of COVID-19. The first chapter mentions the then-snazzy but now-obsolete iPod. Jeez, that seems a bit dated. And an entire chapter is devoted to what we still think was an excellent solution to the problem of making it possible for same-sex couples to marry. Since then, many countries somehow managed to solve that very problem in a way we had not imagined was politically possible. They just passed laws making such marriages legal. So, yeah, maybe some parts of the book could use a bit of tidying up.

So, it came to pass that in the summer of 2020, a summer like no other in our lifetimes, we decided to poke around the manuscript and see if we wanted to make some changes. It helped that Thaler managed to find a set of Microsoft Word files that had been used for what we called the international edition, and those files were (barely) usable. Without those files, this edition would not exist, because we would never have wanted to start over from scratch. We admit to then falling into a bit of a trap. We are supposedly experts on biases in human decision making, but that definitely does *not* mean we are immune to them! Just the opposite.

We are not sure that this particular trap has a name, but it is familiar to everyone. Let's call it the "while we are at it" bias. Home improvement projects are often settings where this bias is observed. A family decides that after twenty years of neglect, the kitchen really needs to be upgraded. The initial to-do list includes new appliances and cabinets, but of course, the floor will be ruined during the construction, so we'd better replace that, and gosh, if we just pushed that wall out a bit, we could add a new window, which looks out on the patio, but oh dear, who wants to look at that patio . . . In the military this is called mission creep. Here we plead guilty to book revision creep. The revision that we planned to knock off during the summer was not given to the publisher until late November.

However, to continue the home remodeling analogy, in spite of our slow pace, what we have here is definitely *not* a gut rehab. The book feels very much like the old one. All the walls remain, and we have not expanded the footprint. But we have gotten rid of a bunch of old pieces of electronics that have been collecting dust and replaced them with newer gadgets.

More specifically, the first four chapters of the book have not much changed. They set out the basic framework of our approach, including the term *libertarian paternalism*, which only its authors love. Examples and references are updated, but the songs remain the same. If it were a record album, we would call this section "remastered," whatever that means. If you have read the original edition, you can probably skim those chapters pretty quickly. After that, however, even previous readers will find many new themes, and perhaps some surprises.

Two important topics are given new chapters early on. The first is what we call *Smart Disclosure*. The idea is that governments should consider the radical thought of moving at least into the twentieth century in the way they disclose important information. Sure, listing ingredients on the side of food packages is useful, especially for those with very good eyesight, but shouldn't Sunstein be able to search online for foods that contain shellfish, given that they can make him very sick? The Internet is not exactly a cutting-edge technology. Widespread use of Smart Disclosure would make it possible to create online decision-making tools that we call *choice engines*, which can make many tasks as

easy as it has become to find the best route to get to a new restaurant.

We have also added a new chapter on what we call *sludge*, which
is nasty stuff that makes it more difficult to make wise choices.
(Sludge is everywhere; you'll see.) The use of Smart Disclosure is
one way to reduce sludge. So is sending everyone a tax return that
has already been completed and can be filed with one click. So is
reducing the length of those forms you have to fill out to get licenses, permits, visas, health care, or financial aid, or to get reimbursed for a trip you take for your employer. Every organization
should create a seek-and-destroy mission for unnecessary sludge.

The rest of the book also has numerous substantive changes
and what we hope is fresh thinking. We introduce several choice
architecture concepts, in addition to "sludge," that are new to this
edition. These include personalized defaults; make it fun; and curation. These concepts play a large role in the chapters about financial decision making. We have increased the space we devote
to climate change and the environment. We highlight both the
limits of choice architecture (preview: we can't solve the problem
just with nudges) and the many ways in which nudges can help us
succeed on a project that demands the deployment of every possible
tool. And, oh, we do have a few things to say about the COVID-19
pandemic.

Some topics that we originally covered get a fresh look. The
passage of years has created the chance to evaluate how policies
work over time. A good example is the Swedish launch (in 2000)
of a national retirement savings program, which allowed investors
to create their own portfolios. In the original edition, we discussed the initial design of that plan. Now, two decades after the
launch, we can provide some insights about how long nudges last.
(Preview: some of them can last almost forever.) We have also re-
written the chapter on organ donation, because everyone thought

we supported a policy we actually oppose. We did state our policy in what we thought was plain language in the first version of the book, and we tried to make it a bit clearer in the paperback editions. But still our message wasn't getting through, so we are trying once again. In case this is as far as you get in the book, please take note: *we do not support the policy called "presumed consent."* Feel free to skip ahead to see why. We really do believe in freedom of choice.

Other topics with fresh looks are devoted to helping consumers make better choices with their money. People have amassed staggering amounts of credit card debt, and then fail to take some simple steps to reduce the costs of maintaining those large balances. Consumers also make demonstrably bad choices in picking mortgages, insurance, and health care plans. You may well be one of the people who could save a lot of money in these domains. But more importantly, we hope that our discussion of these issues will provoke others to make behaviorally informed policy changes in an assortment of domains that we have not explored. We emphasize that the concepts and approaches discussed here are fully applicable to the private sector. Firms should explicitly recognize that their employees and customers and competitors are human beings, and design policies and strategies accordingly. We will offer many specific ideas for how to do this.

It is important to stress what we have not done. We make no attempt to bring readers up to date on the remarkable nudge-related activity, reform, and research that have come about in recent years. Governments all over the world have been nudging, often for good, and the private sector has also been exceptionally inventive. Academic research has grown by leaps and bounds. To explore these developments would take an entirely new book, and in fact many such books have been written, some even by Sunstein. Indeed, Sunstein has coedited a four-volume collection of papers on this topic. (Sunstein thinks editing a four-volume collection of papers on the topic of nudging is fun; Thaler would rather be counting backward from ten million.)

We have some things to say about objections to nudges, and in fact we devote a whole chapter to that topic, but we do not respond systematically to critics. What we hope to offer is a book that will feel fresher, more fun, and less dusty to those reading it for the first time, or even to those returning for another look, as we have spent the past months doing ourselves.

Finally, a word about our decision to call this version of the book the Final Edition. One of the earliest topics to be studied by behavioral economists was self-control problems. Why do people continue to do things they think are dumb (both in foresight and in hindsight)? These include acts such as running up credit card bills, getting more than a bit chubby, and continuing to smoke. One strategy people use to deal with such problems is to adopt *commitment strategies*, in which some tempting (but ill-advised) options are made unavailable. For example, some people with a gambling problem volunteer to put their name on a list of people who will not be allowed into a casino. Using this title is our commitment strategy to prevent us from ever tinkering with this book again. We have loved working on it, and we might even have gotten addicted to it, but we pledge, right here and right now, that there will be no "post-final" edition of *Nudge*. And one of us actually believes that pledge.

RICHARD H. THALER
CASS R. SUNSTEIN
January 2021

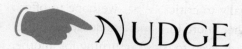
NUDGE

Introduction

The Cafeteria

Imagine that a friend of yours, Carolyn, is the director of food services for a large city school system. She is in charge of hundreds of schools, and hundreds of thousands of kids eat in her cafeterias every day. Carolyn has formal training in nutrition (a master's degree from the state university), and she is a creative type who likes to think about things in nontraditional ways.

One evening, over a good bottle of wine, she and her friend Adam, a statistically oriented management consultant who has worked with supermarket chains, hatched an interesting idea. Without changing any menus, they would run some experiments in her schools to determine whether the way the food is displayed and arranged might influence the choices kids make. Carolyn gave the directors of dozens of school cafeterias specific instructions on how to display the food choices. In some schools the desserts were placed first, in others last, and in still others in a separate line. The locations of various food items varied from one school to another. In some schools the french fries were at eye level, but in other schools it was the carrot sticks that were made more salient.

From his experience in designing supermarket floor plans, Adam suspected that the results would be significant. He was right. Simply by rearranging the cafeteria, Carolyn was able to noticeably increase or decrease the consumption of many food items. From this experience she learned a big lesson: small changes in context can greatly influence schoolchildren, just as they can greatly influence adults. The influence can be exercised for better or for worse. For example, Carolyn knows that she can increase consumption of healthy foods and decrease consumption of unhealthy ones.

With hundreds of schools to work with, and a team of graduate-student volunteers recruited to collect and analyze the data, Carolyn now understands that she has considerable power to influence what kids eat. She is pondering what to do with her newfound power. Here are some suggestions she has received from her usually sincere but occasionally mischievous friends and coworkers:

1. Arrange the food to make the students best off, all things considered.

2. Choose the food order at random.

3. Try to arrange the food to get the kids to pick the same foods they would choose on their own.

4. Maximize the sales of the items from the suppliers who are willing to offer the largest bribes.

5. Maximize profits, period.

Option 1 has obvious appeal, yet it does seem a bit intrusive, even paternalistic. But the alternatives are worse! Option 2, arranging the food at random, could be considered fair-minded and principled, and it is in one sense neutral. But a random order makes no sense in a cafeteria. On efficiency grounds, the salad dressing should be placed next to the salad, not with the desserts. Also, if the orders are randomized across schools, then the children at some schools will have less healthy diets than those at other schools. Is this desirable? Should Carolyn choose that kind of neutrality, if she can easily make most students better off, in part by improving their health?

Option 3 might seem to be an honorable attempt to avoid intrusion: try to mimic what the children would choose for themselves. Maybe that is really the neutral choice, and maybe Carolyn should neutrally follow people's wishes (at least where she is dealing with older students). But a little thought reveals that this is a difficult option to implement. Carolyn's experiment with Adam proves that what kids choose depends on the order in which the items are displayed. What, then, are the "true preferences" of the children? What does it mean to say that Carolyn should try to figure out what the students would choose "on their own"? In a cafeteria, it is impossible to avoid some way of organizing food. And many of the same considerations would apply if she were serving adults rather than children.

Option 4 might appeal to a corrupt person in Carolyn's job, and manipulating the order of the food items would put yet another weapon in the arsenal of available methods to exploit power. But Carolyn is honorable and honest, so she does not give this option any thought. (Not everyone would be this principled, alas.) Like Options 2 and 3, Option 5 has some appeal, especially if Carolyn thinks the best cafeteria is the one that makes the most money. But should she really try to maximize profits if the result is to make children less healthy, especially when she works for the school district?

Carolyn is what we call a *choice architect*. A choice architect has the responsibility for organizing the context in which people make decisions. Although Carolyn is a figment of our imagination, many real people turn out to be choice architects, most without realizing it. Some of them even run cafeterias. If you are a doctor and describe the alternative treatments available to a patient, you are a choice architect. If you create the forms or the website that new employees use to choose among various employee benefits, you are a choice architect. If you design the ballot voters use to choose candidates, you are a choice architect. If you organize a drugstore or a grocery, you are a choice architect (and you confront many of the questions that Carolyn did). If you are a parent describing possible educational options to your son or daughter, you are a choice architect. If you are a salesperson, you are a choice architect (but you already knew that).

There are many parallels between choice architecture and more traditional forms of architecture. A crucial parallel is that there is no such thing as a "neutral" design. Consider the job of designing a new office building. The architect is given some requirements. There must be room for a lobby, 120 offices, thirteen conference rooms of various sizes, a room large enough to have everyone meet together, and so forth. The building must sit on a specified site. Hundreds of other constraints will be imposed—some legal, some aesthetic, some practical. In the end, the architect must come up with an actual building with doors, stairs, windows, and hallways. As good architects know, seemingly arbitrary decisions, such as where to locate the bathrooms, will have subtle influences on how the people who use the building interact. Every trip to the bathroom creates an opportunity to run into colleagues (for better or for worse). A good building is not merely attractive; it also "works."

As we shall see, small and apparently insignificant details can have major impacts on people's behavior. A good rule of thumb is to assume that everything matters. In many cases, the power of these small details comes from focusing people's attention in a particular direction. A wonderful example of this principle comes from, of all places, the men's toilets at Schiphol Airport in Amsterdam. At one point, the authorities etched the image of a black housefly into each urinal. It seems that men often do not pay much attention to where they aim, which can create a bit of a mess, but if they see a target, attention and therefore accuracy are much increased. According to the man who came up with the idea, it works wonders. "It improves the aim," says Aad Kieboom. "If a man sees a fly, he aims at it." Kieboom, an economist, directed Schiphol's building expansion. He reports that etchings reduced "spillage" by 80 percent, a number we are unable to verify. However, we can report that after this example appeared in the first edition of this book, we began seeing those flies in other airports around the world. And yes, we are aware of the availability heuristic, to be discussed later.

The insight that everything matters can be both paralyzing and empowering. Good architects realize that although they can't build the perfect building, they can make some design choices that will have beneficial effects. The location of the coffee machines, for example, may influence workplace interaction. Policymakers can often do the equivalent of painting a fly—for example, by telling people clearly and conspicuously, on their credit card bills, that they might be subject to late fees and overuse fees. If you paint lines on the sidewalk where people wait to enter a supermarket during a pandemic, you can promote social distancing. And just as a building architect must eventually produce the plans for an building, a choice architect like Carolyn must choose a particular arrangement of the food options at lunch, and by so doing she can influence what people eat. She can nudge.*

---

* Please do not confuse *nudge* with *noodge*. As William Safire explained in his "On Language" column in the *New York Times Magazine* (October 8, 2000), the "Yiddishism *noodge*" is "a noun meaning 'pest, annoying nag, persistent complainer.' . . . To *nudge* is 'to push mildly or poke gently in the ribs, especially with the elbow.' One who *nudges* in that manner—'to alert, remind, or mildly warn another'—is a far *geshrei* from a *noodge* with his incessant, bothersome whining." *Nudge* rhymes with *judge*, while the *oo* sound in *noodge* is pronounced as in *book*.

Libertarian Paternalism

If, all things considered, you think that Carolyn should take the opportunity to nudge the kids toward food that is better for them, Option 1, then we welcome you to our movement: *libertarian paternalism*. We are keenly aware that this term is not one that many readers will find immediately endearing. Both words are somewhat off-putting, weighed down by stereotypes from popular culture and politics that make them unappealing to many. Even worse, the concepts seem to be contradictory! Why combine two reviled and contradictory concepts? We argue that if the terms are properly understood, both concepts show a lot of good sense—and they are far more attractive together than alone. The problem with the terms is that they have been captured by dogmatists.

The libertarian aspect of our strategies lies in the straightforward insistence that much of the time, and so long as they are not harming others, people should be free to do what they like—and to opt out of arrangements they deem undesirable if that is what they want to do. To borrow a phrase from the late Milton Friedman, libertarian paternalists urge that people should be "free to choose." We strive to design policies that maintain or increase freedom of choice. When we use the term *libertarian* to modify the word *paternalism*, we simply mean liberty-preserving. And when we say liberty-preserving, we really mean it. Libertarian paternalists want to make it easy for people to go their own way; they do not want to burden those who want to exercise their freedom. (We emphasize that when people are inflicting harm on others, freedom of choice is not the best idea—but even in such cases, nudges can play an important role. We'll get to that. We also acknowledge that if people are making really terrible choices and harming their future selves, nudges might not be enough. We'll get to that, too.)

The paternalistic aspect lies in the claim that it is legitimate for choice architects to try to influence people's behavior in order to make their lives longer, healthier, and better. In other words, we argue for self-conscious efforts, by institutions in the private sector and by government, to steer people's choices in directions that will improve their lives. We are aware that many people, including many philosophers, have devoted a lot of effort to defining the term *paternalism*, and to exploring what might be right or wrong with it. The paternalistic policies that we favor aim to influence choices in a way that will make choosers better off, *as judged by the choosers themselves*. This is a paternalism of means, not of ends; those policies help people reach their own preferred destination.

We know from decades of behavioral science research that people often make poor decisions in laboratory experiments. People also make plenty of mistakes in real life, which reinforces the view well stated by the Beatles: "we get by with a little help from our friends." Our goal, in short, is to help people make the choices that they would have made if they had paid full attention and possessed complete information, unlimited cognitive ability, and complete self-control. (That doesn't mean people shouldn't sometimes stay out late, overeat, and have fun. As they say, "enjoy life now; this is not a rehearsal.")

Libertarian paternalism is a relatively weak, soft, and nonintrusive type of paternalism, because choices are not blocked, fenced off, or significantly burdened. If people want to smoke cigarettes, eat a lot of candy, choose an unsuitable health care plan, or fail to save for retirement, libertarian paternalists will not force them to do otherwise—or even make things hard for them. Still, the approach we recommend does count as paternalistic, because in important contexts, private and public choice architects should not merely track or implement people's anticipated choices. Rather, they should attempt to move people in directions that will make their lives better. They should nudge.

A *nudge*, as we will use the term, is any aspect of the choice architecture that alters people's behavior in a predictable way without forbidding any options or significantly changing their economic incentives. To count as a mere nudge, the intervention must be easy and cheap to avoid. Nudges are not taxes, fines, subsidies, bans, or mandates. Putting the fruit at eye level counts as a nudge. Banning junk food does not.

Many of the policies we recommend can be and have been implemented by the private sector (with or without a nudge from the government). Employers, for example, are important choice architects in many of the examples we discuss in this book. In areas involving health care and retirement plans, we think that employers can give employees far more helpful nudges (for example, through sensible default rules, clear presentation of information, and helpful hints). Private companies that want to make money and to do good can benefit by creating environmentally friendly nudges, helping to reduce air pollution and the emission of greenhouse gases. But, of course, companies can also use the concepts we discuss to increase sales in unsavory ways. They might impose sludge. We strive to reduce the sludge produced in both the public and private sectors. See Chapter 8.

Econs and Humans: Why Nudges Can Help

Those who reject paternalism often claim that human beings do a terrific job of making choices, or if not terrific, certainly better than anyone else would do (especially if that someone else works for the government). Whether or not they have ever studied economics, many people seem at least implicitly committed to the idea of *Homo economicus*, or economic man—the notion that each of us thinks and chooses unfailingly well, and thus fits within the usual depiction of human beings that is offered by economists.

If you look at economics textbooks, you will learn that *Homo economicus* can think like Albert Einstein, store as much memory as Google does in the cloud, and exercise the willpower of Mahatma Gandhi. Really. But the folks we know are not like that. Real people have trouble with long division if they don't have a calculator, sometimes forget their spouse's birthday, and have a hangover on New Year's Day. They are not *Homo economicus*; they are *Homo sapiens*. To keep our Latin usage to a minimum, we will hereafter refer to these imaginary and real species as Econs and Humans.

Consider the issue of obesity. Rates of adult obesity in the United States are over 40 percent,[1] and more than 70 percent of American adults are considered either obese or overweight.[2] Worldwide, there are some 1 billion overweight adults, 300 million of whom are obese. Rates of obesity range from below 6 percent in Japan, South Korea, and some African nations to more than 75 percent in American Samoa.[3] According to the World Health Organization, obesity rates have risen threefold since 1980 in some areas of North America, the United Kingdom, Eastern Europe, the Middle East, the Pacific Islands, Australia, and China. There is overwhelming evidence that obesity increases the risk of heart disease and diabetes, frequently leading to premature death. It would be quite fantastic to suggest that everyone is choosing their best possible diet, or a diet that is preferable to what might be produced with a few nudges.

Of course, sensible people care about the taste of food, not simply about health, and eating is a source of pleasure in and of itself. We do not claim that everyone who is overweight is necessarily failing to act rationally, but we do reject the proposition that all or almost all people are choosing their diet optimally. What is true for diets is true for other risk-related behavior, including smoking and drinking, which produce hundreds of thousands of premature deaths each year in the United States alone. With respect to diet, smoking, and drinking, people's current choices cannot always be said to be the best means of promoting their own well-being (to put it lightly). Indeed, many smokers, drinkers, and overeaters are willing to pay third parties to help them make better decisions.

These findings complement those of the emerging science of choice, consisting of an extensive body of research over the past half-century. Much of the initial research in this field was conducted with laboratory experiments, but a substantial and rapidly growing amount comes from studies of real-world behavior, including archival studies of choices made in natural settings and randomized controlled trials. This research has raised serious questions about the soundness and wisdom of many judgments and decisions that people make. To qualify as Econs, people are not required to make perfect forecasts (that would require omniscience), but they are required to make *unbiased* forecasts. That is, forecasts can be wrong, but they can't repeatedly err in a predictable direction. Unlike Econs, Humans make predictable mistakes. Take, for example, the planning fallacy—the systematic tendency toward unrealistic optimism about the time it takes to complete projects. It will come as no surprise to anyone who has ever hired a contractor to learn that everything takes longer than you think, even if you know about the planning fallacy.*

Thousands of studies confirm that human forecasts are flawed and biased. Human decision making is not so great either. Again, to take just one example, consider what is called the status quo

---

* Knowing about the planning fallacy does not prevent you from making the mistake. This revision took far longer than we anticipated.

bias, a fancy name for inertia. For a host of reasons, which we shall explore, people have a strong tendency to go along with the status quo or default option. When you get a new smartphone, for example, you have a series of choices to make, from the background on the screen to the ringtone to the number of times the phone rings before the caller is sent to voice mail. The manufacturer has picked one option as the default for each of these choices. Research shows that whatever the default choices are, many people stick with them, even when the stakes are much higher than choosing the sound your phone makes when it rings.

We provide many examples of the use of default options, and we will see that defaults are often quite powerful. If private companies or public officials favor one set of outcomes, they can greatly influence people by choosing it as the default. You can often increase participation rates by 25 percent, and sometimes by a lot more than that, simply by shifting from an opt-in to an opt-out design. As we will show, setting default options, and adopting other similar, seemingly trivial menu-changing strategies, can have huge effects on outcomes, from increasing savings to combating climate change to improving health care to reducing poverty. At the same time, we show that there are important situations in which people exercise their freedom and reject defaults. When they feel strongly about something, for example, they might overcome the strength of inertia and the power of suggestion (defaults are often perceived to be hints that they are the recommended option). Changing the default can be an effective nudge, but it is decidedly not the answer to every problem.

The usually large effects of well-chosen default options provide just one illustration of the gentle power of nudges. In accordance with our definition, nudges include interventions that significantly alter the behavior of Humans, even though they would be ignored by Econs. Econs respond primarily to incentives. If the government taxes candy, Econs will buy less candy, but they are not influenced by such "irrelevant" factors as the order in which options are displayed. Humans respond to incentives too, but they are also influenced by nudges.* By properly deploying both incentives and nudges, we can improve our ability to improve people's lives, and help solve many of society's major problems. And we can do so while still insisting on everyone's freedom to choose.

A False Assumption and Two Misconceptions

Many people who favor freedom of choice reject any kind of paternalism. They want the government to let citizens choose for themselves. The standard policy advice that stems from this way of thinking is to give people as many choices as possible, and then let them choose the one they like best (with as little government intervention or nudging as possible). The beauty of this way of thinking is that it offers a simple solution to many complex problems: Just Maximize Choices—full stop!

This policy has been pushed in many domains, from education to health care to retirement savings programs. In some circles, Just Maximize Choices has become a policy mantra. Sometimes the only alternative to this mantra is thought to be a government mandate that is derided as one-size-fits-all. Those who favor Just Maximize Choices don't realize there is plenty of room between

---

* Alert readers will notice that incentives can come in different forms. If steps are taken to increase people's cognitive effort—as by placing fruit at eye level and candy in a more obscure place—it might be said that the "cost" of choosing candy is increased. Some of our nudges do, in a sense, impose cognitive or emotional (rather than material) costs, and in that sense alter incentives. Nudges count as such, and qualify as libertarian paternalism, only if any costs are low. (How low? We leave that judgment to you.)

their preferred policy and a single mandate. They oppose paternalism, or think they do, and they are skeptical about nudges. We believe that their skepticism is based on a false assumption and two misconceptions.

The false assumption is that almost all people, almost all the time, make choices that are in their best interest or at the very least are better than the choices that would be made by someone else. We claim that this assumption is false—indeed, obviously false. In fact, we do not think that anyone actually believes it on reflection.

Suppose a chess novice were to play against an experienced player. Predictably, the novice would lose precisely because he made inferior choices—choices that could easily be improved by some helpful hints. In many areas, ordinary consumers are novices, interacting in a world inhabited by experienced professionals trying to sell them things. More broadly, how well people choose is an empirical question, one whose answer is likely to vary across domains. Generally, people make good choices in contexts in which they have lots of experience, good information, and prompt feedback—say, choosing among familiar ice cream flavors. People know whether they like chocolate, vanilla, coffee, or something else.

They do less well in contexts in which they are inexperienced and poorly informed, and in which feedback is slow or infrequent— say, in saving for retirement or in choosing among medical treatments or investment options. If you are given fifty different insurance policies from which to choose, with multiple and varying features, you might benefit from a little help. So long as people are not choosing perfectly, some changes in the choice architecture could make their lives go better (as judged by them, not by some bureaucrat). As we will try to show, it is not only possible to design choice architecture to make people better off; in many cases, it is easy to do so.

The first misconception is that it is possible to avoid influencing people's choices. In countless situations, some organization or agent *must* make a choice that will affect the behavior of some other people. There is, in those situations, no way of avoiding nudging in some direction, and these nudges will affect what people choose. Choice architecture is inevitable. As illustrated by the example of Carolyn's cafeterias, people's choices are pervasively influenced by the design elements selected by choice architects. No website, and no grocery store, lacks a design. It is true, of course, that some nudges are unintentional; employers may decide (say) whether to pay employees monthly or biweekly without intending to create any kind of nudge, but they might be surprised to discover that people save more if they get paid biweekly, because twice a year they get three paychecks in one month, and many bills come monthly.

It is also true that private and public institutions can strive for one or another kind of neutrality—by, for example, choosing randomly, or by trying to figure out what most people want. But unintentional nudges can have major effects, and in some contexts, these forms of neutrality are unattractive; we shall encounter many examples. It is true as well that choice architects can insist on active choosing—by, for example, saying that if you want to work for the government, you have to specify the health care plan you prefer. But active choosing is itself a form of choice architecture, and it is not one that everyone will prefer, especially when options are numerous and decisions are difficult. In a French restaurant where customers are presented with a cart loaded with what seems like hundreds of varieties of cheese, it can be a blessing to have the option of asking the server to suggest a selection. People do not always like to be told to choose, and if they are forced to do that, they might not be at all happy.

Some people will gladly accept these points for private institutions but strenuously object to government efforts to influence choice with the goal of improving people's lives. They worry that governments cannot be trusted to be competent or benign. They fear that elected officials and bureaucrats will be ignorant, will place their own interests first, or will pay excessive attention to the narrow goals of self-interested private groups. We share these concerns. In particular, we emphatically agree that for government, the risks of mistake, bias, and overreaching are real and sometimes serious. That is why we generally favor nudges over commands, requirements, and prohibitions (except when people are harming others). But governments, no less than cafeterias (which governments frequently run), have to provide starting points of one or another kind. This is not avoidable. As we shall emphasize, they do so every day through the policies they establish, in ways that inevitably affect some choices and outcomes. In this respect, the anti-nudge position is a logical impossibility—a literal nonstarter.

The second misconception is that paternalism always involves coercion. In the cafeteria example, the choice of the order in which to present food items does not force a particular diet on anyone, yet Carolyn, and others in her position, might select some arrangement of food on grounds that are paternalistic in the sense that we use the term. Would anyone object to putting the fruit and salad before the desserts at an elementary school cafeteria if the result were to induce kids to eat more apples and fewer brownies? Is this question fundamentally different if the customers are teenagers, or even adults? Is a GPS device an intrusion on freedom, even if it is paternalistic, in the sense that it tries to tell you how to get to your preferred destination? When no coercion is involved, we think that some types of paternalism should be acceptable even to those who most embrace freedom of choice.

In domains as varied as savings, health, consumer protection, organ donation, climate change, and insurance, we will offer specific suggestions in keeping with our general approach. And by insisting that choices remain unrestricted, we think that the risks of inept or even corrupt designs are reduced. Freedom to choose is the best safeguard against bad choice architecture.

Choice Architecture in Action

Choice architects can make major improvements to the lives of others by designing user-friendly environments. Many of the most successful companies have succeeded in the marketplace for exactly that reason. Sometimes the choice architecture is highly visible, and consumers and employees appreciate the value it provides. Apple's iPhone became an enormous economic success in part because of its elegant style, but mostly because users found it easy to get the device to do what they want. Sometimes the choice architecture is neglected and could benefit from some careful attention.

Consider an illustration from the American workplace. (If you live elsewhere, please take pity on our plight.) Most large employers offer a range of benefits, including such things as life and health insurance and retirement savings plans. Once a year in late fall, there is an open enrollment period when employees are allowed to revise the selections that they made the previous year. Employees are required to make their choices online. They typically receive, by mail, a package of materials explaining the choices they have and instructions on how to log on to make these choices. They also receive various reminders.

Because employees are human, some neglect to log on, so it is crucial to decide what the default options are for these busy, absentminded, and perhaps even overwhelmed employees. Usually, the default is one of two options: employees can be given the same option they chose the previous year, or their choice can be set back to "zero." Call these the "status quo" and "back-to-zero" options. How should the choice architect choose between these defaults?

Libertarian paternalists would like to set the default by asking what thoughtful and well-informed employees would actually want. Although this principle may not always lead to a clear choice, it is certainly better than choosing the default at random, or making either status quo or back to zero the default for everything. For example, it is a good guess that most employees would not want to cancel their heavily subsidized health insurance. So, for health insurance the status quo default (same plan as last year) seems strongly preferable to the back-to-zero default (which would mean going without health insurance).

Compare this to an employee's flexible spending account, a peculiarly cruel "benefit" that we believe exists only in the United States. An employee can contribute money into this account each month that can then be used to pay for certain expenditures (such as uninsured medical or childcare expenses). The cruel feature is that money put into this account has to be spent by March 31 of the following year or it is lost, and the predicted expenditures might vary greatly from one year to the next (for example, medical expenses might go up in a year in which a family welcomes a newborn, or childcare expenses might go down when a child enters school). In this case, the back-to-zero default probably makes more sense than the status quo.

This problem is not hypothetical. Some time ago, Thaler had a meeting with three of the top administrative officers of his employer, the University of Chicago, to discuss similar issues, and the meeting happened to take place on the final day of the open enrollment period. He mentioned this coincidence and teasingly asked whether the administrators had remembered to log on and adjust their benefits package. One sheepishly said that he was planning on doing it later that day and was glad for the reminder. Another admitted to having forgotten, and the third said that he was hoping his wife had remembered to do it! The group then turned to the topic of the meeting, namely what the default should be for an option with the uninviting name "supplementary salary reduction program" (it's better than it sounds; it's actually a tax-sheltered savings program). At that time the default was the back-to-zero option, and Thaler had arranged the meeting hoping to convince the administrators to change the default to "same as last year." After their own absentminded behavior was made salient to them, the administrators quickly agreed to the change. We are confident that many university employees will have more comfortable retirements as a result.

This example illustrates some basic principles of good choice architecture. Choosers are human, so designers should make life as easy as possible. Send reminders (but not too many!) and then try to minimize the costs imposed on those who, despite your (and their) best efforts, space out. As we will see, these principles (and many more) can be applied in both the private and public sectors, and there is much room for going beyond what is now being done. Large companies and governments, please take note. (Also universities and small companies.)

A New Path

We shall have a great deal to say about nudges from private institutions. But many of the most important applications of libertarian paternalism are for governments, and we will offer a number of recommendations for public policy and law. Our hope when we originally wrote this book was that those recommendations might appeal to both sides of the political divide. Indeed, we believed that the policies suggested by libertarian paternalism could be embraced by conservatives and liberals. We are pleased to report that, far more than we could have anticipated, that belief has been vindicated.

In the United Kingdom, former Prime Minister David Cameron, the leader of the Conservative Party, embraced nudging and created the world's first team devoted solely to this effort, officially called the Behavioural Insights Team, but often called the Nudge Unit.* In the United States, former President Barack Obama, a Democrat and a liberal, also embraced the basic idea, directed his agencies to adopt numerous nudges, and created a nudge unit of his own (originally known as the Social and Behavioral Sciences Team, and now called the Office of Evaluation Sciences). The United States Agency for International Development has an assortment of programs that use behavioral science and insights. In the years since the book was originally published, governments around the world, spanning the political landscape, have incorporated these and related ideas in an effort to make their programs more efficient and effective. There are behavioral insights teams or nudge units of various kinds in numerous nations, including Australia, New Zealand, Germany, Canada, Finland, Singapore, the Netherlands, France, Japan, India, Qatar, and Saudi Arabia. A great deal of relevant work is being done by the World Bank, the United Nations, and the European Commission. In 2020, the World Health Organization created a Behavioral Insights Initiative focusing on

---

* The team still exists but is now a "social purpose company" jointly owned by the government, its employees, and a charity called Nesta. By 2020 it had over two hundred employees working in over thirty nations worldwide.

numerous public health issues, including pandemics, vaccination uptake, and risk-taking by young people.

Although the world seems to be becoming increasingly polarized, we continue to believe that libertarian paternalism can be a promising foundation for bipartisanship and for simple problemsolving. Better governance often requires less in the way of government coercion and more in the way of freedom to choose. Mandates and prohibitions have their place (and behavioral science can help to identify them), but when incentives and nudges replace requirements and bans, government will be both smaller and more modest. So, to be clear: this book is not a call for more bureaucracy, or even for an increased role of government. We just strive for better governance. In short, libertarian paternalism is neither left nor right. For all their differences, we hope that people with very different political convictions might be willing to converge in support of gentle nudges.

 **PART I**

HUMANS AND ECONS

I

Biases and Blunders

Have a look, if you would, at the two tables shown in the figure below:

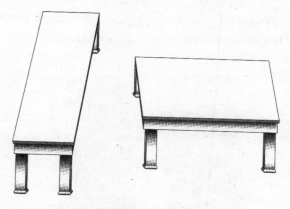

Figure 1.1. Two tables (Adapted from Shepard [1990])

Suppose that you are thinking about which one would work better as a coffee table in your living room. What would you say are the shapes of the two tables? Take a guess at the ratio of the length to the width of each. Just eyeball it.

If you are like most people, you think that the table on the left is much longer and narrower than the one on the right. Typical guesses are that the ratio of the length to the width is 3:1 for the left table and 1.5:1 for the right table. Now take out a ruler and measure each table. You will find that the shapes of the two table-tops are identical. Measure them until you are convinced, because this is a case where seeing is not believing. (When Thaler showed this example to Sunstein at their usual lunch haunt, Sunstein grabbed his chopstick to check.)

What should we conclude from this example? If you see the left table as longer and thinner than the right one, you are certifiably human. There is nothing wrong with you (well, at least not that we can detect from this test). Still, your judgment in this task was biased, and predictably so. No one thinks that the right table is narrower! Not only were you wrong; you were probably confident that you were right. If you like, you can put this visual to good use when you encounter others who are equally human and who are disposed to gamble away their money, say, at a bar.

Figure 1.2. Tabletops (Adapted from Shepard [1990])

Now consider Figure 1.2. Do these two shapes look the same or different? Again, if you are human and have decent vision, you probably see these shapes as being identical, as they are. But these two shapes are just the tabletops from Figure 1.1, removed from their legs and reoriented. Both the legs and the orientation facilitate the illusion that the tabletops are different in Figure 1.1, so removing these distracters restores the visual system to its usual, amazingly accurate state.* These two figures capture the key insight that behavioral economists have borrowed from psychologists. Normally the human mind works remarkably well. We can recognize people we have not seen in years, understand the complexities of our native language, and run down a flight of stairs without falling. Some of us can speak twelve languages, improve the fanciest computers, or create the theory of relativity. However, even Albert Einstein, Bill Gates, and Steve Jobs would probably be fooled by those tables. That does not mean something is wrong with us as humans, but it does mean that our understanding of human behavior can be improved by appreciating how and when people systematically go wrong. Knowing something about the visual system allowed Roger Shepard, a psychologist and artist, to draw those deceptive tables.[1]

In the spirit of those tables, this chapter will spell out some of the most important ways that human judgment and decision making diverge from the predictions of models based on optimization. Before we get started, though, we want to stress that we are not saying that people are irrational. We avoid using that unhelpful and unkind term, and we certainly don't think that people are dumb. Rather, the problem is that we are fallible and life is hard. If every time we went food shopping, we tried to solve the problem of choosing the very best possible combination of items to buy, we would never get out of the store. Instead, we take

---

* One of the tricks used in drawing these tables is that vertical lines look longer than horizontal lines. As a result, the Gateway Arch in Saint Louis looks taller than it is wide, although the height actually equals the width.

sensible shortcuts, and we try to get home before we start eating
the things in our cart. We are human.

Rules of Thumb

To deal with life, we use rules of thumb. They are handy and useful. Their variety is nicely illustrated by Tom Parker's fascinating
1983 book, *Rules of Thumb*. Parker wrote the book by asking friends
to send him examples. These include: "One ostrich egg will serve
24 people for brunch." "Ten people will raise the temperature of
an average size room by one degree per hour." And one to which
we will return: "No more than 25 percent of the guests at a university dinner party can come from the economics department
without spoiling the conversation."

Although rules of thumb can be very helpful, their use can also
lead to systematic biases. This insight, first stated decades ago by
two of our heroes, the psychologists Daniel Kahneman and Amos
Tversky, changed how psychologists (and eventually economists,
lawyers, policymakers, and many others) think about thinking.
Their early work identified three common rules of thumb or
heuristics—anchoring, availability, and representativeness—and
the biases that are associated with each. Their research program
became known as the "heuristics and biases" approach to the
study of human judgment. This approach has been an inspiration
for behavioral economics in general, and especially for this book.

Anchoring

Suppose we were asked to guess the population of Milwaukee, a
city about a two-hour drive north of Chicago, where we both lived

when we wrote the first edition of this book. Neither of us knows much about Milwaukee, but we believe it is the biggest city in Wisconsin. How should we go about guessing? Well, a good thing to do is to start with something we do know, such as the population of Chicago, which is roughly three million. And we know that Milwaukee is a big enough city to have professional baseball and basketball teams, but clearly not as big as Chicago, so, hmmm, maybe it is one-third the size, say one million. Now consider someone from Green Bay, Wisconsin, who is asked the same question. She also doesn't know the answer, but she does know that Green Bay has about one hundred thousand people and that Milwaukee is larger, so she guesses, say, three times larger—three hundred thousand.

This process is called "anchoring and adjustment." You start with some anchor, a number you know, and adjust in the direction you think is appropriate. So far, so good. The bias occurs because the adjustments are typically insufficient. Experiments repeatedly show that in problems similar to our example, people from Chicago are likely to make a high guess (based on their high anchor), while those from Green Bay guess low (based on their low anchor). As it happens, Milwaukee has about 590,000 people.

Even obviously irrelevant anchors creep into the decision-making process. Try this one yourself. Think about the last three digits of your phone number. Write the number down if you can. Now, when do you think Attila the Hun sacked Europe? Was it before or after that year? What is your best guess? Even if you do not know much about European history, you do know enough to know that whenever Attila did whatever he did, the date has nothing to do with your phone number. Still, when we conduct this experiment with our students, we get answers that are more than three hundred years later from students who start with high anchors rather than low ones. (The right answer is 452.)

Anchors can even influence how you think your life is going. In one experiment, college students were asked two questions: (a) How happy are you? (b) How often are you dating? When the two questions were asked in this order, the correlation between the two questions was quite low (.11). But when the question order was reversed, so that the dating question was asked first, the correlation jumped to .62. Apparently, when prompted by the dating question, the students use what might be called the "dating heuristic" to answer the question about how happy they are. "Gee, I can't remember when I last had a date! I must be miserable." Similar results can be obtained from married couples if the dating question is replaced by a lovemaking question.[2]

In the language of this book, anchors serve as nudges. One example comes from tipping behavior in taxicabs. Taxi drivers were initially reluctant to adopt the technology to accept credit cards in their cabs, because the credit card companies take a cut of roughly 3 percent. But those who did install the technology were pleasantly surprised to learn that their tips increased! This was partly due to some anchoring. When customers elected to use their card to pay, they would often be confronted with tip options that looked something like this:

15%
20%
25%
Choose your own amount.

Notice this screen is nudging people toward higher tips by offering precalculated amounts that start at these percentages. (And when in doubt, people often choose the middle option—in this case 20 percent, which is higher than the 15 percent many customers previously chose without this intervention.) Also, the option to choose your own tip is a bit of an illusion. The screen appears only when the trip is over; the customer is ready to leave, others may be waiting to get into the cab, and entering one's own amount requires some calculations and a couple extra steps. By contrast, just clicking one of the buttons is easy!

Nevertheless, it is tricky to figure out what the best defaults would be from the perspective of the driver. This is shown in a careful study by behavioral economist Kareem Haggag. Haggag was able to compare the tips from two cab companies, one of which offered 15, 20, and 25 percent tip suggestions, whereas the other had defaults of 20, 25, and 30 percent. On balance, the screen with the relatively higher default tips significantly increased drivers' earnings, because they increased the average tip. But interestingly, they also provoked an increase in the number of riders who offered no tip at all. Some people were evidently put off by the aggressive defaults, and they refused to give anything.[3] This is connected with the behavioral phenomenon of *reactance*: when people feel ordered around, they might get mad and do the opposite of what is being ordered (or even suggested).

Still, the evidence shows that, within reason, the more you ask for, the more you tend to get. Haggag's headline is that because of the higher on-screen default tips, taxi drivers ended up with a decent increase in their annual earnings. Lawyers who sue companies sometimes win astronomical amounts, in part because they have successfully induced juries to anchor on multimillion-dollar figures (such as a company's annual earnings). Clever negotiators often get amazing deals for their clients by producing an opening offer that makes their adversary thrilled to pay half that very high amount. But keep that notion of reactance in mind. If you get greedy, you might end up with nothing.

Availability

A quick quiz: In the United States, are more gun deaths caused by homicides or suicides?

In answering questions of this kind, most people use what is called the *availability heuristic*. They assess the likelihood of risks by asking how readily examples come to mind. Because homicides are much more heavily reported in the news media, they are more available than suicides, and so people tend to believe, wrongly, that guns cause more deaths from homicide than from suicide. (There are about twice as many gun-inflicted suicides as homicides.) An important lesson can be found here: people often buy a gun thinking they want to protect their family, but it is much more likely that they will increase the chance that a family member successfully commits suicide.

Accessibility and salience are closely related to availability, and they are important as well. If you have personally experienced a serious earthquake, you're more likely to believe that a flood or an earthquake is likely than if you read about it in a weekly magazine. Thus, vivid and easily imagined causes of death (for example, tornadoes) often receive inflated estimates of probability, and less-vivid causes (for example, asthma attacks) receive low estimates, even if they occur with a far greater frequency (here a factor of twenty). So, too, recent events have a greater impact on our behavior, and on our fears, than earlier ones.

The availability heuristic helps to explain much risk-related behavior, including both public and private decisions to take precautions. Whether people buy insurance for natural disasters is greatly affected by recent experiences.[4] In the aftermath of a flood, purchases of new flood insurance policies rise sharply—but purchases decline steadily from that point, as vivid memories recede. And people who know someone who has experienced a flood are more likely to buy flood insurance for themselves, regardless of the flood risk they actually face.[5]

Biased assessments of risk can perversely influence how we prepare for and respond to crises, business choices, and the political process. When technology stocks have done very well, people might well buy technology stocks, even if by that point they've become a bad investment. People might overestimate some risks, such as a nuclear power accident, because of well-publicized incidents such as Chernobyl and Fukushima. They might underestimate others, such as strokes, because they do not get much attention in the media. Such misperceptions can affect policy, because some governments will allocate their resources in a way that fits with people's fears rather than in response to the most likely dangers.

When availability bias is at work, both private and public decisions may be improved if judgments can be nudged back in the direction of true probabilities. A good way to get people to take more precautions about a potential hazard is to remind them of a related incident in which things went wrong; a good way to increase people's confidence is to remind them of a similar situation in which everything worked out for the best.

Representativeness

The third of the original three heuristics bears an unwieldy name: representativeness. Think of it as the similarity heuristic. The idea is that when asked to judge how likely it is that A belongs to category B, people answer by asking themselves how similar A is to their image or stereotype of B (that is, how "representative" A is of B). Like the other two heuristics we have discussed, this one is used because it often works. Stereotypes are sometimes right!

Again, biases can creep in when similarity and frequency diverge. The most famous demonstration of such biases involves the case of a hypothetical woman named Linda. In an experiment, subjects were told the following: "Linda is thirty-one years old, single, outspoken, and very bright. She majored in philosophy. As a student, she was deeply concerned with issues of discrimination and social justice and also participated in antinuclear demonstrations." Then people were asked to rank, in order of the probability of their occurrence, eight possible futures for Linda. The two crucial answers were "bank teller" and "bank teller and active in the feminist movement." Most people said that Linda was less likely to be a bank teller than to be a bank teller and active in the feminist movement.[6]

This is an obvious logical mistake. It is, of course, not logically possible for any two events to be more likely than one of them alone. It just has to be the case that Linda is more likely to be a bank teller than a feminist bank teller, because all feminist bank tellers are bank tellers. The error stems from the use of the representativeness heuristic: Linda's description seems to match "bank teller and active in the feminist movement" far better than "bank teller." As Stephen Jay Gould once observed, "I know [the right answer], yet a little homunculus in my head continues to jump up and down, shouting at me 'but she can't just be a bank teller; read the description!'"[7] Like the availability heuristic, the representativeness heuristic often works well, but it can lead to major errors.

Optimism and Overconfidence

Before the start of Thaler's class in managerial decision making, students fill out an anonymous survey on the course website. One of the questions is "In which decile do you expect to fall in the distribution of grades in this class?" Students can check the top

10 percent, the second 10 percent, and so forth. Since these are MBA students, they are presumably well aware that in any distribution, half the population will be in the top 50 percent and half in the bottom. And only 10 percent of the class can, in fact, end up in the top decile.

Nevertheless, the results of this survey reveal a high degree of unrealistic optimism about performance in the class. Typically less than 5 percent of the class expects their performance to be below the median (the 50th percentile) and more than half the class expects to perform in one of the top two deciles. Invariably, the largest group of students put themselves in the second decile. We think this is most likely explained by modesty. They really think they will end up in the top decile but are too modest to say so.

MBA students are not the only ones overconfident about their abilities. The "above-average" effect is pervasive. In some studies, 90 percent of drivers say they are above average behind the wheel. And nearly everyone thinks they have an above-average sense of humor, including some people who are rarely seen smiling. (That is because they know what is funny!) This applies to professors, too. One study found that about 94 percent of professors at a large university believed they were better than the average professor, and there is every reason to think that such overconfidence applies to professors in general.[8] (Yes, we admit to this particular failing.)

People are unrealistically optimistic even when the stakes are high. In the United States, about 40 to 50 percent of marriages end in divorce, and this is a statistic most people have heard. (The precise number is hard to nail down.) But around the time of the ceremony, almost all couples have been found to believe that there is approximately a zero percent chance that their marriage will end in divorce—even those who have already been divorced![9]

(Second marriage, Samuel Johnson once quipped, "is the triumph of hope over experience.") A similar point applies to entrepreneurs starting new businesses, in which the failure rate is at least 50 percent. In one survey of people starting new businesses (typically small businesses, such as contracting firms, restaurants, or salons), respondents were asked two questions: (a) What do you think is the chance of success for a typical business like yours? (b) What is your chance of success? The most common answers to these questions were 50 percent and 90 percent, respectively, and many said 100 percent in response to the second question.[10]

Unrealistic optimism can explain a lot of individual risk-taking, especially in the domain of risks to life and health. Asked to envision their future, students typically say that they are far less likely than their classmates to be fired from a job, to have a heart attack or get cancer, to be divorced after a few years of marriage, or to have a drinking problem. Older people underestimate the likelihood that they will be in a car accident or suffer major diseases. Smokers are aware of the statistical risks and often even exaggerate them, but most believe that they are less likely to be diagnosed with lung cancer and heart disease than most nonsmokers. Lotteries are successful partly because of unrealistic optimism.[11]

Unrealistic optimism is a pervasive feature of human life; it characterizes most people in most social categories. When they overestimate their personal immunity to harm, people may fail to take sensible preventive steps. During the pandemic of 2020 and 2021, some people failed to take precautions, including maskwearing, because of optimism about their personal risks. If people are running risks because of unrealistic optimism, they might be able to benefit from a nudge. In fact, we have already mentioned one possibility: if people are reminded of a bad event, they may not continue to be so optimistic.

Gains and Losses

People hate losses. In more technical language, people are "loss averse." Roughly speaking, the prospect of losing something makes you twice as miserable as the prospect of gaining the same thing makes you happy. How do we know this?

Consider a simple experiment.[12] Half the students in a class are given a coffee mug with the insignia of their home university embossed on it. The students who do not get a mug are asked to examine their neighbors' mugs. Then mug owners are invited to sell their mugs and nonowners are invited to buy them. They do so by answering this question: "At each of the following prices, indicate whether you would be willing to (give up your mug/buy a mug)." The results show that those with mugs demand roughly twice as much to give them up as others are willing to pay to get one. Thousands of mugs have been used in dozens of replications of this experiment, but the results are nearly always the same. Once you have a mug, you don't want to give it up. But if you don't have one, you don't feel an urgent need to buy one. What this means is that people do not assign specific values to objects; it often matters whether they are selling or buying.

It is also possible to measure loss aversion with gambles. Suppose I ask you whether you want to make a bet. Heads you win $X, tails you lose $100. How much does X have to be for you to take the bet? For many people, the answer to this question is somewhere around $200. This implies that the prospect of winning $200 just offsets the prospect of losing $100.

Loss aversion helps produce inertia, meaning a strong desire to stick with your current holdings. If you are reluctant to give up what you have because you do not want to incur losses, then you will turn down trades you might have otherwise made. In another experiment, half the students in a class received coffee mugs (of course) and half got large chocolate bars. The mugs and the chocolate cost about the same, and in pretests students were as likely to choose one as the other. Yet when offered the opportunity to switch from a mug to a candy bar or vice versa, only one in ten switched.

Loss aversion has a lot of relevance to public policy. If you want to discourage the use of plastic bags, should you give people a small amount of money for bringing their own reusable bag, or should you ask them to pay the same small amount for a plastic bag? The evidence suggests that the former approach has no effect at all, but that the latter works; it significantly decreases use of plastic bags. People don't want to lose money, even if the amount is trivial.[13] (Environmentalists, please remember this point.)

Status Quo Bias

For lots of reasons, people have a general tendency to stick with their current situation. One reason is loss aversion; giving up what we have is painful. But the phenomenon has multiple causes. William Samuelson and Richard Zeckhauser have dubbed this behavior *status quo bias*, and it has been demonstrated in numerous situations.[14] Most teachers know that students tend to sit in the same seats in class, even without a seating chart. But status quo bias can occur even when the stakes are much larger, and it can cost people a lot of money.

For example, in retirement savings plans most participants pick an asset allocation when they join the plan and then forget about it. A study conducted in the late 1980s looked at the decisions of participants in a pension plan that covered many college professors in the United States. The median number of changes in the asset allocation over a lifetime was, believe it or not, zero.[15] In other words, over the course of their careers, more than half of the participants made exactly no changes to the way their contributions were being allocated. Perhaps even more telling, many married participants who were single when they joined the plan still had their mothers listed as their beneficiaries! As we will see, inertia in investing behavior is alive and well in Sweden. (See Chapter 10.)

Status quo bias is easily exploited. A true story: Many years ago, American Express wrote Sunstein a cheerful letter telling him that he could receive, for free, three-month subscriptions to five magazines of his choice.* What a great deal! Free subscriptions seem like a bargain, even if the magazines rarely got read, so Sunstein happily made his choices. What he didn't realize was that unless he took some action to cancel his subscription, he would automatically keep receiving the magazines after the three-month period, automatically paying for them at the normal rate. For more than a decade, he continued to subscribe to magazines that he hardly ever read and that he mostly despised. They tended to pile up around the house. He kept intending to cancel those subscriptions, but somehow never got around to it. It was not until he started working on the original edition of this book that he canceled them.

One of the causes of status quo bias is a lack of attention. Many people often adopt what we call the "yeah, whatever" heuristic. A good illustration is the carryover effect that occurs when people

---

* For young readers, magazines were weekly printed documments that arrived in the mail and featured stale news and nice photographs.

start binge-watching a television series. On most streaming networks if you do nothing when you reach the end of one episode, the next one just starts showing. At that point many viewers (implicitly) say, "yeah, whatever," and keep watching. Many an intended short evening has dragged long into the night as a result, especially on shows with cliffhanger endings. Nor is Sunstein the only victim of automatic renewal of magazine subscriptions, which has now been extended to virtually every online service. Those who are in charge of circulation know that when renewal is automatic, and particularly when people have to make a phone call to cancel, the likelihood of renewal is much higher than it is when people have to indicate that they actually want to continue to receive the magazine. (We will return to this point in Chapter 8 in connection with sludge.) The combination of loss aversion and mindless choosing is one reason why if an option is designated as the default, it will usually (but not always!) attract a large market share. Default options thus act as powerful nudges. For this and other reasons, setting the best possible defaults is a theme we explore often in this book.

Framing

Suppose that you are suffering from serious heart disease and your doctor proposes a grueling operation. You're understandably curious about the odds of surviving this ordeal. The doctor says, "Of one hundred patients who have this operation, ninety are alive after five years." What will you do? That statement might feel pretty comforting, making you confident about having the operation.

But suppose the doctor frames his answer in a somewhat different way. Suppose he says, "Of one hundred patients who have this operation, ten are dead after five years." If you're like most people, the doctor's statement will sound pretty alarming and you might not have the operation. Instinctively, you might think: "A significant number of people are dead, and I might be one of them!" In numerous experiments, people react very differently to the information that "ninety of one hundred are alive" than to "ten of one hundred are dead"—even though the content of the two statements is exactly the same. Even experts are subject to framing effects. When doctors are told that "ninety of one hundred are alive," they are more likely to recommend the operation than if told that "ten of one hundred are dead."[16]

Framing matters in many domains. When credit cards started to become popular forms of payment in the 1970s, some retail merchants wanted to charge different prices to their cash and credit card customers. To prevent this, credit card companies adopted rules that prohibited their retailers from doing so. When a bill was introduced in Congress to forbid credit card companies to impose such rules and the bill seemed likely to pass, the credit card lobby turned its attention to language. Its preference was that if a company charged different prices to cash and credit customers, the credit price should be considered the "normal" (default) price and the cash price a discount—rather than the alternative of making the cash price the usual price and adding a surcharge for credit card customers.

The credit card companies had a good, intuitive understanding of what psychologists would come to call framing. The idea is that choices depend, in part, on the way in which problems are described. The point matters a great deal for public policy. Energy conservation is now rightly receiving a lot of attention, so consider

the following information campaigns: (a) If you use energy conservation methods, you will save $350 per year; (b) If you do not use
energy conservation methods, you will lose $350 per year. There is
evidence that information campaign (b), framed in terms of loss,
might be more effective than information campaign (a). If the government wants to encourage energy conservation, option (b) looks
like a stronger nudge.

   Much like status quo bias, framing effects are exacerbated by
the Human tendency occasionally to be somewhat mindless, passive decision makers. Few of us bother to check to make sure re-
framing the decisions we face would produce a different answer.
One reason why we don't check for consistency may be that we
wouldn't know what to make of a contradiction. This implies that
frames can be powerful nudges, and must be selected with care
and caution.

How We Think: Two Systems

It goes without saying that the biases we have described in this
chapter do not apply to everyone the same way. Yes, most people
are overconfident and optimistic—but not everyone. In fact we
have a good friend who has the opposite traits—he is never confident and is always worried about something, or many things.
That friend happens to be Daniel Kahneman, with whom we have
both had the privilege of being coauthors. A draft of a paper or
book chapter that seemed good last week suddenly can look terrible to him this week. He is constantly rethinking everything.
And this is particularly true of his own work.

   This trait led him to take an unusual step when he won the
Nobel Memorial Prize in Economic Sciences in 2002. Laureates are

asked to deliver a lecture during their week in Stockholm. Most choose to discuss the work that earned the prize in a manner accessible to a lay audience. Kahneman did that, but in his own, unique way. He presented an entirely new way of looking at his joint work with Amos Tversky (who would have shared the prize had he been alive), using a concept from cognitive psychology that had not played even the slightest role in creating the research. Only Kahneman would take the already frantic two months between the announcement of the prize and the ceremony to rethink his life's work completely. This rethinking was later refined and expanded in his bestselling book *Thinking, Fast and Slow*.

The title of the book cleverly states the main idea, to which we devote the rest of this chapter. It is useful to imagine the workings of the brain as consisting of two components or systems. One is fast and intuitive; the other is slow and reflective. Kahneman adopts the terminology of the psychology literature on which he draws, and calls these two components System 1 and System 2. One of us had trouble remembering which one is the fast one (it is 1), so we prefer to use names that remind the reader what they are. We call them the Automatic System and the Reflective System.

Using this framework can help us understand a puzzle about human thought. How can we be so ingenious at some tasks and so clueless at others? Beethoven wrote his incredible Ninth Symphony after he had become deaf, an amazing feat, but one would be hardly surprised to learn that he often misplaced his house keys. Was he a genius or an imbecile? The answer is some of both.

The work of psychologists and neuroscientists on whose work Kahneman relied converged on a description of the brain's functioning that helps us make sense of these seeming contradictions. The approach involves a distinction between two kinds of thinking.[17]

Table 1.1. Two Cognitive Systems

AUTOMATIC SYSTEM	REFLECTIVE SYSTEM
Uncontrolled	Controlled
Effortless	Effortful
Associative	Deductive
Fast	Slow
Unconscious	Self-aware
Skilled	Rule-following

Here is a story that illustrates how the two systems work. Sunstein has a son named Declan, who was, at age nine, unable to resist toy stores. Whenever the two of them passed such a store, Declan would clamor to go inside and buy something, even though he would predictably be bored with the new toy in a day or two. Sunstein, of course, dealt with this dilemma by giving Declan a short primer on the two systems. It was Declan's System 1 that urgently wanted to go into toy stores, although his System 2 fully knew he had enough toys. For a few weeks, the explanation appeared to work, and Declan could pass by toy stores without uttering a word. But one day, he looked seriously at his father and asked, "Daddy, do I even have a System Two?"

As Declan now knows, the Automatic System is rapid and instinctive, and acts without reliance on what we usually associate with the word *thinking*. When you duck because a ball is thrown at you unexpectedly, or get nervous when your airplane hits turbulence, or smile when you see a cute puppy, it is your Automatic System at work. Though the neuroscience is complicated here, brain scientists are able to say that the activities of the Automatic System are associated with the oldest parts of the brain, the parts we share with lizards (as well as puppies).[18]

The Reflective System is more deliberate and self-conscious. We use this system when we are asked, "How much is 411 times 317?" Most people are also likely to use the Reflective System when deciding which route to take for a trip to an unfamiliar place and whether to go to law school or business school. When we are writing this book we are (mostly) using our Reflective Systems, but sometimes ideas pop into our heads when we are in the shower or taking a walk and not thinking at all about the book, and these probably are coming from our Automatic Systems. (Many voters, by the way, seem to rely heavily on their Automatic System.[19] A candidate who makes a bad first impression, or who tries to win votes through complex arguments and statistical demonstrations, may well run into trouble.)*[20]

Most people in the world have an Automatic System reaction to a temperature given in Celsius but have to use their Reflective System to process a temperature given in Fahrenheit; for Americans, the opposite is true. People speak their native languages using their Automatic Systems and tend to struggle to speak another language using their Reflective Systems. Being truly bilingual means that you speak two languages using the Automatic System. Accomplished chess players have pretty fancy intuitions; their Automatic Systems allow them to size up complex situations rapidly and respond with both amazing accuracy and exceptional speed.

One way to think about all this is that the Automatic System is your gut reaction and the Reflective System is your conscious

---

* It is possible to predict the outcome of congressional elections with frightening accuracy simply by asking people to look quickly at pictures of the candidates and say which one looks more competent. These judgments, by students who did not know the candidates, forecast the winner of the election two-thirds of the time!

thought. Gut feelings can be quite accurate, but we often make mistakes because we rely too much on our Automatic System. The Automatic System says, "The airplane is shaking, I'm going to die," while the Reflective System responds, "Plane crashes are extremely rare!" The Automatic System says, "That big dog is going to hurt me," and the Reflective System replies, "Most dogs are quite sweet." The Automatic System starts out with no idea how to kick a ball accurately or shoot a basketball into a faraway hoop. Note, however, that countless hours of practice enable accomplished athletes to avoid reflection and to rely on their Automatic Systems— so much so that good athletes know the hazards of thinking too much and might well do better to "trust the gut," or "just do it."

The Automatic System can be trained with lots of repetition— but such training takes a great deal of time and effort. One reason why teenagers are such risky drivers is that their Automatic Systems have not had much practice, and using the Reflective System is much slower. Sunstein is hopeful that Declan will develop a fully functional Reflective System before he is old enough to get a driver's license.

To see how intuitive thinking works, try the following little test. For each of the three questions, begin by writing down the first answer that comes to your mind. Then pause to reflect.

1. A bat and ball cost $1.10 in total. The bat costs $1.00 more than the ball. How much does the ball cost?

2. You are one of three runners in a race. At the end, you overtake the runner who was in second place. In what place did you finish?

3. Mary's mother had four children. The youngest three are named: Spring, Summer, and Autumn. What is the eldest child's name?

What were your initial answers? Most people say 10 cents, first place, and Winter. But all these answers are wrong. If you think for a minute, you will see why. If the ball costs 10 cents and the bat costs one dollar more than the ball, meaning $1.10, then together they cost $1.20, not $1.10. No one who bothers to check whether his initial answer of 10 cents could possibly be right would give that as an answer, but research by Shane Frederick (who calls series of questions such as these the Cognitive Reflection Test) finds that these are the most popular answers even among bright college students.[21]

The correct answers are 5 cents, second place, and Mary, but you knew that, or at least your Reflective System did if you bothered to consult it. Econs never make an important decision without checking with their Reflective Systems (if they have time). But Humans sometimes go with the answer the lizard inside is giving without pausing to think. If you are a television fan, think of Mr. Spock of *Star Trek* fame as someone whose Reflective System is always in control. (Captain Kirk: "You'd make a splendid computer, Mr. Spock." Mr. Spock: "That is very kind of you, Captain!") In contrast, Homer Simpson seems to have forgotten where he put his Reflective System. (Homer once replied to a gun store clerk who informed him of a mandatory five-day waiting period before buying a weapon, "Five days? But I'm mad now!")

One of our major goals in this book is to see how the world might be made easier, or safer, for the Homers among us (and the Homer lurking somewhere in each of us). If people can rely more on their Automatic Systems without getting into terrible trouble, their lives should be easier, better, and longer. Put another way, let's design policies for *Homer economicus*.

So What?

Our goal in this chapter has been to offer a brief glimpse at human fallibility. The picture that emerges is one of busy people trying to cope in a complex world in which they cannot afford to think deeply and at length about every choice they have to make. People adopt sensible rules of thumb that usually work well but sometimes lead them astray, especially in challenging or unfamiliar situations. Because they are busy and have limited attention, they tend to accept questions as posed rather than trying to determine whether their answers would vary under alternative formulations. The bottom line, from our point of view, is that people are, shall we say, nudge-able. Their choices, even in life's most important decisions, are influenced in ways that would not be anticipated in a standard economic framework. Here is one final example to illustrate.

One of the most scenic urban thoroughfares in the world is Chicago's Lake Shore Drive, which hugs the Lake Michigan coastline that is the city's eastern boundary. The drive offers stunning views of Chicago's magnificent skyline. There is one stretch of this road that puts drivers through a series of S curves. These curves are dangerous. For a long time, many drivers failed to take heed of the reduced speed limit (25 mph) and wiped out. In response, the city adopted a distinctive way of encouraging drivers to slow down.

At the beginning of the dangerous curve, drivers encounter a sign painted on the road warning of the lower speed limit, and then a series of white stripes painted onto the road. The stripes do not provide much if any tactile information (they are not speed bumps) but rather just send a visual signal to drivers. When the stripes first appear, they are evenly spaced, but as drivers reach

Figure 1.3. Lake Shore Drive, Chicago (Courtesy of the city of Chicago)

the most dangerous portion of the curve, the stripes get closer together, giving the sensation that driving speed is increasing (see Figure 1.3). One's natural instinct is to slow down. When we drive on this familiar stretch of road, we find that those lines are speaking to us, gently urging us to touch the brake before the apex of the curve. We have been nudged.

2

Resisting Temptation

Back when he was a graduate student, Thaler was hosting dinner for some guests (other then-young economists) and put out a large bowl of cashew nuts to nibble on with drinks. Within a few minutes it became clear that the bowl of nuts was going to be consumed in its entirety and that the guests might lack sufficient appetite to enjoy all the food that was to follow. Leaping into action, Thaler grabbed the bowl of nuts, and (while sneaking a few more nuts for himself) removed it to the kitchen, where it was put out of sight.

When he returned, the guests thanked him for removing the nuts. The conversation immediately turned to the theoretical question of how they could possibly be happy about the fact that there was no longer a bowl of nuts in front of them. (You can now see the wisdom of the rule of thumb mentioned in Chapter 1 about a cap on the proportion of economists among attendees at a dinner party.) In economics (and in ordinary life), a basic principle is that you can never be made worse off by having more options, because you can always turn them down. Before Thaler removed the nuts, the group had the choice of whether to eat the nuts or not—now they didn't. In the land of Econs, it is against the law to be happy about this!

To help us understand this example, consider how the preferences of the group seemed to evolve over time. At 7:15, just before
Thaler removed the nuts, the dinner guests had three options: A:
eat a few nuts; B: eat all the nuts; and C: eat no more nuts. Their
first choice would be to eat just a few more nuts, followed by eating no more nuts. The worst option was finishing the bowl, since
that would ruin dinner. This means that their preferences were
A > C > B. But by 7:30, had the nuts remained on the table, the
group would have finished the bowl, thereby choosing Option B,
which they had ranked last. Why would the group change its
mind in the space of just fifteen minutes? Or do we really even
want to say that the group has changed its mind?

In the language of economics, the group is said to display behavior that is dynamically inconsistent. Initially people prefer Option A to Option B, but they later choose B over A. We can see
dynamic inconsistency in many places. On Saturday morning,
people might say that they prefer to go for a run later in the day,
but once the afternoon comes, they are on the couch at home
watching the football game or binge-watching the entire season of
a new show.

How can such behavior be understood? Two factors are relevant: temptation and mindlessness. Human beings have been
aware of the concept of temptation at least since the time of Adam
and Eve, but for purposes of understanding the value of nudges,
that concept needs elaboration. What does it mean for something
to be "tempting"?

The American Supreme Court justice Potter Stewart famously
said that although he could not define pornography, "I know it
when I see it." Similarly, temptation is easier to recognize than to
define. And temptations are highly personal. Thaler is a sucker for
a good bottle of wine and has trouble resisting just one more
small glass from a special bottle. Sunstein hates the stuff, but

drinks Diet Coke in large quantities. For us the crucial fact about temptation is that people's state of arousal varies over time.

To simplify things, we will consider just the two end points: hot and cold. When Sally is very hungry and appetizing aromas are emanating from the kitchen, we can say she is in a hot state. When she is thinking abstractly on Tuesday about how much food to eat at dinner on Saturday, she is in a cold state. Late Saturday afternoon, the salad she planned to eat for dinner back on Tuesday now seems skimpy and should perhaps be augmented with a pizza. We call something "tempting" if we consume more of it when we are in a hot state. None of this means that decisions made in a cold state are always better. For example, sometimes we have to be in a hot state to overcome our fears about trying new things. Sometimes dessert really is delicious, and we do best to go for it and hit the gym the next day. Sometimes it is best to fall in love. But it is clear that when we are in a hot state, we can often get into a lot of trouble.

Most people realize that temptation exists, and they take steps to overcome it. The classic example is that of Ulysses, who faced the peril of the Sirens and their irresistible song. While in a cold state, Ulysses instructed his crew to fill their ears with wax so that they would not be tempted by the music. He also asked the crew to tie him to the mast so that he could listen for himself but be restrained from submitting to the temptation to steer the ship closer when the music put him into a hot state.

Thaler removing the cashews and Ulysses tying himself to the mast are examples of commitment strategies. (A reminder: Calling this the Final Edition of this book is a commitment strategy. Really.) Such strategies work well if the risk of submitting to temptation can be anticipated, and removing the temptation is feasible. But in many situations we do not correctly forecast a pending self-control problem because we underestimate the effect of arousal. This is something the behavioral economist George Loewenstein calls the "hot-cold empathy gap," a concept that has heavily influenced our thinking on this subject. Loewenstein's key insight is that even if people realize that they behave differently when aroused, they underestimate the strength of the effect. When in a cold state, we do not appreciate the extent to which our desires and our behavior will be altered when we are "under the influence" of arousal. As a result, our behavior reflects a certain naivete about the effects that context can have on choice.

Consider Luke, who is on a diet but agrees to go out for a business dinner, thinking that it will be easy enough to have just one cocktail and no dessert. But then the host orders a bottle of wine and the waiter brings by the dessert cart, and all bets are off. Or Janet, who plans to go into a department store when it is having a big sale and just see whether it has something on sale that she really needs. Janet ends up with shoes that have no obvious use but look good, and they hurt only a bit (but were 70 percent off). Similar problems affect those who have problems with smoking, alcohol, a compulsion to exercise, and shopping as "therapy."

Self-control problems can be illuminated by thinking about an individual as containing two semiautonomous selves: a farsighted "Planner" and a myopic "Doer." You can think of the Planner as speaking for your Reflective System, or the Mr. Spock lurking within you, and the Doer as heavily influenced by the Automatic System, or everyone's Homer Simpson. The Planner is trying to promote your long-term welfare but must cope with the feelings, mischief, and strong will of the Doer, who is exposed to the temptations that come with arousal. Research in neuroeconomics has found evidence consistent with this two-system conception of self-control. Some parts of the brain get tempted, and other parts are prepared to enable us to resist temptation by assessing how we should react to it.[1] Sometimes the two parts of the brain can be in severe conflict—a kind of battle that one or the other is bound to lose. (We are not trying to make controversial claims here about neuroscience; the brain is complicated.)

Self-Control Strategies

Since we are at least partly aware of our weaknesses, we sometimes take steps to engage outside help. We make lists to help us remember what to buy (and not buy) at the grocery store. We buy an alarm clock to help us get up in the morning. We ask friends to stop us from having dessert or to fortify our efforts to quit smoking. We buy cars that have all sorts of nudges, warning us when we are in a dangerous situation. In these cases, our Planners are taking steps to control the actions of our Doers, often by trying to change the incentives that Doers face.

Unfortunately, Doers are often difficult to rein in (think of controlling Homer Simpson), and they can foil the best efforts of Planners. Alarm clocks, even those embedded in our phones, are illuminating examples. The optimistic Planner sets the alarm for 6:15 A.M., hoping for a full day of work, but the sleepy Doer turns off the alarm and goes back to sleep until 9:00. This can lead to fierce battles between the Planner and the Doer. Some Planners put the alarm clock on the other side of the room, so the Doer at least has to get up to turn it off, but if the Doer crawls back into bed, all is lost. Fortunately, enterprising firms sometimes offer to help the Planner out.

Consider the Clocky alarm clock, pictured in Figure 2.1. Clocky is the "alarm clock that runs away and hides if you don't get out of bed." With Clocky, the Planner sets the number of snooze minutes the Doer will be permitted in the morning. When that

PRODUCT

Clocky® (patent pending) is an alarm clock that runs away and
hides if you don't get out of bed on time. The alarm sounds, you
press the snooze, and Clocky will roll off of the bedside table,
jump to the floor, and wheel away, bumping mindlessly into
objects until he finds a spot to rest. When the alarm sounds
again, you must awaken to search for him. Clocky will find new
spots everyday, kind of like a hide-and-seek game.

Clocky alarm clocks were designed to reinterpret the common
alarm clock into something that is not stressful and obnoxious
but amusing and a better fit between humans and technology.

Figure 2.1. Clocky advertisement

number runs out, the clock jumps off the nightstand and dashes
around the room making annoying sounds. The only way to turn
the damn thing off is to get out of bed and find it. By that time,
even a groggy Doer is awake.*

Planners have a number of available strategies to control recal-
citrant Doers, but they can sometimes use some help from outsid-

---

* We discovered Clocky when first writing *Nudge*. At that time Sunstein's
daughter, Ellyn, was in high school, and sometimes had trouble getting up in
time for school. Sunstein thought Clocky would be a great solution, but once
Ellyn realized how it worked, she threw it at her loving father.

ers. We will be exploring how private and public institutions can provide that help. In daily life, one strategy involves informal bets. Many years ago Thaler helped a young colleague by using this strategy. The colleague (let's call him David) had been hired as a new faculty member with the expectation that he would complete the requirements for his Ph.D. before he arrived, or at worst within his first year as a faculty member. David had lots of incentives to finish his thesis, including a strong financial incentive: until he graduated, the university treated him as an instructor rather than an assistant professor and did not make its normal contributions to his retirement plan, which amounted to 10 percent of his salary. David's inner Planner knew that he needed to stop procrastinating and get his thesis done, but his Doer was involved in many other more exciting projects and always put off the drudgery of writing up the thesis. (Thinking about new ideas is usually more fun than writing up old ones.)

That is when Thaler intervened by offering David the following deal. David would write Thaler a series of checks for $100, payable on the first day of each of the next few months. Thaler would cash that month's check if David failed to put a copy of a new chapter of the thesis under Thaler's office door by midnight of the deadline day. Furthermore, Thaler promised to use the money to have a party to which David would not be invited. (One hundred dollars went further back then.) David completed his thesis on schedule four months later, never having missed a deadline (though time stamps revealed that most chapters were printed within minutes of being due). It is instructive that this incentive scheme worked even though David's monetary incentive from the university was greater than $100 a month.

The scheme worked because the pain of having Thaler cash the check and have a party at David's expense was more salient than the rather abstract and pallid forgone contribution to his retirement savings plan. When they heard this story, some of Thaler's colleagues threatened to go into business competing with him on this incentive plan, though Thaler points out that in order to succeed in this business you have to be known as a big enough jerk to cash the check.

Sometimes friends can adopt such betting strategies together. John Romalis and Dean Karlan, two economists, adopted an ingenious arrangement for weight loss. When John and Dean were in graduate school studying economics, they noticed that they were putting on weight, and worried that this would get worse when they were on the job market, when they hoped to be wined and dined by potential employers. They made a pact. Each agreed to lose thirty pounds over a period of nine months. If either failed, he had to pay the other $10,000, which was a lot of money to them. The bet was a big success; both met their target.

They then turned to the more difficult problem of keeping the weight off. The rules they adopted were that on one day's notice, either one could call for a weigh-in. If either was found to be over the target weight, he would have to pay the other an agreed-upon sum. In four years, there were several weigh-ins, and only once was either one over target (the resulting fine was paid in full immediately). Notice that as in the case of David's thesis bet, Dean and John were acknowledging that without the bet to encourage them, they would have eaten too much, even though they still would have wanted to lose the weight. At some point they called off their bet, but Karlan went on to help create a company called Stickk.com that facilitates similar friendly commitments. The company's website reports that it currently has about $50 million in bets on the line and has created more than half a million commitments over the life of the site.

In some situations, people may want the government to help them deal with their self-control problems. Some items such as heroin are banned outright; a possible explanation is that people would be unable to resist the lure of the drugs. There are laws requiring people to buckle their seatbelts, save for retirement, and refrain from texting while driving. Requirements and bans of this kind are pure rather than libertarian paternalism, though third-party interests are often also at stake. When those interests are absent, we prefer a less intrusive role for the government. For example, smokers might benefit from cigarette taxes, which discourage consumption without forbidding it. Interest in taxes based on sugar content can be explained in similar terms; they might combat "internalities," understood as the harms that we inflict on our future selves. Some governments have attempted to help gamblers by creating a mechanism through which they can put themselves on a list of people who are banned from casinos. Since no one is required to sign up, and since a refusal to do so is close to costless, this approach really can be counted as libertarian as we understand the term.

An interesting example of a government-imposed self-control strategy is daylight saving time (or summer time, as it is called in many parts of the world). Surveys reveal that many (though by no means all) people think that daylight saving time is a great idea, primarily because they enjoy the "extra" hour of daylight during summer evenings. Of course, the number of daylight hours on a given day is fixed, and setting the clocks ahead one hour does nothing to increase the amount of daylight. The simple change of the labels on the hours of the day, calling "six o'clock" by the name "seven o'clock," just nudges us into waking up an hour earlier. Along with having more time to enjoy an evening stroll, we end up saving energy, too.

In many cases, markets provide self-control services, and government is not needed at all. Companies such as Stickk.com can make money by helping Planners in their battle with Doers. An interesting example is a distinctive financial services institution that used to be quite popular and that continues to have a small following: the Christmas savings club. Here is how a Christmas club typically works. In November (around Thanksgiving in the United States), a customer opens an account at her local bank and commits herself to depositing a given amount (say $10) each week for the next year. Funds cannot be withdrawn until a year later, when the total amount is redeemed, just in time for the Christmas shopping season. The usual interest rate on these accounts was close to zero even back in the days in which banks actually paid interest on money in savings accounts.

Think about the Christmas club in economic terms. This is an account with no liquidity (you can't take your money out until the end of the year), high transaction costs (you have to make deposits every week), and a near-zero rate of return. It is an easy homework exercise in an economics class to prove that such an institution cannot exist. Yet for many years Christmas clubs were widely used, with billions of dollars in investments, and they remain popular with smaller, local banks, and community-based credit unions.[2]

How come? If we realize that we are dealing with Humans rather than Econs, it is not hard to explain the appeal of such clubs. Households lacking enough money for Christmas giving would commit themselves to solving the problem by joining a Christmas club. The inconvenience of making the deposits and the loss of money paid in interest would be small prices to pay in return for the assurance of having enough money to buy gifts. And think back to Ulysses, tying himself to the mast—the fact that money could not be withdrawn was a plus, not a minus. Christmas clubs are in many ways an adult version of a child's piggy bank, designed to make it easier to put money in than to take money out. The fact that it is hard to withdraw money is entirely the point of the device.

It is hard to find a Christmas club now because they have been made unnecessary for most households by the advent of credit cards.* Since Christmas shopping can now be financed, households no longer find it necessary to save up in advance. This is not to say, of course, that the new regime is in all respects better. Saving at a zero percent interest rate with no opportunity to withdraw the funds may seem dumb, and it is clearly worse than just depositing the money into an interest-bearing account, but earning a zero-interest rate may well be preferable to paying 18 percent or more on credit card debt.

The market battle between credit cards and Christmas clubs is a good illustration of a more general point, one to which we return. Markets provide strong incentives for firms to cater to the demands of consumers, and firms will compete to meet those demands, whether or not those demands represent the wisest choices. One firm might devise a clever self-control device such as a Christmas club, but that firm cannot prevent another firm from offering to lend people money in anticipation of the receipt of those funds. Credit cards and Christmas clubs compete, and indeed both are offered by the same institutions—banks. While competition usually does drive down prices, it does not always lead to an outcome that is best for consumers. Even so, a large number of apps are specifically designed to help people to resist temptation: current examples include Daily Budget, Lose It!, Flipd, and Mute.

---

* Although Christmas clubs have become unpopular, most Americans still make use of a non–interest bearing savings vehicle that might be called the Easter account. Three-quarters of Americans get refunds when they file their tax return, with the average refund being more than $3,000. If these refunds were described as interest-free loans to the government, they would probably not be so popular. Although taxpayers could adjust their withholding rates to reduce the size of their refund, and in principle could earn interest on these funds throughout the year, many prefer to get the refund as a way of being forced to save. When the refund comes, it feels like a windfall.

But even when we're on our way to making good choices, competitive markets find ways to get us to overcome our last shred of resistance to bad ones. At O'Hare Airport in Chicago, two food vendors compete across the aisle from each other. One sells fruit, yogurt, and other healthy foods. The other sells Cinnabons, tempting cinnamon buns that have a whopping 880 calories and 37 grams of fat. Your Planner may have set the course for the yogurt and fruit stand, but the Cinnabon outlet intentionally blasts the aromas from their ovens directly into the walkway in front of the store. Care to guess which of the two stores always has the longer line?

Mental Accounting

Alarm clocks and Christmas clubs are external devices people use to solve their self-control problems. Another way to approach these problems is to adopt internal control systems, otherwise known as *mental accounting*. Mental accounting is the system (sometimes implicit) that households use to evaluate, regulate, and process their home budget. Almost all of us use mental accounts, even if we're not aware that we're doing so.

The concept is beautifully illustrated by an exchange between the actors Gene Hackman and Dustin Hoffman that you can find online.[3] Hackman and Hoffman were friends back in their starving artist days, and Hackman tells the story of visiting Hoffman's apartment and having his host ask him for a loan. Hackman agreed to the loan, but then they went into Hoffman's kitchen, where several mason jars were lined up on the counter, some stuffed with money. One jar was labeled "rent," another "entertainment," and so forth. Hackman asked why, if Hoffman had so much money in jars, he would possibly need a loan, whereupon Hoffman pointed to the food jar, which was empty.*

According to economic theory (and simple logic), money is *fungible*, meaning that it doesn't come with labels. Twenty dollars in the rent jar can buy just as much food as the same amount in the food jar. But households adopt mental accounting schemes that violate fungibility for the same reasons that organizations do: to control spending. Most organizations have budgets for various activities, and anyone who has ever worked in such an organization has experienced the frustration of not being able to make an important purchase because the relevant account is already depleted. The fact that there is unspent money in another account is considered no more relevant than the money sitting in the rent jar on Dustin Hoffman's kitchen counter.

At the household level, violations of fungibility are everywhere. One of the most creative examples of mental accounting was invented by a finance professor we know. At the beginning of each year, he designated a certain amount of money as his intended gift to a local charity called United Way. Then if anything bad happened to him during the year—a speeding ticket, for example—he mentally deducted the fine against the United Way gift. This provided him with a form of "mental insurance" against minor financial mishaps.†

You can also see mental accounting in action at the casino. Watch a gambler who is lucky enough to win some money early in the evening. You might see him take the money he has won and put it into one pocket and put the money he brought with him to gamble that evening (yet another mental account) into a different

---

* Here is the URL for this clip: https://youtu.be/t96LNX6tkoU.

† You might think this deprives the United Way of money, but not so. The professor has an incentive to make sure his intended gift is large enough to cover all his mishaps.

pocket. Gamblers even have a term for this. The money that has recently been won is called "house money" because in gambling parlance the casino is referred to as the house. Betting some of the money that you have just won is referred to as "gambling with the house's money," as if it were somehow different from some other kind of money. Experimental evidence reveals that people are more willing to gamble with money that they consider house money.[4]

This same mentality affects people who never gamble. When investments (say, in the stock market) pay off, people are willing to take big chances with their "winnings." For example, mental accounting contributed to the large increase in stock prices in the 1990s, as many people took on more and more risk with the justification that they were playing only with their gains from the past few years. The same thing happened with speculative real estate investors a few years later. Similarly, people are far more likely to splurge impulsively on a big luxury purchase when they receive an unexpected windfall than they are with savings that they have accumulated over time, even if those savings are fully available to be spent.

Mental accounting matters precisely because the accounts are treated as nonfungible. True, the mason jars used by Dustin Hoffman (and his parents' generation) have largely disappeared in modern economies (though they remain in some poor countries). But many households continue to designate accounts for various uses: children's education, vacations, rainy day, retirement, and so forth. In many cases, these are literally different accounts, as opposed to entries in a mental ledger. The sanctity of these accounts can lead to seemingly bizarre behavior, such as simultaneously borrowing and lending at very different rates. We discuss these issues further in Chapter 11.

Of course, many people do not suffer from an inability to save.

Some people actually have trouble spending! If their problem is extreme, we call such people misers, but even regular folks can find that they don't give themselves enough treats in life. We have a friend named Dennis who adopted a clever mental accounting strategy to deal with this problem. At some point Dennis started collecting Social Security payments, although both he and his wife were still working full-time. Since he had been a good saver over the years (in part because his employer has a mandatory and generous retirement plan), Dennis wanted to be sure he would do the things he enjoys (especially trips to Paris with lots of fine dining) while he was still healthy and not be put off by the expense. So he opened a special savings account into which his Social Security checks were directly deposited. He designated this to be a "fun account." We hear that a spiffy electric bike was the latest purchase from that account.

For each of us, using mental accounts can be extremely valuable. They make life both more pleasurable and more secure. Many of us could benefit from both a near sacrosanct "rainy day" account for emergencies and an "entertainment and fun" account. Understanding mental accounts would also improve public policy. Governments can benefit from understanding the concept of mental accounting. As we will see, if we want to encourage savings, it will be important to direct the increased savings into a mental (or real) account where spending it will not be too big a temptation.

3

Following the Herd

Econs (and some economists we know) are pretty unsociable creatures. They communicate with others only if they can gain something from the encounter, they care about their reputations (because a good reputation is valuable), and they will learn from others if actual information can be obtained, but Econs are not followers of fashion. Their hemlines do not go up and down except for practical reasons, they do not wear ties, and if they did they would not grow narrower and wider simply as a matter of style. (By the way, ties were originally used as napkins; they actually had a function.) Humans, on the other hand, are often influenced by other Humans, even when they shouldn't be.

Sometimes massive social changes, in markets and politics alike, start with a small and even serendipitous social nudge. A prominent person might state an opinion or engage in an action, which gives a kind of signal, a green light or a permission slip, to others, who do the same. Or the opinion or action might come from someone who is not so prominent, but who is committed and who manages to come to the public's attention, and who ends up turning a business or even a culture around. The issue might involve a product, a book, an idea, a political candidate, or a cause.

And occasionally, a trickle becomes a flood, especially when social media is involved.

In this chapter, we try to understand how and why social influences work. An understanding of those influences is important to choice architects for two reasons. First, most people learn from others. This is usually good, of course. Learning from others is how individuals and societies develop. But many of our biggest misconceptions also come from others. The problem is that what we learn from such interactions may not actually be true. When social influences have caused people to have false or biased beliefs, then some nudging may help. A second reason this topic is important for our purposes is that one of the most effective ways to nudge (for good or evil) is via social influence.

In 2020, in the places where we were living during the spring and summer (Northern California and Boston), most people chose to wear masks in public places in response to the COVID-19 pandemic—but in other places in the United States, many people (including prominent political leaders) made a point of *not* wearing masks. Social influences both promoted and discouraged mask wearing. A point worth remembering: Telling people that *a new norm is emerging*—say, in the domain of sustainability—can create a self-fulfilling prophecy.[1] Many do not want to be on the wrong side of history, and if they learn that people are increasingly doing something, they might think that what seemed difficult or even impossible is achievable, maybe even inevitable.

Social influences come in two basic categories. The first involves information. If many people do something or think something, their actions and their thoughts convey information about what is best for you to do or think. If people are picking up after their dogs, buckling their seatbelts, driving under the speed limit, saving for retirement, treating people equally, or wearing masks, you might think that is the right thing to do. The second involves peer pressure. If you care about what other people think about you (perhaps in the mistaken belief that they are paying some attention to what you are doing—see below), then you might go along with the crowd to avoid their wrath or curry their favor. In some places during the COVID-19 pandemic, you'd get a cold stare or worse, if you weren't wearing a mask in a public place—and in some places, you'd get a cold stare or worse if you were wearing a mask.

For a quick preview of the power of social nudges, consider just a few research findings:

1. Teenage girls who see that other teenagers are having children are more likely to become pregnant themselves.[*2]

2. Employees are far more likely to file suit against their employers if members of the same work group have also done so.[3]

3. Broadcasters mimic one another, producing otherwise inexplicable fads in programming.[4] (Think reality television, game shows, singing and dancing contests that come and go, the rise and fall and rise of science fiction, and so forth.)

4. The academic effort of college students is influenced by their peers, so much so that the random assignments of first-year students to dormitories or roommates can have big consequences for their grades and hence on their future prospects.[5] (Maybe parents should worry less about which college their kids go to and more about which roommate they get.)

---

* For this and all the other examples in this list, we leave out the implied phrase "holding everything else constant." So, what we mean here is that controlling for other risk factors that predict teenage pregnancy, girls are more likely to get pregnant if they see other girls doing so.

5. In the American judicial system, federal judges on three-
    judge panels are affected by the votes of their colleagues.
    The typical Republican appointee shows pretty liberal voting
    patterns when sitting with two Democratic appointees, and
    the typical Democratic appointee shows pretty conservative
    voting patterns when sitting with two Republican appoin-
    tees. Both sets of appointees show far more moderate voting
    patterns when they are sitting with at least one judge ap-
    pointed by a president of the opposing political party.[6]

The bottom line is that Humans are easily nudged by other Humans. Why? One reason is that we like to conform.

Doing What Others Do

Imagine that you find yourself in a group of six people, engaged in
a test of visual perception. You are given a ridiculously simple
task. You are supposed to compare a line, shown on a large white
card, to three other lines and match it to the one that is identical
in length.

In the first three rounds of this test, everything proceeds
smoothly and easily. People make their matches aloud, in se-
quence, and everyone agrees with everyone else. The task is not
hard. But on the fourth round, something odd happens. The five
other people in the group announce their matches before you—
and each one makes an obvious error. They choose the wrong
line! It is now time for you to make your announcement. What
will you do?

If you are like most people, you think it is easy to predict your
behavior in this task: You will say exactly what you think. You'll

call it as you see it. You are independent-minded, and so you will tell the truth. But if you are a Human, and you really participated in the experiment, you might well follow those who preceded you and say what they said, thus defying the evidence of your own senses.

In the 1950s, Solomon Asch, a brilliant social psychologist, conducted a series of experiments in just this vein.[7] When asked to decide on their own, without seeing judgments from others, people almost never erred, since the task was easy. But when everyone else gave an incorrect answer, people erred more than one-third of the time. Indeed, in a series of twelve questions, nearly three-quarters of people erroneously went along with the group at least once, defying the evidence of their own senses. Notice that in Asch's experiment, people were responding to the decisions of strangers, whom they would probably never see again. They had no particular reason to want those strangers to like them.

Asch's findings seem to capture something universal about humanity. Conformity experiments have been replicated and extended in more than 130 studies from seventeen countries, including Zaire (now known as Democratic Republic of the Congo), Germany, France, Japan, Lebanon, and Kuwait.[8] The overall pattern of errors—with people conforming to a clearly mistaken judgment between 20 and 40 percent of the time—does show intriguing differences across nations, but in every nation, the level of conformity is pretty high. And though 20 to 40 percent of the time might not seem large, remember that in this task the correct answer was obvious. It is almost as if people can be nudged into identifying a picture of a dog as a cat as long as other people before them have done so.

Why, exactly, do people sometimes ignore the evidence of their own senses? We have already sketched out the two main answers. The first involves the information that seems to be conveyed by other people's answers; the second involves peer pressure and the desire not to face the disapproval of the group. In Asch's own studies, several of the conformists said, in private interviews, that their initial perceptions must have been wrong. If everyone in the room accepts a certain proposition, or sees things in a certain way, you might conclude that they are probably right. Remarkably, brain-imaging work has suggested that when people conform in Asch-like settings, they actually *see* the situation as everyone else does.[9]

On the other hand, social scientists have found less conformity, in the same basic circumstances as Asch's experiments, when people are asked to give anonymous answers. People become more likely to conform when they know that others will see what they have to say. Sometimes people will go along with the group even when they think, or know, that everyone else has blundered. Unanimous groups are able to provide the strongest nudges— even when the question is an easy one and people ought to know that everyone else is wrong.[10]

Asch's experiments involved evaluations with pretty obvious answers. Most of the time, it isn't hard to assess the length of lines. What if the task is made a bit more difficult? The question is especially important for our purposes, because we are particularly interested in how people are influenced, or can be influenced, in dealing with problems that are both hard and unfamiliar. Some key studies were undertaken back in the 1930s by the psychologist Muzafer Sherif.[11] In Sherif's experiments, people were placed in a dark room, and a small pinpoint of light was positioned at some distance in front of them. The light was actually stationary, but because of a perceptual illusion called the autokinetic effect, it appeared to move. On each of several trials, Sherif asked people to estimate the distance that the light had moved. When polled individually, subjects did not agree with one another, and their answers varied significantly from one trial to another. This is not surprising; because the light did not move, any judgment about distance was a stab in the literal dark.

But Sherif found big conformity effects when people were asked to act in small groups and to make their estimates in public. Here the individual judgments converged and a group norm, establishing the consensus distance, quickly developed. Over time, the norm remained stable within particular groups, thus leading to a situation in which different groups made, and were strongly committed to, quite different judgments. There is an important clue here about how seemingly similar groups, cities, and even nations can converge on very different beliefs and actions simply because of modest and even arbitrary variations in starting points.

Sherif also tried a nudge. In some experiments, he added a confederate—his own ally, unbeknownst to the people in the study. When he did that, something else happened. If the confederate spoke confidently and firmly, his judgment had a strong influence on the group's assessment. If the confederate's estimate was much higher than those initially made by others, the group's judgment would be inflated; if the confederate's estimate was very low, the group's estimate would fall. A little nudge, if it was expressed with confidence, could have major consequences for the group's conclusion. Decades after Sherif's work, social scientists uncovered the confidence heuristic: people tend to think that confident speakers must be correct. The clear lesson here is that consistent and unwavering people, in the private or public sector, can move groups and practices in their preferred direction. An important implication is that if senior members of a group want to obtain the actual beliefs of their junior coworkers, they will ask for those beliefs independently (so coworkers don't influence each other) and, most important, before they state their own opinion.

More remarkably still, the group's judgments became thoroughly internalized, so that people would adhere to them even when reporting on their own—indeed even a year later, and even when participating in new groups whose members offered different judgments. Significantly, the initial judgments were also found to have effects across the laboratory equivalent of "generations." Even when enough fresh subjects were introduced and others retired so that all the participants were new to the situation, the original group judgment tended to stick, although the person who was originally responsible for it was long gone.[12] In a series of experiments, people using Sherif's basic method have shown that an arbitrary "tradition," in the form of some judgment about the distance, can become entrenched over time, which means that many people end up following it notwithstanding its original arbitrariness.[13]

We can see here why many traditions are robust over decades or centuries, even if they really are arbitrary, in the sense that they make no sense and serve no purpose. We can also see why many groups fall prey to what is known as "collective conservatism": the tendency of groups to stick to established patterns even as new needs arise. Once a practice (like wearing ties) has become established, it can be perpetuated, even if there is no reason for it. To be sure, many traditions persist because they help the people who live by them. But sometimes a tradition can last for a long time, and receive support or at least acquiescence from large numbers of people, even though it was originally the product of a small nudge from a few people or perhaps even one. Of course, a group might shift if it can be shown that the practice is causing serious problems. But if there is uncertainty on that question, people might well continue doing what they have always done. "It's a tradition!"

Many experiments, growing out of Asch's basic method, find large conformity effects for judgments of many different kinds.[14] Consider the following finding. People were asked, "Which one of the following do you feel is the most important problem facing our country today?" Five alternatives were offered: economic recession, educational facilities, subversive activities, mental health, and crime and corruption. Asked privately, a mere 12 percent chose subversive activities. But when exposed to a group that unanimously selected that option, 48 percent of people made the same choice![15]

In a similar finding, people were asked to consider this statement: "Free speech being a privilege rather than a right, it is proper for a society to suspend free speech when it feels threatened." Asked this question individually, only 19 percent of the control group agreed, but confronted with the shared opinion of only four others, 58 percent of people agreed. These results are closely connected with one of Asch's underlying interests, which was to understand how Nazism had been possible. Asch believed that conformity could produce a very strong nudge, ultimately generating behavior (such as that which led to the Holocaust) that might seem (and still seems) unthinkable.

Whether or not Asch's work provides an adequate account of the rise of fascism, or any other surprising movement, there is no question that social pressures nudge people to accept some pretty odd conclusions—and those conclusions might well affect their behavior. An obvious question is whether choice architects can use this fact to move people in better directions. We now turn to that question.

Cultural Change, Political Change, and Unpredictability

Do you ever wonder how some performer, dance, or catchphrase suddenly becomes popular? Often it is a powerful combination of random chance and social influence. This is illustrated by a brilliant experiment involving music downloads conducted by Matthew Salganik, Peter Dodds, and Duncan Watts. For their study, the researchers created an artificial music market, involving thousands of participants who were visitors to a website popular with young people.[16] The participants were given a long list of previously unknown songs from obscure bands. They were each asked to listen to any songs that interested them and to decide which songs (if any) to download. About half of the participants were asked to make their decisions independently, based on the names of the bands, the titles of the songs, and their own judgment about the quality of the music. The other half could see how many times each song had been downloaded by other participants. The key question was whether that information would affect people's decision to download.

Each participant in this second group was also randomly assigned to one of eight possible "worlds," each of which evolved on its own; those in any particular world could see only the downloads of those in their own world. You might predict that in the end, social influences would not really matter, and that quality (as measured by the choices of those in the control group) would win out. Salganik and his colleagues asked these questions: Would people be affected by the choices of others? Would different songs become popular in the different worlds? Would people be nudged by what other people did?

There is not the slightest doubt. In all eight worlds, individuals were far more likely to download songs that had been previously downloaded in significant numbers, and far less likely to download songs that had not been as popular. For that reason, initial popularity greatly mattered; it could make all the difference between success and failure. While the least popular songs in the control group never went to the top, and while the most popular songs never fell to the bottom, *almost anything else could happen.*

The songs that did well or poorly in the control group, where people did not see other people's judgments, could perform very differently in the "social influence worlds." In those worlds, the ultimate success or failure of songs depended strongly on whether they attracted initial popularity. The identical song could be a hit or a failure simply because of the judgments of the people who heard it early in the process. For that reason, the success of songs was quite unpredictable and varied considerably across worlds.

What Salganik and his coauthors found was an "informational cascade," which occurs when people receive information from the choices of others. Suppose that there is a group of eight people, deciding whom to hire for a new position in a small business. The three candidates are Adam, Barbara, and Charles. If the first speaker says that Adam is clearly best, the second might agree, not because she prefers Adam, but because she trusts the first speaker and it is not clear that he is wrong. Once the first two speakers have spoken in favor of Adam, they have created a strong nudge on his behalf, and the third speaker might simply go along. The fourth speaker, and those who follow, might agree too, at least if they do not feel strongly; they are in a cascade. The popularity of music (and movies, and books) is often a result of this sort of cascade effect. Of course, informational cascades can be accompanied by "reputational cascades," in which people go along with others not because they have learned from them, but because they do not want to incur their wrath or disapproval.

The music downloads experiment has implications for unpredictable change in many other domains, including business and politics. Building directly on that experiment, sociologist Michael Macy of Cornell University and his collaborators asked whether the visible views of other people could suddenly make particular political positions popular among Democrats and unpopular among Republicans—or vice versa.[17]

Here's how the experiment worked. All participants (consist-ing of thousands of people) were initially asked whether they identified with Republicans or Democrats. They were then di-vided into ten groups: two "independence" groups and eight "in-fluence" groups. In the independence groups, participants were asked what they thought about twenty separate issues—without receiving any information about how members of either political party stood on those issues. In the eight influence groups, partici-pants could see whether Republicans or Democrats were more likely to agree with some political claim. The authors carefully se-lected issues for which it would not be obvious which side parties would favor. For example: "Companies should be taxed in the countries where they are headquartered rather than in the coun-tries where their revenues are generated."

The authors hypothesized that in the influence condition, it would be especially hard to predict where Republicans and Dem-ocrats would end up. If the early Republican participants in one group ended up endorsing a position, other Republicans would be more likely to endorse it as well—and Democrats would be more likely to reject it. But if the early Republicans rejected it, other Re-publicans would reject it as well—and Democrats would endorse it. That's exactly what happened! Across groups, Democrats and Republicans often flipped positions, depending on what the early voters did. As the researchers put it, "Chance variation in a small number of early movers" can have major effects in tipping large populations—and in getting both Republicans and Democrats to embrace a cluster of views that actually have nothing to do with each other. These findings help explain how members of both parties flip over short periods of time, and also how issues sud-denly, and surprisingly, become polarizing across political lines.

In many domains people are tempted to think, after the fact, that the success of a musician, actor, author, or politician was inevitable in light of his or her skills and characteristics. Beware of that temptation. Small interventions and even coincidences, at a key stage, can produce large variations in the outcome. Today's hot singer is probably indistinguishable from dozens and even hundreds of equally talented performers whose names you've never heard. We can go further. Most of today's political leaders are hard to distinguish from dozens or even hundreds of others whose candidacies badly fizzled. Much the same can be said for professors and for companies and products of all kinds. Social influences matter, and so does luck.

The effects of social influences may or may not be deliberately planned by particular people. For a vivid and somewhat hilarious example of how social influences can affect beliefs even if no one plans anything, consider the Seattle Windshield Pitting Epidemic.[18] In late March 1954, a group of people in Bellingham, Washington, noticed some tiny holes, or pits, on their windshields. Local police speculated that the pits had resulted from the actions of vandals, using BBs or buckshot. Soon thereafter, a few people in cities south of Bellingham reported similar damage to their windshields. Within two weeks, the apparent work of vandals had gone even farther south, to the point where two thousand cars were reported as damaged—these evidently not the work of vandals. The threat appeared to be approaching Seattle. The Seattle newspapers duly reported the risk in mid-April, and soon thereafter, several reports of windshield pits came to the attention of local police.

Before long, those reports reached epic proportions, leading to intense speculation about what on earth, or elsewhere, could possibly be the cause. Geiger counters found no radioactivity. Some people thought that an odd atmospheric event must have been responsible; others invoked sound waves and a possible shift in the earth's magnetic field; still others pointed to cosmic rays from the sun. By April 16 no fewer than three thousand windshields in the Seattle area were reported to have been pitted, and Seattle's mayor promptly wrote to the governor as well as President Dwight Eisenhower: "What appeared to be a localized outbreak of vandalism in damaged auto windshields and windows in the northern part of Washington State has now spread throughout the Puget Sound area. . . . Urge appropriate federal (and state) agencies be instructed to cooperate with local authorities on emergency basis." In response, the governor created a committee of scientists to investigate this ominous and startling phenomenon.

Their conclusion? The damage, such as it was, was probably "the result of normal driving conditions in which small objects strike the windshields of cars." A later investigation, supporting the scientists' conclusion, found that brand-new cars lacked pits. The eventual judgment was that the pits "had been there all along, but no one had noticed them until now." (You might have a look at your car right now; if you've had it for a while, there's probably a pit or two, or more. It's not the work of space aliens.)

Here's a less dated example of social influences. In 2012, authorities in Colombia introduced a school-based immunization program to deal with HPV (sometimes called genital warts), with the effect of reaching about 90 percent of the relevant population in its initial year. So far, so good. But in 2014, several adolescent girls in one school seemed to have adverse reactions to the vaccine, and they were admitted to a local hospital. Soon thereafter, videos of adolescent girls with all sorts of symptoms—twitching, fainting, falling unconscious—appeared on social media platforms and in national newspapers. About six hundred cases were reported. The health authorities found that the HPV vaccine was not responsible and that what had happened was a mass psychogenic reaction. This finding did not alleviate public concerns. Fear spread rapidly through relevant communities, and by 2016, HPV vaccine uptake among eligible girls fell to 14 percent for the first dose and 5 percent for the complete course, where the corresponding numbers had been 98 percent and 88 percent in 2012.[19]

The Seattle Windshield Pitting Epidemic and the Colombia psychogenic reactions are extreme examples of unintentional social nudging, but every day we are influenced by people who are not trying to influence us. Most of us are affected by the eating habits of our dining companions, whatever their intentions. If you find yourself nudged by your friends' dietary choices, it is unlikely to be because your friends decided to nudge you. More likely you just thought, Oh, that looks good. Nevertheless, social influences are often used strategically. In particular, advertisers are entirely aware of the power of those influences. Frequently they emphasize that "most people prefer" their own product, or that "more and more people" are switching from another brand, which was yesterday's news, to their own, which represents the future. They try to nudge you by telling you what most people are now doing, or what people are increasingly doing.

In many nations, candidates for public office, or political parties, do the same thing: they emphasize that "most people are turning to" their preferred candidates, hoping that the very statement can make itself true. Nothing is better than a perception that voters are shifting to a candidate in droves. In the United States, a perception of that kind helped to account for the election of Barack Obama in 2008, for that of Donald Trump in 2016, and for his defeat at the hands of Joe Biden in 2020. When voters flock to one candidate or another, they are each making what they believe to be an independent judgment on the successful candidate's behalf. Maybe they were, but maybe not; their judgment might be strongly driven by the widespread perception that other people are flocking to that candidate.

Identity: What People Like You Do

Of course, it is important to recognize that people's identity, or their self-understanding, can greatly matter. If people in one part of the world are told that people in another part of the world are recycling, becoming vegetarians, or wearing masks, they could think: "Oh, I should do that too!" But they might also react this way: "Well, thank goodness I'm not like those people!" For choice architects who want to use social influences, a challenge is to work with, rather than against, people's sense of who they are. That sense might have to do with nationality, culture, region, ethnicity, religion, politics, or a favorite team. We might even give it a name: identity-based cognition.

Consider Texas's now classic and stunningly successful effort to reduce littering on its highways. State officials were frustrated with the failure of their well-funded and highly publicized advertising campaigns, which attempted to convince people that it was their civic duty to stop littering. Many of the litterers were men between the ages of eighteen and twenty-four, who were not exactly impressed by the idea that a bureaucratic elite wanted them to change their behavior. Public officials decided that they needed "a tough-talking slogan that would also address the unique spirit of Texas pride." Explicitly targeting the unresponsive audience, the state enlisted popular Dallas Cowboys football players to participate in television ads in which they collected litter, smashed beer cans in their bare hands, and growled, "Don't mess with Texas!" Other spots included popular singers, such as Willie Nelson.

People can now get all kinds of "Don't Mess with Texas" products, from decals to shirts to coffee mugs. One popular decal offers patriotic colors, reflecting both the U.S. flag and—perhaps more important—the Texas flag!

The overwhelming majority of Texans now know this slogan. At one point, "Don't Mess with Texas" was voted America's favorite slogan by a landslide and was honored with a parade down New York City's Madison Avenue. (We are not making this up. Only in America, to be sure.) More to the point: Within the first year of the campaign, litter in the state had been reduced by a remarkable 29 percent. In its first six years, there was a 72 percent reduction in visible roadside litter.[20] All this happened without the use of any mandates, threats, or coercion but rather via a creative nudge.

In one or another way, many governments have enlisted identity-based cognition and thus used a broadly similar approach. A public health initiative in India, designed to increase use of toilets, has emphasized Mahatma Gandhi's commitment to cleanliness and so appealed directly to national pride. To encourage citizens

Figure 3.1. Don't Mess with Texas logo (Used with permission of Don't Mess with Texas, Texas Department of Transportation)

of Montana to wear face masks, Governor Steve Bullock launched a campaign with pictures of Montanans fishing, skiing, and bow-hunting, with the caption MONTANANS WEAR FACE COVERINGS ALL THE TIME. We need evidence, of course, to know when and how well such appeals work. But if nudges use social influences and social norms, they are most likely to be promising if people are asked to learn from and act like people who are like them—and whom they trust.

Pluralistic Ignorance

For those who want to enlist social influences, an important challenge, as well as a real opportunity, is *pluralistic ignorance*—that is, ignorance, on the part of all or most, about what other people think. We may follow a practice or a tradition not because we like it or even think it defensible, but merely because we think that most other people like it. Many social practices persist for this reason, which means a small shock, or nudge, can dislodge them.[21] A dramatic example is Communism in the former Soviet bloc, which lasted in part because people were unaware of how large a share of the population despised the regime. As people became aware of what others actually thought, they were emboldened to say what they believed, and to act accordingly.

There is a clue here to understanding how large-scale social change comes about. Often people are authorized or nudged to speak and act in accordance with their actual views. Think of the wonderful Hans Christian Andersen story "The Emperor's New Clothes." The nudge is emphatically social; it often turns out to be a kind of permission slip. If a child says out loud that the emperor is naked, the people in a crowd might suddenly feel licensed to say so too. Dramatic changes, rejecting long-standing practices, are often produced by a nudge that starts a kind of cascade or band-wagon effect, because it gives people a sense of what others actually think, and thus authorizes them to say what they actually think too. Consider, for example, the rise of gay marriage, #MeToo, and #BlackLivesMatter. All of these movements were fueled by visible actions, including vigorous social media campaigns, that permitted or encouraged people to reveal long-silenced anger and outrage. People who had shut themselves up, or suffered or grieved or raged in silence, suddenly saw a kind of green light.

A vivid example comes from an experiment in Saudi Arabia. In that country, there has long been a custom of "guardianship," by which husbands are allowed to have the final word on whether their wives work outside the home. Asking a large group of young married men in private whether they are in favor of female labor force participation, economist Leonardo Bursztyn and his colleagues learned that the overwhelming majority answer yes.[22] At the same time, they found that those men are profoundly mistaken about the social norm; they wrongly think that other, similar men, even those in their local community, do not want their wives to join the labor force.

Bursztyn and his colleagues randomly corrected the beliefs of half of those young men about what other young men believed. As a result, they became far more willing to authorize their wives to work (recall the custom of guardianship)—and there was a significant impact on what women actually did. Four months after the intervention, the wives of men in the experiment who had received the information about others' beliefs were more likely to have applied and interviewed for a job. Here's the broader lesson: if people wrongly think that most people are committed to a long-standing social norm, a small nudge correcting that misperception can inaugurate large-scale change.

Social Norms as Nudges

The general lesson from this line of research is clear. If choice architects want to shift behavior and to do so with a nudge, they might be able to achieve this by simply informing people about what others are thinking and doing. Sometimes the thoughts and practices of others are surprising, and hence people are much affected by learning what they are. A voluminous body of research finds that informing people about the social norm can be extremely effective. Here as elsewhere, there is no substitute for actually testing hypotheses. Populations are not all alike. (Some nudge units have a good slogan: "Test, test, test.") But consider just a few examples.

In the context of tax compliance, an experiment conducted by officials in Minnesota produced big changes in behavior.[23] Groups of taxpayers were given four kinds of information. Some were told that their taxes went to various good works, including education, police protection, and fire protection. Others were threatened with information about the risks of punishment for noncompliance. Others were given information about how they might get help if they were confused or uncertain about how to fill out their tax forms. Still others were just told that more than 90 percent of Minnesotans already complied in full with their obligations under the tax law.

Only one of these interventions had a significant effect on tax compliance, and it was the last. Apparently, some taxpayers are more likely to violate the law because of a misperception—plausibly based on the availability of media or other accounts of cheaters—that the level of compliance is pretty low. When informed that the actual compliance level is high, they become less likely to cheat. It follows that either desirable or undesirable

behavior can often be increased, at least to some extent, by drawing public attention to what others are doing. (Note to political
parties: If you would like to increase turnout, please do not la-
ment the large numbers of people who fail to vote. But do tell
people that many of their neighbors vote!)

Using this strategy can save the government a lot of money, as
illustrated by one of the first experiments conducted by the UK's
Behavioural Insights Team. The goal of the experiment was to see
whether taxpayers who owed money could be nudged to pay off
their debts more quickly. The results were analyzed by team member Michael Hallsworth in collaboration with three academic economists. The subjects (who did not know they were part of an
experiment) were taxpayers, such as business owners, who had income that was not subject to the withholding tax and had not paid
in full. Several different letters were tried and compared to a control letter just reminding people of how much money they owed.

The winning formulation was to say, "Nine out of ten people in
the UK pay their tax on time. You are currently in the very small
minority of people who have not paid us yet." Notice this short
message conveys (truthfully) both that most people pay on time
and that you are in the minority of those who don't. A follow-up
experiment found that the message could be further strengthened
by making it local, as in "Nine out of ten taxpayers in Manchester
pay on time." The impact of these letters was substantial, increasing the number of people paying within the first twenty-three
days by as much as five percentage points.[24] That may not sound
like a large effect, but as with many such interventions, the costs
are negligible. The government was already sending reminder letters, so why not nudge people at the same time?

Indeed, it turns out that regardless of the context, *whose* norm
people are being asked to follow matters. Celebrities and so-called
influencers might believe that they are best positioned to inspire

regular people like us to change our ways. But in fact, people seem simply to respond best to norms set by others in similar settings and circumstances. A 2008 study determined how best to nudge hotel-goers to reuse their towels.[25] You've probably already guessed that asking guests to save the environment by reusing their towels wasn't as effective as a message communicating a social norm: "Join your fellow guests in helping to save the environment. Almost 75 percent of guests . . . help by using their towels more than once."

The "guests" part turned out to be key. The researchers also tested messages highlighting reuse rates of people matching different aspects of the guest's identity (for example, gender), as well as the behavior of people who had stayed in the same room. Although participants reported that other identities were more important to them, their behavior was ultimately influenced most by people who had stayed in the same room! The researchers called such specific in-grouping "provincial norms." As any adolescent will tell you, peer pressure is real.

With respect to both public opinion and law, much of the world witnessed a cascade on an issue that motivated a whole chapter of the original edition of this book: same-sex marriage. When that edition was published in 2008, many nations, including ours, were badly torn on the issue. Lots of people felt strongly that same-sex marriage should be allowed and recognized; indeed, they thought this was quite obvious. In the United States, interracial marriage had once been illegal in many states, but in 1967 such laws were declared unconstitutional. Supporters of same-sex marriage believed that the same arguments should apply in this case. Yet others felt equally strongly that same-sex marriage was abhorrent. It is noteworthy that in 2008, the official position of Barack Obama, a left-of-center mixed-race presidential candidate committed to civil rights and equality for all, was that marriage is between a man and a woman. We thought that we had discovered a solution, very much in the spirit of libertarian paternalism: privatize marriage.

We argued that governments should get out of the business of defining marriage as a legal category. Instead, we suggested, they should simply regulate legal domestic partnerships just as they do business partnerships. In the United States, such partnerships are called civil unions. At the time, many governments (states and countries) did allow same-sex couples to get civil unions, but such couples justifiably felt that they were being discriminated against, since only opposite-sex couples were eligible for *marriage*, a term that bestowed both legal and social status. (In the United States, civil partners also did not qualify for many legal rights, including tax benefits bestowed upon spouses.) In our proposed regime, all such legal provisions would be defined by the status granted by governments, but marriages would be purely private affairs, conducted by religious groups or others according to whatever rules they wished to use. Marriage, as such, would not be an official category defined by the government. We hoped this approach would soften an intense disagreement: if the government got out of the marriage business, the whole area would become less contested.

We actually still like that idea, but twelve years of history has rendered it largely moot. Much to our (pleasant) surprise, over that period, many nations took a different and much simpler approach. They would just allow and recognize same-sex marriage! In the United States, which was our particular focus, this happened exceptionally quickly. In 2012, President Barack Obama said that he had changed his mind, announcing that "same-sex couples should be able to get married."[26] In 2015, the Supreme Court of the United States ruled that under the U.S. Constitution, same-sex couples have a right to get married.[27] To the surprise of many people (in-

cluding us), the court's decision did not produce much of a backlash. In every state of the union, same-sex marriage is now legal.

Around the world, there has been an uncommonly rapid movement toward the same conclusion. As of 2021, same-sex marriages
were recognized in about thirty countries. They include Argentina
(2010), Australia (2017), Austria (2019), Brazil (2013), Canada (2005),
Denmark (2012), England and Wales (2013), Finland (2015), France
(2013), Germany (2017), Iceland (2010), Ireland (2015), Mexico
(2009), the Netherlands (2000), New Zealand (2013), Norway
(2008), Portugal (2010), South Africa (2006), Spain (2005), and
Sweden (2009).[28]

Linger over those dates, if you would. Every nation on the list
had long refused to recognize same-sex marriages; for generations, most of their citizens would have ridiculed or abhorred the
idea. Yet in a short period, all of them came to treat same-sex
couples the same as opposite-sex couples, and generally did so
without a lot of controversy. How did that happen? Why did so
many people (including us) fail to anticipate it?

A full answer would take a book of its own. But we already
have two major clues. First, many gays and lesbians who had not
disclosed their sexual orientation, and who had never sought even
to ask for same-sex marriage, came out of the closet. Every time
someone shared, "I am gay," or "I am a lesbian," or "I am bisex-
ual," a small nudge was put in place. Once people began revealing
their sexual orientation to friends and family, the floodgates
started to open, perhaps especially when their family members
were politicians who were members of a party opposed to this
change.

Openness about sexual orientation in the workplace also had an
effect, particularly when that workplace was the United States Supreme Court. Justice Lewis Powell Jr.—who cast the decisive vote
in a 1986 case that set back the gay rights movement—famously

told his fellow justices that he had never met someone who was gay. In fact, one of his law clerks that term was gay. But in 2013, two years before the decision that legalized gay marriage nationwide, thirty members of the National LGBT Bar Association were admitted to practice in the Supreme Court—the first time openly gay lawyers were admitted to the Supreme Court bar as a group.[29]

Second, social influences were crucial. With respect to same-sex marriage, cities, states, and nations witnessed both informational and reputational cascades. Increasing numbers of individuals joined a swelling chorus, amplifying the volume of the message to which they were themselves responding. A statement that was long punished by old norms ("I am in favor of same-sex marriage") was suddenly rewarded by new ones. As we have seen, a norm or practice that is understood to be emerging, or to be increasingly supported, can operate as a powerful nudge, even if it is not yet supported by a majority.[30] In the relevant period, the emerging norm was unambiguously in favor of same-sex marriage. That created a kind of self-fulfilling prophecy. And we must say that as much as we liked our idea, we are very pleased with this outcome.

The social influences that we have emphasized here can easily be enlisted by private and public choice architects. Both businesses and governments can use the power of social influences to promote many good (and bad) causes. In fact, they are doing that every day. With respect to the good, much more remains to be done.

 **PART II**

THE TOOLS OF THE CHOICE ARCHITECT

4

When Do We Need a Nudge?

We have seen that people perform amazing feats, but they also commit ditzy blunders. What's the best response? Choice architecture and its effects cannot be avoided, and so the short answer is an obvious one. Call it the golden rule of libertarian paternalism: offer nudges that are most likely to help and least likely to inflict harm.[*1] A slightly longer answer is that people are most likely to need nudges when decisions require scarce attention, when decisions are difficult, when people do not get prompt feedback, and when they have trouble translating aspects of the situation into terms that they can easily understand. When people are in situations that are unfamiliar or rare, they might well need a nudge. If you are trying to drive from your home to the local grocery store, you probably do not need to rely on a GPS device. If you are trying to find your way around a town you have never visited, that device might be indispensable.

In this chapter we try to put some flesh on these points. We begin by specifying the kinds of situations in which people are

---

* Colin Camerer and his colleagues call for "asymmetric paternalism," which they define as taking steps to help the least sophisticated people while imposing minimal harm on everyone else. Our golden rule is in the spirit of their formulation.

most likely to make poor choices. We then turn to questions about what some people think to be the potentially magical powers of markets. We ask whether and when free markets and open competition tend to exacerbate rather than mitigate the effects of human frailty. The key point is that for all their virtues, markets often give companies a strong incentive to cater to (and profit from) our frailties, rather than to try to eradicate them or to minimize their effects.

Fraught Choices

Suppose you are told that a group of people will have to make some choice in the near future. You are the choice architect. You are trying to decide how to design the choice environment, what kinds of nudges to offer, and how subtle the nudges should be. What do you need to know to design the best possible choice environment?

Spacing Out

Perhaps the single most common mistake any of us make is simply to forget something. As with self-control problems, we all know that we have limited attention and can be absentminded. That is why we make lists of what to do and what to buy at the store, and why we have calendar apps on our phones that send us reminders. Much good can come from such cues to pay attention. This is one of many domains in which technology has made it easier to nudge, both ourselves and others. When nearly everyone is carrying a phone in their pocket that can receive a text message, as is often true even in poor countries, it is feasible to send well-timed prompts. Most businesses have learned this lesson. We get reminders of upcoming appointments with our doctors or hairstylists, as well as of restaurant reservations. We are told that a bill is due. Alas, some businesses that make money from our forgetting, such as credit card companies, which charge a steep fee if you fail to make a payment on time, do not provide these courtesy reminders unless you figure out how to ask for them. Funny how that works.

Although reminders have become ubiquitous and can work as terrific nudges, that does not mean there are not new ways of helping people keep track of their appointments and obligations. Here are just two examples.

Get out the vote: For as long as anyone could remember, campaigns used the same formula to encourage turnout on election day. Voters who were judged likely to be supporters of their candidate would be called and asked whether they planned to vote (for that candidate). If the answer was yes, the call was over. That changed after the presidential election in the United States in 2008. Political scientist David Nickerson and behavioral scientist Todd Rogers had run some experiments during the primary season in which they posed a three-question follow-up to the initial inquiry about voting intentions: 1) "What time do you expect you'll head to the polls?" 2) "Where do you expect you'll be coming from?" and 3) "What do you think you'll be doing before you head out?"

The idea for these follow-up questions came from research by psychologist Peter Gollwitzer, who found that people were more likely to fulfill their goals if they had made explicit "implementation intentions." The theory worked well in this situation. Prompting voters to make a plan increased turnout by 4.1 percentage points! Interestingly, the effect was much stronger for single-person households. Remembering is only half the battle if plans also have to be coordinated. Eliciting implementation intentions, or asking something like those three questions, can have a large impact in many domains.

Checklists: Although commercial pilots have flown hundreds or possibly thousands of times, they always go through a formal ritual before every takeoff, which is to go over a checklist of things that have to be ready before the plane leaves the gate. They don't want to forget to top up the fuel before taking off! In his bestselling book *The Checklist Manifesto*, surgeon Atul Gawande details the value of a similar ritual in the operating room. The danger that Gawande wants to reduce is infections to the patient that can be introduced during the procedure. It turns out that if everyone involved thoroughly washes their hands, infections can be cut to zero, but surgeons can space out too!

One interesting key to the success of such programs is to authorize everyone in the room to remind absentminded offenders. Lower-status members of the team, such as nurses, might normally be reluctant to pipe up if a famous surgeon has skipped a step, but if it is considered part of their job, they do it. By the way, this is a completely general principle. All organizations work better if everyone is empowered to speak up when the boss is about to make a mistake. And checklists can provide a kind of choice architecture for choice architects: when he worked in the White House, Sunstein helped create a "regulatory impact analysis checklist," consisting of just over one page, to remind government agencies of the concrete things they needed to do before they finalized a regulation.

Benefits Now, Costs Later

We have seen that predictable problems arise when people must make decisions that test their capacity for self-control. Many choices in life, such as whether to wear a blue shirt or a white one, lack important self-control elements. Self-control issues are most likely to arise when choices and their consequences are separated in time. At one extreme are what might be called investment goods, such as exercising, flossing, and healthy eating (meaning, healthy foods, and not too much of them). For these goods the costs are borne immediately, but the benefits are delayed. When it comes to investment goods, people tend to err on the side of doing too little. Although there are some exercise nuts and flossing freaks, it seems safe to say most people are not resolving on New Year's Eve to floss less next year and to stop using the exercise bike so much.

At the other extreme are what might be called temptation goods: smoking, drinking a lot of alcohol, binge-watching old episodes of *Friends*, and eating jumbo chocolate doughnuts are in this category. We get the pleasure now and suffer the consequences later. (The consequences from binge-watching are the deadlines missed because we were procrastinating.) Again, we can use the New Year's resolution test: How many people vow to smoke more cigarettes, drink more alcohol, watch more sitcoms, or have more chocolate doughnuts next year? Both investment goods and temptation goods are prime candidates for nudges. Most people do not need any special encouragement to eat another brownie, but they could use some help exercising more.

Degree of Difficulty

Nearly everyone over the age of six knows how to tie shoelaces, can play a respectable game of tic-tac-toe, and easily spells the word *cat*. But only a few of us can tie a decent bow tie, play a masterly game of chess, or spell (much less pronounce) the name of the psychologist Mihály Csíkszentmihályi. Of course, we learn to cope with the harder problems. We can buy a pre-tied bow tie, read a book about chess, and look up the spelling of Csíkszentmihályi on the web (then copy and paste every time we have to use his name). We use spellcheckers and spreadsheets to help with harder problems. But many problems in life are quite difficult, and sometimes no technology as easy as a spellchecker is available to help. We are more likely to need more help picking the right mortgage than choosing the right loaf of bread.

Frequency

Even hard problems become easier with practice; solving them can even become automatic. Both of us have managed to learn how to serve a tennis ball into the service court with reasonable regularity (and in Sunstein's case, even a bit of velocity, at least on a good day), but it took some time. The first time people try to execute this motion, they are lucky if the ball goes over the net, much less into the service box. Practice makes perfect (or at least better).

Unfortunately, some of life's most important decisions do not come with many opportunities to practice. Most students choose a college only once. Outside of Hollywood, most of us choose a spouse, well, not more than two or three times. Few of us get to try many different careers. And outside of science fiction, we get one chance to save for retirement (though we can make some adjustments along the way). Generally, the higher the stakes, the less often we are able to practice. Most of us buy houses and cars not more than once or twice a decade, if that, but we are really practiced at grocery shopping. Most families have mastered the art of milk inventory control, not by solving the relevant mathematical equation but through trial and error.*[2]

None of this is to say that the government should be telling people whom to marry or what to study. This is a book about libertarian paternalism. At this stage we just want to stress that difficult and rare choices are good candidates for nudges.

Feedback

Even practice does not make perfect if people lack good opportunities for learning. Learning is most likely if people get immediate, clear feedback after each try. Suppose you are practicing your golf putting skills on the practice green. If you hit ten balls toward the same hole, it is easy to get a sense of how hard you have to hit the ball. Even the least talented golfers will soon learn to gauge the speed of the green under these circumstances. Suppose instead you are putting the golf balls but you are not getting to see where they stop rolling. In that environment, you could putt all day and never get any better at distance control.

---

* There is a deep irony here. In the early days of behavioral economics, many tradition-bound economists dismissed the findings from psychology experiments on the grounds that the experiments were only for "low stakes" and that people were often not given sufficient opportunities to learn. These economists argued that if the stakes were raised and subjects were given practice trials, then people would get it "right." There are at least two problems with this argument. First, there is little evidence that performance improves when the stakes go up. To a first approximation, the stakes just don't seem to matter much. Second, and more important, economics is certainly supposed to help explain life's big decisions, and these are the decisions that come without many practice trials. There might be a lower divorce rate if people had several "practice marriages" in their twenties and thirties before settling down to the real thing (though we are not confident about that prediction), but the fact is that in the real world, choosing a life partner is hard and people often fail. Similarly, there might be fewer philosophy Ph.D.'s driving cabs if choices about graduate school came with practice trials, but at age thirty-five it is hard to ask for a do-over.

Alas, many of life's choices are like practicing putting without being able to see where the balls end up, and for one simple reason: the situation is not structured to provide good feedback. For example, we usually get feedback only on the options we select, not the ones we reject. Unless people go out of their way to experiment, they may never learn about alternatives to the familiar ones. If you take the longer route home every night, you may never learn there is a shorter one. Long-term processes rarely provide good feedback. Someone can eat a high-fat diet for years without having any strong warning signs until they have a heart attack. When feedback is ineffective, we may benefit from a nudge.

Knowing What You Like

Most of us have a good sense of whether we prefer coffee ice cream to vanilla, Bruce Springsteen to Bob Dylan, and basketball to football (of either variety). These are examples for which we have had the time to sample the alternatives and learn about our tastes. But suppose that you have to forecast your preferences for the unfamiliar, such as when dining for the first time in a Burmese restaurant, or in a country with an exotic cuisine. Smart tourists often rely on others (waiters, for example) for help: "Most foreigners like x and hate y." Even in less exotic locales, it can be smart to let someone else choose for you. Many of the best restaurants in the world give their diners very few choices. You might be asked whether you want the two-hour or three-hour treatment, and whether you have any dietary restrictions. The benefit of having so little choice is that the chef is authorized to serve you things you would never have thought to order. At the best sushi bars, the tradition is to let the chef decide what you eat. Just ask for "omakase" and you will eat well. If there are things foreigners often dislike, the chef will sometimes ask, "Are you sure you want the uni?" That is personalized omakase.

It is particularly hard for people to make good decisions when they have trouble translating the choices they face into the experiences they will have. A simple example is ordering a dish from a menu in a language you do not understand. But even when you do know the meaning of the words being used, you may not be able to translate the alternatives you are considering into terms that make the slightest sense to you.

Take the problem of choosing a mutual fund for your retirement portfolio. Most investors (including us) would have trouble knowing how to compare a "capital appreciation" fund with a "dynamic dividend" fund, and even if the use of those words were made comprehensible, the problem would not be solved. What an investor needs to know is how a choice between those funds affects her spending power during retirement under various scenarios. That is something even an expert armed with a good software package and complete knowledge of the portfolios held by each fund can have trouble analyzing. (As they say in the required disclaimers, "Past returns are not always a good predictor of future returns.") The same problem arises for the choice among health plans; we may have little understanding of the effects of our selection. If your daughter gets a rare disease, will she be able to see a good specialist? How long will she have to wait to be seen by that doctor? Choosing a car isn't the hardest decision in the world, but exactly which features do you want your car to have? Traction control? Adaptive headlights? Blind-spot warning? Rear cross-traffic alert? When people have a hard time predicting how their choices will end up affecting their lives, they have less to gain from having numerous options and perhaps even from choosing for themselves. A nudge might be welcomed.

Markets: A Mixed Verdict

The discussion thus far suggests that people may most need a good nudge for choices that require memory or have delayed effects; those that are difficult, are infrequent, and offer poor feedback; and those for which the relationship between choice and experience is ambiguous. A natural question is whether free markets can solve people's problems, even under such circumstances. Often market competition will do a lot of good. But can markets perform miracles? We should always be suspicious of miracles.

A colorful and illustrative example is the sale of bogus medical treatments, a practice that can be found in various forms around the world. In movies depicting the American Wild West, the magic elixir was often called "snake oil," perhaps to discourage competitors from entering the market. Snake oil was said to cure many aliments, ranging from acne to arthritis to impotence. Modern versions still exist in the "natural health" sector (which is, in many countries, only lightly regulated), but for the sake of this brief discussion let's focus on snake oil, because the marketing strategy often employed helps make a more general point about markets and their limitations.

The setup in the classic western movie version shares features of many scams and swindles that regularly reemerge in slightly different forms over the years. A "doctor" in a covered wagon comes into town and opens for business somewhere near the local saloon. He offers to sell bottles of his special brew of snake oil, which can cure whatever ails you. As it happens, someone in the crowd on crutches soon emerges and challenges the doctor, calling him a fraud. Pointing to his gimpy leg that prevents him from walking, he says, "I bet you can't cure this, doc!" The doctor generously offers the poor man a free sample, and miraculously, the next night his leg is healed! Many bottles are sold and early the next morning, the doctor and his partner, who played the part of the man on crutches, head out of town to their next destination. Some version of the same scam can still be seen in crowded city locations popular with tourists, though instead of snake oil they may be peddling the chance to win some easy money playing three-card monte or spot the pea. (The accomplice wins some early money in this variation.)

Although these sorts of scams seem extreme, they are just a few examples of the many products that appeal to Humans but not Econs. You can find a whole bunch of them on the internet, and if you watch late-night television in some countries, there's a lot of snake oil for sale. As we discuss in our exciting (some critics even say thrilling) chapter on insurance, many products in that space should be avoided just like snake oil. Here is a preview: just say no to extended warranties. But the question we want to discuss here is larger: whether competitive markets protect consumers from such scams. Sadly, the answer is no.

Entry into the snake oil business, though not free, was nevertheless unregulated. Any two people with a wagon, some bottles, and a gift for fast talking could enter this business. It would help to have a knack for brazen lying, and no qualms about taking money from innocent bystanders. To be sure, there was always the risk that someone would recognize them and they would get in trouble with the local sheriff. But here is the key point. No one could make any money telling people not to buy snake oil! Few of us are in such perfect health that we wouldn't be happy to spend a few dollars for a bottle of a magic elixir. Does it cure COVID-19? Tennis elbow? Bad back? Writer's block (or sore fingers)?

Snake oil is just an extreme version of any ill-advised purchase. Many people become addicted to gambling, and for them casinos can be as dangerous as heroin or crack. And although they are regulated and entry can be limited, casinos do compete with one another as well as with other forms of gambling, such as sports betting or do-it-yourself options trading. They compete by offering enticing environments, free drinks, and sometimes better odds. But no one has gotten rich by convincing people not to gamble. We hope that the chapters in the section on money will help you avoid some frequent mistakes Humans make in the financial sector, but we won't charge extra to read those chapters, and we do not expect our writing to eliminate the extended warranty business.

In the modern era, it's easier than ever to sell snake oil. People can go online and sell products that are said to reduce the risk of cancer, to cure diabetes, to save you money, to make your skin clear, and to fight anxiety and depression. We are fans of the actress Gwyneth Paltrow (check out the underrated *Country Strong*), but her website, Goop, has been selling products that might actually contain small amounts of snake oil. With respect to health, romance, and money, it is not at all hard to exploit people's lack of information. If one of those things is at stake, companies have a strong incentive to exploit behavioral biases, including availability, unrealistic optimism, and anchoring. And they certainly try to create informational cascades. Sometimes they succeed.

There is a general lesson here. Much of the time, more money can made by catering to human frailties than by helping people to avoid them. Bars make a lot more money than Alcoholics Anonymous. So, if Humans have problems, they might benefit from a well-chosen nudge.

5

Choice Architecture

Design is not just what it looks like and feels like. Design is how it works.

—Steve Jobs

Early in Thaler's career, he was teaching a class to business school students who would sometimes leave early to go for job interviews (or maybe a nap) and would try to sneak out of the room as unobtrusively as possible. Unfortunately for them, the only way out of the room was through a large double door in the front, in full view of the entire class (though not directly in Thaler's line of sight). The doors were equipped with large, handsome wood handles—vertically mounted cylindrical pulls about three feet in length. When the students came to these doors, they were faced with two competing instincts. One instinct says that to leave a room you push the door. The other instinct says that when faced with large wooden handles that are obviously designed to be grabbed, you pull. It turns out that the latter instinct trumps the former, and every student leaving the room began by pulling on the handle. (There is a reason such handles are called pulls.) Alas, the door opened outward.

At one point in the term, Thaler pointed this out to the class, as an embarrassed student was pulling on the door handle while trying to escape the classroom. Thereafter, whenever a student got up to leave, the rest of the class would eagerly wait to see if the student would push or pull. Amazingly, most still pulled! Their Automatic Systems triumphed; the signal emitted by that big wooden handle simply could not be screened out. (And when Thaler would leave that room he would, on occasion, sheepishly find himself pulling too.)

Those doors are bad architecture because they violate a simple psychological principle with a fancy name: *stimulus response compatibility*. The idea is that you want the signal you receive (the stimulus) to be consistent with the desired action. When there are inconsistencies, performance suffers and people blunder.

Consider, for example, the havoc that would be created by placing a large red octagonal sign along the road that read GO. The difficulties induced by such incompatibility are easy to show experimentally. One of the most famous such demonstrations is the Stroop test.[1] In the modern version of this experiment, people see words flashed on a computer screen and then are given a very simple task. They press the right button if they see a word that is displayed in red, and press the left button if they see a word displayed in green. People find the task easy and can learn to do it quickly and with great accuracy. That is, until they are thrown a curveball, in the form of the word *green* displayed in red, or the word *red* displayed in green. For these incompatible signals, response time slows and error rates increase.

A key reason is that the Automatic System reads the word faster than the color-naming branch of the Reflective System can decide the color of the text. See the word *green* in red text and the nonthinking Automatic System rushes to press the left button, which is, of course, the wrong one. You can try this for yourself. Just use a bunch of colored crayons to write a list of color names, making sure that most of the names are not the same as the color they are written in. (Better yet, get a nearby kid to do this for you.) Then name the color names as fast as you can (that is, read the words and ignore the color). Easy, isn't it? Now, as fast as you can, say the color that each word is written in, and ignore the word itself. Harder, isn't it? In tasks like this, Automatic Systems often win over Reflective ones. (Know the old expression "You can't fight city hall"? Within the human mind, the Automatic System is city hall.)

Although we have never seen a green stop sign, doors such as the ones previously described are frustratingly commonplace, and they violate the same principle. Flat plates shout "push me" and big handles yell "pull me," so architects should not expect people to push things that are meant to be grabbed! This is a failure of design to accommodate basic principles of human nature. Life is full of products that suffer from such defects. Isn't it obvious that the largest buttons on a television remote control should be the power, channel, and volume controls? Yet how many remotes do we see that have the volume control the same size as the input control button (which, if pressed accidentally, can cause the picture to disappear, sometimes until a teenager can be found to fix things)?

The world does not have to be full of door handles that scream "pull" but need to be pushed. Instead, it is possible to incorporate human factors into design, as Don Norman's wonderful book, *The Design of Everyday Things*, illustrates. In fact, the idea of the book is illustrated by its brilliant cover, which has the image of a teapot with its handle and the spout on the same side. Pause and think about it.

Another of Norman's examples of bad design may now be sitting in your kitchen: a basic four-burner stove (Figure 5.1). Most such stoves have the burners in a symmetric arrangement, as in the stove pictured at the top, with the controls arranged in a linear fashion below. In this setup, it is easy to get confused about which knob controls the front burner and which controls the back, and many pots and pans have been burned as a result. The other two designs we have illustrated are only two of many better possibilities. The spirit of this chapter is that good design is often no more expensive than bad design. In fact, a simple plate that is labeled "push" has to be less expensive than an elaborate bronze or wooden pull.

The same principles of good design and functional architecture apply in the world of choices as well. Our primary mantra is a simple one: if you want to encourage some action or activity, Make It Easy. This insight falls into the category of what the great psychologist Kurt Lewin called "channel factors," a term he used for small influences that could either facilitate or inhibit certain be-

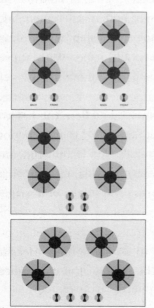

Figure 5.1. Three designs of four-burner stovetops

haviors.[2] Think about the channel as similar to the path a river takes after the spring snow melts. The path can be determined by seemingly tiny changes in the landscape. For people, Lewin argued that similarly tiny factors can create surprisingly strong inhibitors to behavior that people want to take. Often we can do more to facilitate good behavior by removing some small obstacle than by trying to shove people in a certain direction.

An early illustration of Lewin's idea was produced by Howard Leventhal, Robert Singer, and Susan Jones on the campus of Yale University.[3] The subjects were Yale seniors who were given some persuasive education about the risks of tetanus and the importance of going to the health center to receive an inoculation. Most of the students were convinced by the lecture and said that they planned to go get the shot, but these good intentions did not lead to much action. Only 3 percent actually went and got the shot.

Other subjects were given the same lecture but were also given a copy of a campus map with the location of the health center circled. They were then asked to look at their weekly schedules, make a plan for when they would go and get the shot, and look at the map and decide what route they would take. With these nudges, 28 percent of the students managed to show up and get their tetanus shot. Notice that this manipulation was very subtle. The students were all seniors and surely knew where the health center was located (Yale is not a huge campus), and they were not given an actual appointment. Still, nine times as many students got shots, illustrating the potential power of channel factors. This is the same principle that was used in the get-out-the-vote study mentioned earlier.

So, if you remember just one thing from this book, let it be this. If you want to encourage people to do something, *Make It Easy.* If you're so inclined, hum it to the tune of the old Eagles song: "Take It Easy."

Defaults: Padding the Path of Least Resistance

For reasons we have discussed, many people will take whatever option requires the least effort, or the path of least resistance. Recall the discussion of inertia, status quo bias, and the "yeah, whatever" heuristic. All these forces imply that if, for a given choice, there is a default option—an option that will prevail if the chooser does nothing—then we can usually expect a large number of people to end up with that option, whether or not it is good for them. And as we have also stressed, these behavioral tendencies toward doing nothing will be reinforced if the default option comes with some implicit or explicit suggestion that it represents the normal or the recommended course of action.

Defaults are ubiquitous and powerful. They are also unavoidable in the sense that for any node of a choice architecture system, there must be an associated rule that determines what happens to the decision maker if she does nothing. Usually the answer is that if I do nothing, nothing changes; whatever is happening continues to happen. But not always. Some dangerous machines, such as chain saws and lawn mowers, are designed with "dead man switches," so once you are no longer gripping the machine, it stops. When you leave your computer alone for a while when taking a call, nothing is likely to happen until you have talked long enough to trigger the computer to lock itself and display the screen saver. Of course, you can choose how long it takes before your screen saver comes on, but implementing that choice takes some action. Your computer probably came with a default time lag and a default screen saver. Chances are good that those are the settings you still have.

Choice architects (such as Carolyn the cafeteria director) have many opportunities to choose defaults, and they can do so in ways that are self-serving or welfare enhancing. This is true in both the public and private sectors. In 1938, Germany held an election in which voters were asked, "Do you approve of the reunification of Austria with the German Reich accomplished on 13 March 1938 and do you vote for the list of our Führer, Adolf Hitler?" As shown in Figure 5.2, the option "ya" was more than gently nudged.[4] Similarly, in the private sector, firms often can and do choose defaults that are either well-meaning guesses about what their customers would prefer or self-serving grabs of privacy data or money. They might, for example, automatically enroll people in programs that are not at all in their customers' interests. We have more to say about this when we discuss the topic of sludge in Chapter 8, but for now we should be clear that we are not naive optimists about the intentions of choice architects in any sector. Whenever Thaler is asked to sign a copy of *Nudge*, he signs it "Nudge for good!" This is meant as a plea, not an expectation.

We should reiterate that defaults are not always sticky, and we will see examples of that later. For example, people will be more

Figure 5.2. German election ballot, 1938

likely to override the default if the outcome is obviously bad and the cost of opting out is low. When most cars are started, the default setting for the sound system is to play the previous source at the volume setting last used. That works well enough if the car has only one driver, but a parent whose normal choice is a news station at a low volume will quickly change the volume, source, or both if the last user was a teenager who listens to hip-hop at high volume. In fact, the two drivers are likely to adopt the habit of immediately changing the music as soon as they enter the car (the same way that they alter the position of the driver's seat and mirrors if they are very different heights). Modern cars allow the second adjustments to be automatic if the keys electronically identify the drivers. Maybe music will be next?

There is a broader lesson here. If people know their preferences, and know that they dislike the outcome that is embedded in the default, they will probably change it. Here's a simple demonstration. A change in the default thermostat setting had the expected effect on employees at the Organisation for Economic Co-operation and Development (OECD). During winter, a 1°C decrease in the default caused a significant reduction in the average setting. But when choice architects reduced the default setting by 2°C, the reduction in the average setting was actually smaller. The reason? A lot of employees thought that it was too cold, and promptly returned the setting to the one that they preferred. The general rule appears to be that even Humans will reject a default if it makes them really uncomfortable.[5]

We have emphasized that default rules are inevitable—that private institutions and the legal system cannot avoid choosing them. In some cases, though not all, there is an important qualification to this claim. The choice architect can force the choosers to make their own choice! This approach has various names, including "required choice," "mandated choice," and "active choosing."[6] In setting up a new app, for example, required choice would be implemented by leaving all the possible options unchecked and requiring that at every opportunity, people select one of the options before being allowed to proceed to the next step. Government forms often have this characteristic. For benefits programs in the United States, you might be asked to answer a bunch of questions, and if you leave an answer blank, you might not be allowed to go on to the next page.

Active choosing is not uncommon. In many contracts, some issues are considered so important, and so easily overlooked, that people are required explicitly to consent that they have agreed to the specified terms, because we do not want them to make such decisions inadvertently or mindlessly. Active choosing has the advantage of overcoming inertia, inattention, and procrastination; choice architects can find out what people actually prefer, without having to guess. You can think of requirements of explicit consent as a behaviorally informed policy, one that reflects an effort to protect people not only against their own inattention but also against manipulation. (In fact many such policies can be understood to reflect an emerging legal right: the right not to be manipulated.) Active choosing can be designed to ensure that people really do consent to something. When the University of Chicago reopened its buildings in the fall of 2020 following the COVID-19 shutdown, both students and employees were required to complete a "COVID attestation" that said they were familiar with all the rules and agreed to follow them.

There is a kind of intermediate option: prompted choice. If you are buying some product online, you might be prompted to buy some ancillary service, too (such as insurance). With prompted choice, you are not required to choose at all; you can simply ignore the prompt and click "next screen." To work, prompted choice has to have a default (to establish what happens if you disregard the prompt). In one particularly charged issue, organ donation, we will have some nice things to say about prompted choice. In a sense, it is softer and less intrusive than required choice, which really forces people to say what they want.

We believe that required choice, favored by many who like freedom, is often the best way to go. But consider two objections to that approach. First, Humans will often consider required choice to be a nuisance or worse, and would much prefer to have a good default. In the software example, it is really helpful to know what the recommended settings are. Most users do not want to have to read an incomprehensible manual to determine which arcane setting to select. When choice is complicated and difficult, people might greatly appreciate a sensible default. It is hardly clear that they should be forced to choose.

Second, required choosing is often more appropriate for simple yes-or-no decisions than it is for more complex choices. At a restaurant, the default option is to take the dish as the chef usually prepares it, with the option to ask that certain ingredients be added or removed. In the extreme, required choosing would imply that the diner has to give the chef the recipe for every dish she orders! When choices are highly complex, required choosing may not be a good idea; it might not even be feasible. See Chapter 10 about the Swedish pension system to see what can go wrong if people are strongly urged to choose for themselves.

Expect Error

Humans make mistakes. A well-designed system expects its users to err and is as forgiving as possible. Some examples from the world of real design illustrate this point.

■ For decades in the Paris subway system, Le Métro, users would buy a packet of small tickets that were inserted into a machine that read the ticket, printed a record on it that rendered it used, and then spit it out from the top of the machine. (Locals now just use an electronic card that they wave at a sensor.) The tickets had a magnetic strip on one side but were otherwise symmetrical. On Thaler's first attempt to navigate the Métro, he was not sure how to use the system, so he tried putting the card in with the magnetic strip faceup and was pleased to discover that it worked. He was careful thereafter always to insert the card with the strip faceup. Many years and trips to Paris later, Thaler was proudly demonstrating to visiting friends the correct way to use the Métro system when his wife started laughing. It turns out that it didn't matter which way you put the ticket into the machine! The only reason Thaler never made a mistake was that it was impossible to do so.

In stark contrast is the system still used in most Chicago parking garages. When entering the garage, you put your credit card into a machine that reads it and remembers you. Then, when leaving, you must insert the card again into a machine at the exit. This requires reaching out of the car window and inserting the card into a slot. Because credit cards are not symmetrical, there are four possible ways to put the card into the slot (faceup or facedown, strip on the right or left). Exactly one of those ways is the right way. And in spite of a diagram above the slot, it is very easy to put the card in the wrong way, and when the card is spit back out but the gate does not go up, it is not immediately obvious what caused the card to be rejected or to recall which way it was inserted the first time. Both of us have been stuck for several painful minutes behind some idiot who was having trouble with this machine, and we both have to admit to having occasionally been the idiot who makes all the people behind him start honking.

■ Over the years, automobiles have become much friendlier to their Human operators. In fact they are full of nudges. If you do not buckle your seat belt, you are buzzed. If you are about to run out of gas, a warning sign appears and you might be beeped. If you wander into another lane, your car makes an unpleasant sound. If you back up and are close to hitting something, you hear a loud warning. If you drive for three hours or more without stopping, your car might ask you if you would like to stop for a cup of coffee. Any remotely sensible car comes with an automatic switch for the headlights that turns them on when you are operating the car and off when you are not, eliminating the possibility of leaving your lights on overnight and draining the battery. Nudges of these kinds are saving lives, and we can expect many more of them in the future.

But some error-forgiving innovations are surprisingly slow to be adopted. Take the case of the gas tank cap. On most cars, the gas cap is now attached by a piece of plastic, so that when you remove the cap you cannot possibly drive off without it. Our guess is that this bit of plastic cannot cost more than 10 cents. Once some carmaker had the good idea to include this feature, what excuse can there ever have been for building a car without one?

Leaving the gas cap behind is a special kind of mistake psychologists call a "postcompletion" error.[7] The idea is that when you have finished your main task, you tend to forget things relating to previous steps. Other examples include leaving your ATM card in the machine after getting your cash or leaving the original in the photocopier after getting your copies. Most ATMs (but still not all!) no longer allow this error because you get your card back immediately. Another strategy, suggested by Don Norman, is to use what he calls a "forcing function," meaning that in order to get what you want, you have to do something else first. So if you have to remove the card in order to get your cash, you will not forget to do so. Unless, of course, you forget why you came to the ATM.

- Another automobile-related bit of good design involves the nozzles for different varieties of gasoline. The nozzles that deliver diesel fuel are too large to fit into the opening on cars that use gasoline, so it is not possible to make the mistake of putting diesel fuel in your gasoline-powered car (though it is still possible to make the opposite mistake). The same principle has been used to reduce the number of errors involving anesthesia. One study found that human error (rather than equipment failure) caused 82 percent of "critical incidents."[8] A common error was that the hose for one drug was hooked up to the wrong delivery port, so the patient received the wrong drug. This problem was solved by designing the equipment so that the connectors were different for each drug. It became physically impossible to make this previously frequent mistake.

- A major problem in health care is medication adherence and drug compliance. Many patients are on medicines they must take regularly and in the correct dosage. In the United States, more than 125,000 people die annually because they do not take their prescribed medicines.[9] In principle, all of those deaths ought to be preventable. Nudges should be able to help, which brings us to an interesting choice-architecture question: If you are designing a drug and you have complete flexibility, how often would you want your patients to have to take their medicine?

  If we rule out a onetime dose administered immediately by the doctor (which would be best on all dimensions but is often technically infeasible), then the next-best solution is a medicine taken once a day, preferably in the morning. It is clear why once a day is better than twice (or more) a day, because the more often you have to take the drug, the more opportunities you have to forget. But frequency is not the only concern; regularity is also important. Once a day is *much* better than once every other day, because it can be incorporated into the morning routine. And since people tend to take more pills as they age, adding another is not a problem. (Pill container boxes, one for each day, are useful nudges.) By contrast, remembering to take your medicine every other day is beyond most of us. (Similarly, meetings that occur every week are easier to remember than those that occur every other week.) Some medicines are taken once a week, and many patients take such medicines on Sundays (because that day is different from other days for most people and thus easy to associate with taking one's medicine). Take the pill before going to church, turning on the game, doing the puzzle, or what have you.

Birth control pills present a special problem along these lines, because they are generally taken every day for three weeks and then skipped for one week. To solve this problem and to make the process automatic, the pills are sold in a special container that contains twenty-eight pills, each in a numbered compartment. Patients are instructed to take a pill every day, in order. The pills for days twenty-two through twenty-eight are placebos whose only role is to facilitate compliance for Human users. There is room for a lot more thinking about effective nudges to promote medication adherence; they could save numerous lives.[10]

■ While working on the first edition of this book, Thaler sent an email to his economist friend Hal Varian, who works for Google. Thaler intended to attach a draft of the introduction to give Hal a sense of what the book was about, but he forgot the attachment. When Hal wrote back to ask for the missing attachment, he noted with pride that Google was experimenting with a new feature of its email program, Gmail, that would solve this problem. A user who mentions the word *attachment* but does not include one would be prompted: "Did you forget your attachment?" Thaler sent the attachment along and told Hal that this was exactly what the book was about.

Google caught on and now has an assortment of nudges specifically designed to address forgetfulness. As the company put it in 2018, "When your inbox is flooded with emails, some will inevitably slip through the cracks. Luckily, the new Gmail can help. It will now 'nudge' users to reply to emails they may have missed and to follow up on emails for which they haven't received a response."[11] As both of us have found, the feature is useful. With respect to an email sent to Sunstein about one of his writing commitments, for example, the program said, "Sent 6 days ago. Follow up?" To its credit, Google practices libertarian paternalism. The company adds: "Nudging is on by default for users with the new Gmail enabled, but they can turn it off from their Gmail settings menu if they choose." Hurray!

■ Visitors to London who come from the United States or other parts of Europe have a problem being safe pedestrians. They have spent their entire lives expecting cars to come at them from the left when they cross the street, and their Automatic System knows to look that way. But in the United Kingdom, automobiles drive on the left-hand side of the road, so the danger often comes from the right. Many pedestrian accidents occur as a result. The city of London tries to help with good design. On many corners, especially in neighborhoods frequented by tourists, the pavement has signs that say, "Look right!" After the initial publication of this book, Thaler became a frequent visitor to London and was always grateful to those signs for preventing unhappy collisions with oncoming traffic.

Give Feedback

An excellent way to help Humans improve their performance is to provide feedback. Well-designed systems tell people when they are doing well and when they are making mistakes.

■ An important type of feedback is a warning that things are going wrong or, even more helpful, are about to go wrong. Our laptops warn us to plug in or shut down when the battery is dangerously low. A Tesla will alert a driver on a trip whether there is enough power left in the battery to reach the destination, and if not, it will alter the GPS directions to include a stop at a charging station. Health alerts can tell you all sorts of things, increasingly in real time. But warning systems have to avoid the problem of offering so many warnings that they are ignored. If our computer constantly nags us about whether we are sure we want to open that attachment, we begin to click "yes" without thinking about it. The warnings are thus rendered useless.

■ Feedback can be improved in many activities. Consider the simple task of painting a ceiling. This task is more difficult than it might seem because ceilings are usually painted white, and it can be hard to see exactly where you have painted. Later, when the paint dries, the patches of old paint will be annoyingly visible. How to solve this problem? Some helpful person invented a type of ceiling paint that goes on pink when wet but appears white when dry. Unless the painter is so colorblind that she can't tell the difference between pink and white, this solves the problem.

Understanding "Mappings": From Choice to Welfare

Some tasks are easy, like choosing a flavor of ice cream; other tasks are hard, like choosing a medical treatment. Consider, for example, an ice cream shop where the varieties differ only in flavor, not calories or other nutritional content. Selecting which ice cream to eat is merely a matter of choosing the one that tastes best. If all of the flavors are familiar, most people will be able to predict with considerable accuracy the relation between their choice and their ultimate consumption experience. Call this relation between choice and welfare a *mapping*. Even if there are some exotic flavors, the ice cream store can solve the mapping problem by offering a free taste.

Choosing among treatments for some disease is quite another matter. Suppose you are told that you have been diagnosed with early-stage prostate cancer and must choose among three options: surgery, radiation, and "watchful waiting," which means doing nothing for now. Watchful waiting can be an attractive option because prostate cancer usually progresses slowly. Each of these options comes with a complex set of possible outcomes regarding side effects of treatment, quality of life, length of life, and so forth. Comparing the options involves making such trade-offs as the following: Would I (hypothetically) be willing to risk a one-third chance of impotence or incontinence in order to increase my life expectancy by about three years? This is a hard decision on two levels. First, the patient is unlikely to know the data about the relative risks and benefits of each option, and second, he may have difficulty forecasting what life would be like if he were incontinent.

And here are two scary facts about this scenario. First, many patients are asked to decide which course of action to take in the very meeting at which their doctor breaks the bad news about the diagnosis. Second, the treatment option they choose depends strongly on the type of doctor they see.[12] (Some specialize in surgery, others in radiation. None specialize in watchful waiting. Guess which option we suspect might be underutilized.) Note that in an attempt to increase the number of patients who elect watchful waiting, it has been reframed as "active surveillance," which sounds less passive.

The comparison between ice cream and treatment options illustrates the concept of mapping. A good system of choice architecture helps people to improve their ability to map choices onto outcomes and hence to select options that will make them better off. One way to do this is to make the information about various options more comprehensible, by transforming numerical information into units that translate more readily into actual use. If I am buying apples to make into apple cider, it helps to know the rule of thumb that it takes three apples to make one glass of cider. If you are told that a tire's safety rating is 4 on a scale of 1 to 10, it would be valuable to give you a sense of what that means, in terms of what actually matters to you. (And yes, this example comes from actual deliberations within the U.S. government, about how best to convey the safety ratings of tires.)

Structure Complex Choices

People adopt different strategies for making choices depending on the size and complexity of the available options. When we face a small number of well-understood alternatives, we tend to examine all the attributes of all the alternatives and then make trade-offs when necessary. But when the choice set gets large, we must use alternative strategies, and these can get us into trouble.

Sometimes the choice architect provides a function similar to that of a curator at a museum. To the two of us, the most enjoyable art exhibits are rich enough to offer a meaningful experience but also small enough to be enjoyed in less than two hours, about the length of most movies. The old expression that less is more rings true here. Good choice architects often winnow the choice set down to a manageable size.

Often, however, people are their own choice architects; they even nudge themselves. A self-nudge can be called a "snudge," and for most of us, life can be improved via well-chosen snudges. People might limit the amount of food in their refrigerators; they put some money they don't want to spend into a one-year certificate of deposit that has a penalty for early withdrawal; they might delete Facebook or Twitter from their smartphones; they might program their computer so that they cannot receive email during certain hours. People work to counteract their own self-control problems, often by redesigning the architecture within which they make choices—for example, by making certain options harder or less fun, or by eliminating them together.[13]

For a more elaborate example, consider Jane, who has just been offered a job at a company located in a large city far from where she is living now. Compare two choices she faces: which office to select at her workplace and which apartment to rent as her home. Suppose Jane is offered a choice of three available offices. A reasonable strategy for her to follow would be to look at all three offices, note the ways they differ, and then make some decisions about the importance of such attributes as size, view, neighbors, and distance to the nearest restroom. This is described in the choice literature as a compensatory strategy, since a high value for one attribute (big office) can compensate for a low value for another (loud neighbor).

Obviously, the same strategy cannot be used to pick an apartment. In a large city, thousands of apartments might be available. If Jane ever wants to start working, she will not be able to visit each apartment and evaluate them all. Instead, she is likely to simplify the task in some way. One strategy to use is what Amos Tversky called "elimination by aspects." Someone using this strategy first decides what aspect is most important (say, commuting distance), establishes a cutoff level (say, no more than a thirty-minute commute), then eliminates all the alternatives that do not come up to this standard. The process is repeated, attribute by attribute (no more than $2,500 per month; a functional kitchen; dogs permitted), until either a choice is made or the set is narrowed down enough to switch over to a compensatory evaluation of the finalists.

When people are using a simplifying strategy of this kind, alternatives that do not meet the minimum cutoff levels may be eliminated even if they are fabulous on all other dimensions. So, for example, an apartment that is a thirty-five-minute commute will not be considered even if it has a dynamite view and costs $500 a month less than any of the alternatives.

Social science research reveals that as the choices become more numerous or vary on more dimensions, people are more likely to adopt simplifying strategies. The implications for choice architecture are related. As alternatives become more numerous and more complex, choice architects have more work to do, and are much more likely to influence choices (for better or for worse). For an ice cream shop with three flavors, any menu listing those flavors in any order will do just fine, and effects on choices (such as the order in which they are listed) are likely to be minor because people know what they like. As choices become more numerous, though, good choice architecture should provide structure, and structure will affect outcomes.

Consider the example of a paint store. Even ignoring the possibility of special orders, paint companies often sell thousands of colors that you can apply to the walls in your home. It is possible to think of many ways of structuring how those paint colors are offered to the customer. Imagine, for example, that the colors were listed alphabetically. Arctic White might be followed by Azure Blue, and so forth. While alphabetical order is a satisfactory way to organize a dictionary or a workplace directory, it is a horrible way to organize a paint store.

Instead, paint stores have long used something like a paint wheel, with color samples organized by similarity: all the blues are together, next to the greens, and the reds are located near the oranges, and so forth. The problem of selection is made considerably easier by the fact that people can see the actual colors, especially since the names of the paints are spectacularly uninformative. (On the Benjamin Moore Paints website, three similar shades of beige are called Roasted Sesame Seed, Oklahoma Wheat, and Kansas Grain.) Thanks to modern computer technology and online shopping, many problems of consumer choice have been made far simpler. A good paint website not only allows the consumer to browse through dozens of shades of beige but also permits the consumer to see (within the limitations of the computer monitor) how a particular shade will work on the walls with the ceiling painted in a complementary color.

Of course, the variety of paint colors is tiny compared to the number of books sold by Amazon (zillions) or websites covered by Google (many zillions). Successful online companies succeed in part because of immensely helpful choice architecture. Customers looking for a movie or television show to stream can easily search movies by actor, director, genre, and more, and they can also get recommendations based on the preferences of other movie lovers with similar tastes, the method called "collaborative filtering." Algorithms use the judgments of other people who share your tastes to filter through the vast number of books or movies available in order to increase the likelihood of picking one you like. Collaborative filtering is an effort to solve a problem of choice architecture. If you know what people like you tend to like, you might well be comfortable in selecting products you don't know, because people like you tend to share your tastes. For many of us, collaborative filtering is making difficult choices easier.

A cautionary note: Surprise and serendipity can be fun for people, and good for them too, and it may not be entirely wonderful if our primary source of information is about what people like us like. Sometimes it's good to learn what people unlike us like—and to see whether we might even like that. If you like the mystery writer Harlan Coben (and we agree that he's great), collaborative filtering will probably direct you to other mystery writers (we suggest trying Lee Child, by the way), but why not try a little Joyce Carol Oates or A. S. Byatt, or maybe even Henry James? If you think of yourself as a progressive, and you like books that fit your predilections, you might want to see what conservatives think; if nothing else, you will fare better when arguing with your relatives at family gatherings. Public-spirited choice architects—those who provide our various sources of news, for example—know it's good to nudge people in directions that they might not have specifically chosen in advance. Structuring choice sometimes means helping people to learn, so they can later make better choices on their own.

Incentives

We now turn to the topic with which most economists would have started: prices and incentives. Though we have been stressing factors that are often neglected by traditional economic theory, we do not intend to suggest that standard economic forces are unimportant. This is as good a time as any to state for the record that we believe in supply and demand. If the price of a product goes up, suppliers will usually produce more of it and consumers will usually want less of it. So choice architects must think about incentives when they design a system. Sensible architects will align the incentives of the most important decision makers. One way to start to think about incentives is to ask four questions about a particular choice architecture:

Who chooses?
Who uses?
Who pays?
Who profits?

When one person chooses, uses, and pays for a good or service provided by a single supplier, things are pretty simple and incentives are well aligned. If you go somewhere for lunch, you choose what you want and pay for it. If you don't like what you got, you can pick something else next time, or go to a different restaurant. It is a little more complicated when a group dines together and shares the bill. If the group is large, some people might be inclined to order more expensive items than they would alone, since they are paying only a small share of the extra cost. Others might do just the opposite. Thaler might enjoy an expensive bottle of wine but would feel bad about Sunstein having to pay for his share of it. When the answers to the first three questions above is one person, markets tend to work reasonably well, at least so long as people have adequate information and are not suffering from behavioral biases. (We ignore externalities for now but will return to them in Chapter 14, on climate change.)

The opposite is true of the notorious U.S. health care system. In this system, patients receive health care services that are often chosen by their physicians and (for most people) paid for by an insurance company or government. The fees are then divided up among a host of providers, from medical workers to equipment manufacturers to hospitals to drug companies to malpractice lawyers. Two patients receiving identical services can pay wildly different prices. It is no surprise, then, that the United States has the most expensive health care system in the world, with only mediocre health care outcomes.

Aligning incentives is very standard economics. But as usual, it is possible to elaborate and enrich the standard analysis by remembering that the agents in the economy are Humans. To be sure, even mindless Humans demand less when they notice that the price has gone up. But will they notice the price change?

The most important modification that must be made to a standard analysis of incentives is salience. Do choosers actually notice the incentives they face? In free markets, the answer is usually yes, but in important cases it can be no. Consider the example of members of an urban family deciding whether to buy a car. Suppose their choices when they are unable to walk or bike are to take taxis, ride-share services, and public transportation or to spend a significant amount of their savings to buy a used car, which they can park on the street in front of their home for a small fee. Once they acquire the car, the only salient costs of owning will be the stops at the gas station, occasional repair bills, and a yearly insurance bill. The opportunity cost of money spent on the car is likely to be neglected. (In other words, once they purchase the car, they tend to forget about the up-front payment and stop treating it as money that could have been spent on something else.) In contrast, every time the family uses a taxi, the cost will be in their face, with the meter clicking every few blocks. So a behavioral analysis of the incentives of car ownership will predict that people will underweight the opportunity costs of car ownership and possibly other less salient aspects, such as depreciation, and may overweight the very salient costs of using a taxi.*

An analysis of choice architecture systems must make similar adjustments. It is common to use the tax system to alter incentives—but which taxes are salient? In many countries, retirement savings are encouraged through tax incentives, such as making contributions and earnings tax-free until the money is withdrawn. Do such incentives work? The best study we know finds that they have little effect, especially when compared to (drum roll, please) defaults![14] Rich savers are more likely to pay attention to tax incentives, in part because they have hired advisers to attend to such things, so they will switch money into tax-exempt accounts, but that is mostly just moving money around rather than increasing savings. Worse, these kinds of incentives given via tax breaks are not very visible to the public. In the United States they are called tax expenditures, but no one gets a bill for the money that the government is not collecting. Behaviorally sound public policy would evaluate policies based on how efficient they are at achieving their goals and also on the visibility of their costs. Unfortunately, politicians often do not find it in their best interest to make the costs of their activities transparent.[15]

Of course, salience can be manipulated, and good choice architects can take steps to direct people's attention to incentives.

---

* Companies that specialize in short-term rentals could profitably benefit by helping people solve these mental accounting problems.

Before Ronald Reagan was elected President of the United States, he served as governor of California. In 1967, California was the only state with an income tax that did not withhold money regularly from employees' paychecks. Instead, people had to pay the entire amount once a year when taxes were due. There was a bill in the state legislature to join all the other states and start withholding money from each paycheck, but Reagan, a fiscal conservative, opposed it. In justifying his position, he famously said, "Taxes should hurt." However, the Democrat-controlled state legislature went against his wishes.[16]

In some domains, people may want the salience of gains and losses treated asymmetrically. For example, no one would want to go to a health club that charged its users on a "per step" basis on the treadmill. At the same time, many treadmill users enjoy watching the "calories burned" meter while they work out (especially since those meters seem to give generous estimates of calories actually burned). For some people, even better might be a pictorial display that indicates the calories one has burned in terms of food: after ten minutes, a user would only see a small bag of carrots, but after forty minutes, a large cookie.

When to Take a Break

One tool in the choice architect's arsenal can be easy to neglect: when to schedule an intermission. In theatrical plays, operas, and concerts there is usually at least one break in the performance that allows both the performers and the audience a chance to stretch their legs, use the toilets, get a snack, and, at least for audience, an opportunity to realize that there are more comfortable places to nap. Good choice architects realize that the timing of the break can be an important part of the design. Some plays are designed to be performed in one sitting because there is simply no place in performance where an intermission can be added without ruining the experience.

The authors of books have similar decisions to make. How long should the chapters be? Action-packed thrillers tend to have short chapters, but our favorite writers somehow manage to end each of those chapters with us dying to find out what happens next. Many a long night has been created that way, with us sleepily thinking, Oh, just one more chapter. You have probably noticed that this book is neither a thriller or a concert, but we are die-hard choice architects and we feel like this might be a good time to take a short break. We can promise you that the next chapter, which wraps up what we have to say about the tools of choice architecture, is really fun. Really! Furthermore, taking a break is your choice. To opt out, just turn the page.

6

But Wait, There's More

In the United States, there is an old tradition of late-night commercials that hawk some kind of gadget that performs kitchen miracles or some new form for snake oil. These commercials inevitably utilize a simple mental accounting principle, which is to "segregate gains," meaning that rather than immediately describing all the products being offered in the sale, some are held out and offered as a special bonus "if you call right now." In that spirit, in this chapter we offer two bonus tools of choice architecture: curation and "make it fun." Furthermore, you can read this short chapter right now, or wait. It is up to you.

Curation

When we were working on the original version of this book, we would often meet at our favorite lunch haunt and then wander into a nearby bookstore to continue our chat. There are many good bookstores in the University of Chicago neighborhood, Hyde Park. It may surprise some readers to find us using the present tense in the previous sentence, but many remain in business. (No longer a Chicagoan, Sunstein misses the bookstores of Hyde Park, but he cherishes the Concord Bookshop in Massachusetts.) How can a brick-and-mortar bookstore survive in the post-Amazon age, even in the midst of a pandemic? Although some bookstores have branched out into selling coffee and knickknacks, in Hyde Park and Concord they still concentrate on books. What do successful bookstores (and other small retail establishments) have in common? They are good *curators*.

Curation is essential for any business that wants to compete with online giants. Amazon sells, essentially, every book that is in print, and many that are not, and it can deliver to your home quickly or to your tablet in less than a minute. This means that a traditional retailer cannot compete by offering *more* choices. It is hard to beat "anything you want." In fact, the prospect of wandering around a gigantic warehouse crammed with (only) a million books is completely unattractive. Yet shopping on Amazon is simple and easy (and even during COVID-19, you never needed to wear a mask). How do both options survive? The answer, of course, is choice architecture. Small shops compete via curation, while online megastores use navigation tools to make finding and choosing among so many options easy.

There is not a single recipe for curation, any more than there is a single way to run a successful business. Some great bookstores prosper not only because they curate well but also because they give customers a terrific experience, full of surprises, serendipity, and delight, as they wander from the fiction section to the mystery corner. Other successful bookstores specialize in travel or science fiction or art. Similarly, some great restaurants are great because they are good at one thing, and they keep doing that thing. The best places to get ramen, hot dogs, tacos, pizza, and ribs are often storefronts that sell just one thing. Singapore is famous for its hawker centers, where each stall focuses on one type of dish. Two of these food stalls have even won Michelin stars, although a meal only costs a few dollars and the stalls look like any other small street food stall.[1] They are curating.

For many years, Thaler's favorite wine shop in Chicago was a tiny place with boxes piled to the ceiling in no apparent order. But the owner, who was always there, knew every bottle of wine in the store and knew the tastes of his customers about as well as a good algorithm would. Maybe better, because he would say to try a bottle of something because it was novel, and Thaler would not mind bearing a bit of risk. Serendipity can be fun, for books, music, and movies, as well as wine. Good curation combines getting rid of bad options and introducing novel ones.

These ideas will be a recurring theme in the chapters that follow. Choice architecture in domains from human resource departments to social security to health care must use some combination of curation and navigation tools. If they don't, people will flounder. As we have mentioned, some people have a simple philosophy: Just Maximize Choices. That's not always a bad idea, but it can be problematic without sophisticated choice architecture tools. Instead, a well-curated small selection and/or a good default can produce quite satisfactory outcomes.

Fun

Fun is the final element of good choice architecture that we discuss. As you know, the first mantra of nudging is to make it easy to take the desired action. A good complement to this advice is to make the desired activity fun.

The idea is well illustrated by a famous passage in Mark Twain's novel *Tom Sawyer*. Tom, a mischievous young boy, has been punished by Aunt Polly for some act of misbehavior. The punishment is that he has to whitewash (paint) Polly's fence along the front sidewalk. Tom, who would rather be off playing with his friends, dreads not only the tedious task at hand but also the ridicule he will face from buddies who pass by and see his plight. When the first such friend, Ben Rogers, approaches with a delicious apple in hand, Tom turns a neat trick. He paints with such care and relish that Ben is soon convinced that whitewashing the fence is in fact a thrilling privilege. He soon gives Tom his apple for the right to take a turn at painting. By the end of the afternoon, the fence has been painted three times by a series of Tom's friends, each of whom gives up some bit of treasure for the chance to take a turn. Twain writes, "If he hadn't run out of whitewash he would have bankrupted every boy in the village."

Twain said that "work consists of whatever a body is obliged to do. Play consists of whatever a body is not obliged to do."[2] Whenever we can make some activity seem like play, pique our curiosity, or build excitement or anticipation, we will find that people are not only willing to undertake that activity; they even may be willing to pay for the opportunity!

This principle is put to good use by the Volkswagen Group in a series of videos it has produced with the advertising agency DDB Stockholm as part of what it calls its Fun Theory. The idea is that people can be encouraged to be more environmentally and health conscientious if the desired behavior is made to seem fun. In the best-known video, viewed more than twenty-three million times, a crew is shown building a gigantic set of piano keys on a stairway adjacent to an escalator that takes passengers up to the street from a Stockholm subway station. When the project is complete, the stairs have been transformed into a musical instrument, and passengers are soon seen hopping, skipping, and dancing up the stairs in pure joy. The ad claims that 66 percent more people used the stairs after they were made fun. We have no idea whether these data are accurate, and furthermore we very much doubt that building working pianos in stairwells is an economically viable strategy, but we do believe in the principle. In fact, when we were deciding whether to take on the task of doing this revision, we adopted a simple rule: we would do it if and only if the process was fun.

Realizing that the musical stairs were more amusing than practical, the Fun Theory folks sponsored a contest to generate other ideas. The winning entry suggested offering both positive and negative reinforcement to encourage safe driving. Specifically, a camera would measure the speed of passing cars. Speeders would be issued fines, but some of the fine revenues would be distributed via lottery to drivers who were observed obeying the speed limit. A short test of the idea offered promising results.[3]

This example illustrates an important behavioral point: many people love lotteries. Some governments are already using this insight. Most colorfully, New Taipei City in Taiwan initiated a lottery as an inducement for dog owners to clean up after their pets. Owners who deposited dog waste into a special depository were made eligible for a lottery to win gold ingots, thus literally turning dog waste into gold. The top prize was worth about $2,000. The city reports that it halved the fecal pollution in its streets during the initiative.[4]

Over in mainland China, lotteries are used for a different purpose: tax compliance. As in many parts of the world, China has a thriving cash economy, and it is common for small businesses like restaurants to evade paying sales tax. To combat this behavior, the government printed up special receipts that are supposed to be given to restaurant customers when they pay. Cleverly, each receipt includes a scratch-off lottery ticket, giving customers an incentive to ask for a receipt, which then makes the transaction reportable to the government. Finance ministers around the world should take note.

Lotteries may also serve as effective motivators toward better health. A group of scholars including Kevin G. M. Volpp, a physician and social scientist at the University of Pennsylvania, ran an experiment to encourage the employees at a health care management company to undertake a health risk assessment. One group of employees was offered a 25 percent chance to win $100 as an inducement to participate. The lottery was an effective motivator, increasing participation by about 20 percent.[5]

When lotteries are used to motivate people, it is important to get the details right. Participants are likely to find a lottery more enticing if they find out whether they would have won. The Dutch government uses this principle very effectively. One of its state lotteries is based on postal codes. If your postal code is announced as the winner, you know that you would have won had you only bought a ticket. The idea is to play on people's feelings of regret.

Lotteries are just one way to provide positive reinforcement. Their power comes from the fact that the chance of winning the prize is overvalued. Of course, you can simply pay people who do the right thing, but if the payment is small, it could well backfire. (If the total prize money had been divided evenly among all those dog owners who turned in their baggies, we estimate that the price paid would have been about 25 cents per bag. Would anyone bother for that?)

An alternative to lotteries is a frequent-flyer-type reward program, in which the points can be redeemed for something fun. A free goody can be a better inducement than cash because it offers that rarest of commodities: a guilt-free pleasure. This sort of reward system has been successfully used in England to encourage recycling. In the Royal Borough of Windsor and Maidenhead, a London suburb, citizens could sign up for a rewards program in which they earned points depending on the weight of the material they recycled. The points were good for discounts at merchants in the area. Recycling increased by 35 percent.[6]

A pandemic is not a lot of fun, but New Zealand's prime minister, Jacinda Ardern, has a terrific sense of humor, and she injected fun into the effort to combat COVID-19. At a critical point, she announced severe restrictions on people's mobility. But she solemnly informed the people of New Zealand that the Easter Bunny would be exempt from the restrictions, and so too for the tooth fairy. She made people smile and laugh while nudging, and occasionally mandating, behavior that would eliminate the disease from her nation.

The moral here is simple. Make it fun. And if you don't know what fun is, then you are not having enough of it.

7

Smart Disclosure

Suppose that you decide to buy a new smartphone and have to select both a phone and a service provider. Do you think you have all the information that you need to make a good choice? For us, the only aspects of the decisions about which we would feel even remotely confident are the phone's color and size, because for those decisions we can do a physical inspection. After that we would be flummoxed. How many GB of storage do we need? What is a GB anyway? What in the world does "1792-by-828-pixel resolution at 326 ppi" mean?

Choosing a phone plan is even worse. How many calls or texts will we make? What will it cost to use when we travel? How much data do we use? Will that change if we get this new phone? Yikes! Can we go back to choosing the color?

Choosing a phone and accompanying plan is hardly the biggest or most complicated decision that consumers have to make. What credit card(s) to use? What kind of mortgage to get? Where to go on vacation? The good news is that we can improve decision making in these and other domains, and in so doing, make the market for goods and services much more transparent, competitive, and fair. We can do all that by improving one aspect of the choice architecture: how information is collected and made available to consumers. We call this Smart Disclosure. But before we get into the details of how that would work, let's back up a bit.

Measurement

It is easy to take for granted the solutions to many problems that societies faced before it was possible to have anything resembling a modern market-based economy. For example, a starting point is the creation of standardized units of *measurement*. If I want to buy your grain, we need to agree on the quantity you are going to give me. Ancient societies invented standard units to measure length, weight, and time, among other things. As a matter of history, the rise of money is a complex and fascinating matter.[1] In whatever manner it came to be, the adoption of money, or other measures of value, allowed for greater efficiency because relying on barter is highly limiting. If you have some fish and want to trade them for apples, it helps not to have to find someone with apples who happens to want fish.

To create organized commodity markets, such as those that exist for oil, soybeans, or cotton, it is also necessary to have standardized units of quality. Someone who buys a barrel of West Texas crude oil knows what sort of oil to expect and how much is in a barrel (42 U.S. gallons, or 159 liters). Naturally, as societies evolve, new units of measurement are necessary. Download speeds are measured (for now) in megabits per second. In 1980, consumers had no need for this particular statistic.

An ongoing useful role for governments is the creation of standardized units to make comparisons easier for consumers. This is not as easy as it seems. Consider measures of fuel economy. Intuitively, we understand that a vehicle is more fuel efficient if it can travel farther on a given unit of fuel, but under what conditions? Cars use less fuel driving on the highway than in city traffic, for example. If automobile manufacturers are allowed to calculate their own measures of fuel economy and each picks an idiosyncratic (and self-serving) definition, then it is impossible for consumers to compare the numbers reported by competing firms.

To solve this problem in the United States, the Environmental Protection Agency uses a uniform way to report fuel economy in units of miles per gallon (mpg). Interestingly, in Europe, fuel economy is reported in liters per one hundred kilometers.* Aside from the conversion to metric from the archaic English measurement units still used in the United States, notice that this number is the inverse of the other. In the United States, consumers see how far you go on a unit of fuel, while in Europe they see how much fuel you need to go a particular distance. Can it matter if you report a/b rather than b/a?

A clever paper by Rick Larrick and Jack Soll shows that it does—and that the European approach is better.[2] To see why, try this little test: Alice replaces a car that gets 34 mpg with one that gets 50 mpg. Bob trades his guzzler that gets only 18 mpg for one that gets 28 mpg. Who saves more money on fuel? Most people guess Alice, since she is increasing miles per gallon by 14 instead of 10, but actually Bob will decrease his fuel consumption by more than twice as much! The mistake is in thinking that fuel economy is a linear function of miles per gallon. It isn't. So good choice architects not only have to pick a standardized way to measure but also need to think carefully about how to report the findings, so that Humans do not get confused. (Econs know that the right

---

* We are sidestepping the questions raised by the rise of electric cars; if the issue is greenhouse gas emissions, those questions raise tricky standardization problems of their own, because the evironmental impact of an electric car depends on the source of the electricy.

answer is Bob.) Even Humans can understand that a car that reports 16 liters per 100 kilometers uses twice as much fuel as one that reports just 8.

Another regulatory domain in which standardization was important was in lending markets. One might think that reporting the interest rate charged for a loan is a simple matter, but that is not the case. Until 1968, U.S. lenders had considerable flexibility in the way they quoted the interest rate they charged. To remedy this problem, Congress enacted a law called the Truth in Lending Act, which required all lenders to report interest rates using the same formula. This method of calculating an interest rate was dubbed the annual percentage rate (APR). To the extent that the law worked as intended, this was excellent choice architecture because borrowers could compare the cost of borrowing by looking at just one number: the quoted APR.

Alas, this simple method breaks down when lending instruments get complicated. For example, the cost of a mortgage is not fully captured by the interest rate, especially for a variable rate mortgage, in which the rate can change when market conditions change. Along with the initial interest rate, borrowers need to know how quickly rates can change, which market interest rates trigger payment increases (do you know what LIBOR means?*), and a host of other details likely hidden in the fine print. What can we do about that?

One step is for the government to create a standard contract in which all the fine print is regularized and departures are highlighted. Standard-form leases for apartment rentals are a good example. These establish what is considered normal, such as a

---

* LIBOR, which stands for London Inter-Bank Offered Rate, is the benchmark interest rate at which major global banks lend to one another. LIBOR is administered by the Intercontinental Exchange, which asks major global banks how much they would charge other banks for short-term loans.

deposit of one month's rent, which must be returned within two weeks of the tenant's departure. Deviations from the normal contract must be added manually and agreed upon by both parties, thus avoiding the mindless use of the "yeah, whatever" heuristic. The benefit is that through regularization, consumers can easily compare the offers from competing suppliers. This is an idea that can be used in many domains. We will come back to it when we discuss mortgages in Chapter 11.

Smart Disclosure

The term *fine print* is an interesting one. In some sense, its meaning is quite literal. The fine print in a contract is printed in a smaller font than the rest of the agreement. But the phrase has a more general meaning, because the intended goal of putting something in a smaller font is to make it less salient and harder to process. The fine print contains that information the seller is required to tell you but does not want you to read. The fine print is where you can find the *disclosures*.

If you have a secret that you do not want anyone to know about (say, a crush on a particular movie star), you have every right to keep that fact to yourself. But if you want to sell your house, there is a long list of things you cannot keep secret. Any lead pipes? A leaky roof? A large family of very friendly rodents living in the attic? All these things have to be disclosed, to use the fancy legal word for informing others of pertinent information. Governments devote enormous amounts of time to deciding what has to be disclosed in almost every conceivable legal situation. Indeed, in his role as administrator of the Office of Information and Regulatory Affairs during the Obama administration, Sunstein had the opportunity to oversee many such disclosure rules. As he saw frequently, there is an initial question whether to require certain information to be disclosed. Maybe markets are working plenty well enough, and a mandatory disclosure is unnecessary. Then there is a second question, which is *how* to require that information be disclosed. The second question is always one of choice architecture. A mandated disclosure may not do any good at all if it is presented in a tiny font using technical terms that consumers do not understand.

Disclosure rules have an ancient history, but here's something surprising. With a few notable exceptions, especially in the financial sector, the technology used to make disclosures has barely changed. Admittedly, we now use computers, but we might as well be using quills and scrolls. Those who are required to make disclosures still put them into documents, either printed or online. The technical specifications for a pair of headphones are available online, but do you know how to interpret numbers on frequency response and sensitivity?

Here we make the radical suggestion that it is time for disclosure rules to make use of at least twentieth-century technology. For bold thinkers, enlisting current-century tools would make things work even better. In the original edition of this book, we made a proposal along these lines under the clunky name RECAP. It was an acronym whose unabbreviated meaning even we can't remember. Some folks in the Obama administration had the idea to rebrand this idea Smart Disclosure, a term we are happy to adopt.

A document released by the White House and still very much in effect says this:[3]

As used here, the term "smart disclosure" refers to the timely release of complex information and data in standardized, machine readable formats in ways that enable consumers to make informed decisions. Smart Disclosure will typically take the form of providing individual consumers of goods and services with direct access to relevant information and data sets. Such information might involve, for example, the range of costs associated with various products and services, including costs that might not otherwise be transparent. In some cases, agencies or third-party intermediaries may also create tools that use these data sets to provide services that simplify consumer decision-making. Such decision-making might be improved, for example, by informing consumers about the nature and effects of their own past decisions (including, for example, the costs and fees they have already incurred).

It may not be poetry but you get the idea. In short, Smart Disclosure is a set of policy rules meant both to solve the problem of the fine print and to facilitate better decisions by consumers. Building on the preceding quotation, it can be taken to have two main components. First, complex information should be disclosed and made available in a format that is both standardized and machine readable. Think of a spreadsheet to get an idea of what form these disclosures might take. Second, any organization, public or private, that keeps track of information involving the behavior of individuals or households should generally make that data accessible to them. In particular, any company that keeps track of past service and usage data for its customers (for example, smartphone plans, streaming services at Netflix, and anything sold by Amazon) should make that data accessible to those customers. The idea is that people would own their purchase history data. (Of course, there might be exceptions, as in the case of national security for governments.)

We will say a bit more about both of these ideas. But we should stress up front that we expect that only the most obsessive and tech-savvy consumers would ever make use of such files themselves. Rather, the data would be imported into software designed to help people make better choices.

Make All Disclosures Machine Readable

Perhaps the most useless of disclosures (a ridiculously strong claim, we concede) are the "terms and conditions" that all online service providers must share with their customers. We are sure that well-meaning regulators had very good intentions in requiring each one of the items in the list of terms and conditions. But in so doing, the regulators have rendered the disclosures useless. We are told by our friends at the Behavioural Insights Team in London that the terms and conditions for using PayPal have a total of 36,275 words. That is a bit more than one-third the length of this book. We have a strong hunch that there is no one in the world, including any of the employees at PayPal, who has read all those words. In what meaningful sense does such a document deserve to be called disclosure? Obfuscation would seem to be more appropriate. To be clear, we in no way wish to single out PayPal. It was our colleagues at the Behavioural Insights Team who did that. The curious thing about these disclosures is that they are available online but might as well be a large pile of paper. They are not (easily) readable on a computer. The goal of Smart Disclosure is to solve that problem. The way we now shop for travel illustrates how that could improve things.

Readers of a certain age, perhaps over forty, may remember a time when there were many people with the job title of "travel agent." If you wanted to fly from New York to Paris to Berlin to Rome and then back home, for example, you would call the travel agent, who would arrange flights and hotel reservations. Arranging the trip would entail multiple phone calls. We are not making this up; ask your parents.

Of course, travel agents are still around, but they have become an endangered species. Anyone with a computer or smartphone can book the trip just described, possibly making use of one or more travel websites such as Egencia, Expedia, or Booking.com. We call companies that help consumers to search among various options *choice engines*. A key thing to note about choice engines is that their ability to function depends crucially on their access to timely and accurate data on prices and availability. Because airlines post the relevant data online (in part because the government requires them to do so), travel websites can instantly search all the available flights.

One might worry about whether choice engines should be trusted. Like any business, we think that they should be subject to the usual laws regarding fraud or self-dealing, and the appropriate regulators should monitor their behavior. But there are also sites such as Kayak that are choice engine aggregators, with which users can easily search across the various choice engines in order to make sure they are getting the lowest prices. The existence of such meta–choice engines can help consumers monitor the prices being offered by the choice engines themselves.

Travel websites are pretty good at what they do, but there can be gaps, because they do not always provide or even have access to all relevant information. For example, airlines were at one point not required to disclose, in the prices they posted online, information about the taxes that consumers would have to pay in order to buy tickets. Informed by behavioral economics, the U.S. Department of Transportation issued a regulation mandating fuller disclosure; as a result, consumers were greatly helped, as the share of those taxes that airlines passed on to them fell substantially.[4] In some countries, alas, airlines are not required to post all pertinent fees, which means that searching for a price for two people traveling with large suitcases is not as simple as it might be.

True, it's not the biggest problem in the world, but it can be hard to find out how much it costs to park your car at a hotel. The result can be sticker shock when visiting a big city. A larger problem is that many hotels and resorts use two fiendish practices: partitioned pricing, which is to divide a price into components without disclosing the total, and drip pricing, which is to advertise only part of a price up front and withhold other parts until customers move toward finalizing their choices (or even until they check out). Both of these practices exploit consumer inattention and they might disappear if Smart Disclosure was comprehensive in this space.

Still, travel shopping is a breeze compared to shopping for a mortgage. Mortgages have numerous technical details that can be very important but hard for consumers to process, and lenders do not post the full details of their prices online. This is one reason there is still an active profession of people called mortgage brokers, while travel agents are disappearing.

Another category for which data can be surprisingly hard to find is the ingredients of foods. In the United States, food producers are required to list all of their ingredients on the package, but that can be a long list! What if your child has a nut allergy? To make it easier to see whether a food contains potential allergens, producers are also required to list separately, in bold, the presence of any of the top eight allergens.[5] That's good. But examining products one by one, looking for the absence of a particular ingredient, is quite literally a pain in the neck. Wouldn't it be nice if this aspect of life, and of parenting, were made easier?

You Should Own Your Usage Data

Have you noticed that music and video streaming services have gotten pretty good at predicting what you might like? It can almost feel like they know you better than you know yourself. But here's the thing: in some ways they do!

Consider a streaming service such as Netflix. In its early days, back when it was sending customers DVDs in the mail, Netflix would try to guess your tastes by getting you to rate a bunch of movies or shows that you had seen. They don't bother with that anymore because they can infer what you like by what you watch! Did you watch the entirety of *Breaking Bad* or did you quit after three episodes? Did you start and stop or did you binge your way through three seasons during one long rainy weekend? And if you have been subscribing for some time, they have one big advantage over you: they remember everything that you watched or even started to watch! We Humans can sometimes get all the cop shows confused.

There is a general point here. Netflix has possession of something valuable, which is your own past behavior. That gives them an advantage over any competitor that is starting fresh. Obviously, Netflix owns whatever algorithms it has created in order to convert your viewing history into useful recommendations. It need not (and should not) be required to share that bit of intellectual property. But shouldn't you have a right to make use of your past viewing behavior as well?

Let's return to the plight of the parents of the child with a nut allergy. Suppose they do most of their shopping at a large supermarket in their neighborhood. If it is part of a chain, there is a good chance this supermarket has some kind of "shopper's club" that keeps track of what each household buys. We think that parents—and all other customers—should have the right to access that shopping history, including from online shopping services. Why might they want that data? Well, suppose that with just a couple of clicks, they could download all their purchases over the past six months in a format that allows them to be uploaded to a website that offered to search through all their purchases and find the ones that they might want to take off their future shopping lists (on the basis of specified criteria, such as nuts, high calories, lots of sugar, or high prices). The website might even recommend good substitutes.

Of course, to do what we are suggesting, the No-Nuts website (as it might be called) would need access to a database of all the ingredient lists for every product in the store, but that would be possible once the first of our proposals was adopted. If ingredients that are printed on the package are also retrievable online, it should be easy to create a database of product ingredients. The matching with purchase data would be simple since purchases are scanned at checkout, and each item has a unique identifier. If food producers were required to keep their ingredient lists up-to-date in an online database, all of this would be easy. Surely, we can do better than scanning each potential purchase with a phone to make sure there are no ingredients on the do-not-buy list.

Similarly, shopping for a new smartphone and accompanying plan would be much easier for a choice engine that had access both to all the pricing features of a plan *and* to the consumer's past usage data. A good choice engine would even be able to anticipate how usage changes when people upgrade to a new phone or tablet. If consumers gave the choice engine continued access to their usage, they could also get suggestions on switching to a new plan.

Smart Disclosure is not just an idea. In both the United States and Britain, there has been a lot of progress in beginning to turn the idea into a reality. There's much more to be done, and throughout the rest of the book we highlight opportunities to employ this tool, but here are two examples from the United Kingdom to whet your appetite.

Many people now use their bank account to make regular payments for such things as rent, utilities, and credit card bills. Setting up one of these payments is reasonably straightforward and takes just a few minutes, but it is a mild hassle. Suppose that a customer is unhappy with her bank and would like to switch to another. That itself is a hassle that creates quite a bit of inertia in retail banking, but it is compounded by the prospect of setting up a new batch of automatic payments. Just reading these sentences is making Sunstein break into a sweat. But all would be fine if he moved to London!

Since 2018, all UK-regulated banks have to let you share your financial data, such as your spending habits, regular payments, and companies you use (bank, credit card, or savings statements), with authorized providers offering budgeting apps, or other banks—as long as you give your permission. Every provider that uses Open Banking to offer products and services must be regulated by the appropriate authority. At the moment, the nine biggest banks and building societies are enrolled in the Open Banking Directory, and others are coming soon. One example of this is the personal finance app Lumio, which allows you to connect all your bank accounts, pensions, and investments in one place. Smart Disclosure makes that possible.

The other UK example comes from the energy sector, in which consumers have a choice of energy providers. Having such a choice sounds wonderful to anyone who lives in California, where the public utilities have become notorious, first for causing wildfires, and later for preemptive power outages to prevent a recurrence of the same threat. However, as we have seen, having choices is one thing; making good choices is another.

The key innovation in the UK energy industry was to require energy suppliers to provide their customers with usage data in a machine-readable format on energy bills (via QR codes) and then to work with third-party intermediary companies to create choice engines. One example of this is the Uswitch app, which allows you to scan your energy bill with your phone and then suggests a list of energy deals tailored to your usage habits.

More like that, please!

8

#Sludge

Sludge. noun. Thick, soft, wet mud or a similar viscous mixture of liquid and solid components, especially the product of an industrial or refining process.[1]

Perhaps the most basic principle of good choice architecture is our mantra: Make It Easy. If you want to encourage some behavior, figure out why people aren't doing it already, and eliminate the barriers that are standing in their way. If you want people to obtain a driver's license or get vaccinated, make it simple for them, above all by increasing convenience.

Of course, this principle has an obvious corollary: if you want to discourage some behavior, make it harder by creating barriers. If you want to make it harder for people to vote, forbid voting by mail and early voting, and reduce the number of polling stations (and place them far away from public transportation stops). While you're at it, try to make people spend hours in line before they can vote. If you don't want people to immigrate to your country, make them fill out a lot of forms and wait for months for good news in the mail (not by email), and punish them for answering even a single question incorrectly. If you want to discourage poor people from getting economic benefits, require them to navigate a baffling website and to answer a large number of questions (including some that few people can easily understand).

All around the world, governments are keenly interested in reducing cigarette smoking, but they have not banned cigarettes. Instead, they have taken steps to make smoking increasingly difficult. In our youth, every bar and restaurant had a cigarette vending machine to accommodate smokers who ran out during the meal. First, those machines were removed, then smokers were segregated into smoking sections, then smoking in restaurants was banned altogether. Naturally, tobacco companies opposed these regulations. Back when television commercials for cigarettes were permitted, the creators used every tool in the nudge arsenal to make smoking more attractive, especially to young people, who could be induced to become lifetime addicts. Models in cigarette ads were attractive and sexy. Somehow, they never appeared to be foul-smelling or ill.

Our point is that nudges, and behavioral science more generally, can be and have been used for good and for evil. We have mentioned the ballot that nudged voters to vote for Hitler. People can be defaulted into programs that do not help them. In this chapter we delve briefly into the dark side of choice architecture. The term that has come to be used to capture some of that dark side is *sludge*. We believe that the term was originally used by Cait Lamberton and Benjamin Castleman in a 2016 article in the *Huffington Post*.[2] Independently, and using that prestigious academic outlet called Twitter, Thaler later expressed outrage at a particular business practice we will discuss below and called it sludge. The term has taken off and now is often used with the hashtag symbol.

What exactly is sludge? Not surprisingly, it turns out that Twitter is not the ideal medium to produce a carefully defined academic term, especially when it was (obviously) chosen in part because of the rhyme. Academics have vigorously debated the best formulation. Nevertheless, the term has stuck, and we will use it here in part because it is fun, without getting too bogged down on definitions. If you want to dig into this topic, Sunstein has an entire (short) book devoted to the subject. (Take a guess at its title?)

We use the term to mean this: any aspect of choice architecture consisting of friction that makes it harder for people to obtain an outcome that will make them better off (by their own lights). If you cannot get financial aid without filling out a twenty-page form, you have been subjected to sludge. If you cannot obtain a student visa without having four rounds of interviews, you are facing sludge. If you cannot get a COVID-19 test or vaccination without navigating a baffling website, dealing with a lot of online forms and paperwork, and driving a long distance to some hospital where you have to wait for two hours, sludge is in your way.

Some choice architects intentionally impose sludge, inserting friction into a process in order to achieve goals of their own. Making it hard to cancel a membership or a subscription is an example. Making it hard for poor people to vote, qualify for job training, or get contraceptives is another. The term *dark patterns* refers to an assortment of online practices that are specifically designed to manipulate people (in order to take their money). Some dark patterns count as sludge; they impose a lot of friction if people want to avoid certain charges.

Other types of sludge are the inevitable by-product of a well-intended administrative process, designed to ensure that people actually qualify for or are entitled to something they want. The software our publishers provided when we were proofreading the galleys of this book was so sludge-ridden that Sunstein gave up and typed up a list of changes. We couldn't help but wonder whether this bit of sludge was designed to reduce the number of last-minute changes we introduced, such as this one. In the United

States the technical term for such provisions is *program integrity*, and sludge can be a by-product of efforts to ensure it. Suppose that you have to submit an assortment of forms and wait months for approval in order to get a visa or to open a new business. Or suppose that to get emergency health care, you have to fill out a bunch of forms that you cannot understand. Or suppose that to work for the U.S. Department of State, you have to compile a lot of information about your travel over the past twenty years and about your friends in foreign countries.

Some forms of sludge, particularly common in government settings, have come to be called red tape. A more formal term for red tape is *administrative burdens*, which Sunstein adores but Thaler thinks is itself a form of sludge. But as is known to anyone who has ever worked in a large private organization—from corporations to universities—governments do not have a monopoly on red tape. Many companies, and many nonprofits (including universities), impose a lot of sludge, including on their own employees.

As long as there has been commerce, there have been scoundrels and scammers, and as long as there have been organizations* with more than a dozen participants, there has been self-imposed sludge introduced in the name of good governance. Our goal here is to make readers a bit more aware of when sludge is most likely to be lurking, and how it can be reduced if not eradicated. We are well aware that we are exploring the tip of a large iceberg, and our treatment is not meant to be exhaustive. We don't want to create sludge in our own book!

---

* Writing this sentence makes us realize that the term *organization* is kind of amusing.

Private Sector Sludge: External Facing

Thaler is a self-declared expert in misbehaving. He even wrote a book with that title. When the book was published, he was excited to get an email from his editor sharing a link to the first review of the book, in a prestigious London newspaper, no less. When he excitedly clicked on the link he ran into a paywall. Aargh! But wait, the newspaper was offering a trial subscription for a month that cost only £1. What a deal! Of course, the fact that it did cost a pound meant that he would have to provide a credit card, and he knew that inevitably he would be automatically renewed at the end of the month, so he figured he'd better check the dreaded fine print.

As he suspected, once the trial period was over, his subscription would be automatically renewed. No surprise there. But the price was a bit stiff: £27 a month for an online subscription. Still, a pound was not a lot to read the first review of a book he had managed to write without Sunstein's help. Ready to splurge on the trial deal, he checked into how to go about unsubscribing, which he planned to do as soon as he had finished reading the review, to avoid the risk of a lifetime subscription. Here he ran into a bit of a shock. It turns out that to unsubscribe he would have to give the newspaper fourteen days' notice, meaning that the "one-month" trial subscription only lasted two weeks. Worse, it was not possible to cancel online. You had to call the London office, not on a toll-free line, during London business hours!

This is the experience that led to the Twitter term #sludge.

The Unsubscribe Trap

The story about the London newspaper is sadly far from unique, although it is a bit extreme. The problem, as we see it, is not with the automatic renewals per se. Those can, in fact, reduce sludge. For any subscription, the presumption that the customer wants to continue the service each month seems reasonable. (Just imagine if your electricity or internet were turned off once a month unless you actively renewed your service!) When billing is annual, then we think a courtesy email reminder is the way we would like to be treated, and some of our favorite information providers do this. Doing so is a good way to create loyal customers.

The sludge comes in when the procedures for subscribing and unsubscribing significantly differ. Why can you subscribe just by entering your credit card but have to call long-distance to unsubscribe? This practice uses sludge as an intentional retention policy, which is unfortunately quite common. We asked a spokesperson for that newspaper why they had this requirement and were told that before readers abruptly ended their subscription, the newspaper wanted to be sure that they were made aware of the vast scope of its coverage. The spokesperson pointed to the paper's sports coverage as an example. Yup, missing out on those cricket match reports would be a shame. (We are happy to report that this particular newspaper has changed its policy to allow readers to cancel by sending an email. That is not as good as a one-click cancellation, but we tested it and found the rest of the process to be sludge-free.)

Many organizations appear to make this asymmetry between the ease of joining and the pain of leaving an important part of their business model. At least in the United States, gyms and cable companies are notorious practitioners of this strategy. We have heard of one case in which a gym, just reopening after a prolonged COVID-19 shutdown, required members to come to the gym in person if they wanted to cancel their membership. This is sludge with an extra helping of germs! In the case of the London newspaper, it was at least possible to find out the rules pretty easily on the webpage, but in many cases the withdrawal costs are hidden deep in the fine print. At the very least we think firms should be required to disclose the cancelation terms, and in a full-sized font. Some U.S. states have gone further. California and New York now require that any subscription that is initiated online can also be canceled online.[3] We can also see some value in a type of "standard form subscription," in which quitting is easy and free, and exceptions have to be made salient.

Rebates

Another common sludgy business practice involves mail-in rebates. In the usual setup the seller of some product offers to return a portion of the sales price to the customer after the sale. The standard economic analysis of this kind of promotion is that it is a way to practice price discrimination. Although the term makes it sound nasty and possibly illegal, in many contexts price discrimination is common and well accepted. If you book your airline ticket or hotel room well in advance of your trip, you pay a lower price. This policy "discriminates" between highly price-sensitive consumers who are willing to plan and commit ahead of time, and those who are less price sensitive, such as those on expense accounts. There is nothing pernicious about price discrimination as such, and in fact the practice lowers the cost to price-sensitive consumers because they are cross-subsidized by the last-minute travelers who pay full price.

The way price discrimination usually works is that in order to get the lower price, the consumer has to do something, such as book early or take a flight at an inconvenient time. Think of this as a hurdle the consumer has to jump over to get the deal. In the case of rebates, the hurdle consists of the sludge involved in redeeming the coupon. The amount of sludge involved can be considerable. It is not uncommon for the seller to require the consumer to send by mail (yes, with a stamp) the original receipt for the purchase plus the part of the packaging that includes the bit of scanner code used to identify the product. Often this piece of cardboard is located in a particularly inconvenient spot. Keep your box cutter handy.

After mailing in your materials (better make a copy, just in case) and waiting a couple of months, if you have done everything right and your letter did not get "lost," you will receive a check in the mail, which of course you need to remember to deposit. Not surprisingly, only a small proportion of rebates are successfully redeemed, roughly 10 to 40 percent.

Why do firms bother to offer rebates? Or put another way, why do customers fall into this trap? A good analysis of this question appears in a paper we would nominate in a contest for best title of an academic paper: "Everyone Believes in Redemption."[4] In an experimental study, the authors found that people were unrealistically optimistic about the likelihood that they would jump through all the necessary hoops. People thought there was about an 80 percent chance that they would do so within the thirty days they were given. The actual redemption rate was around 30 percent. It is an overstatement to say that everyone believes in redemption—but most people certainly do.

In the same study, the researchers made three efforts (with different groups of people) to de-bias people—that is, reduce the massive difference between their predicted and actual redemption rates. In the first intervention, they informed participants, very clearly, that in previous groups redemption rates were below one-third. In the second, they issued two clear reminders, one soon after purchase and another when the deadline for redemption was near. In the third, they made redemption far simpler by eliminating the requirement that people print out and sign a certification page.

As it turned out, none of the three interventions reduced people's optimism! In all conditions, people still thought there was about an 80 percent chance that they would mail in the forms. Moreover, the first two interventions had no effect on what people actually did. When hearing about the behavior of other groups, people apparently thought, "Jeez, those other groups are idiots. I would never do that." There is a general (sad) lesson here. Telling people that some activity is dangerous (running up large credit card bills, binge drinking, unprotected sex) is like informing someone that people often oversleep. It is not much help. To wake up on time they need an alarm—maybe even a Clocky.

The only effective intervention was to use our magic elixir: Make It Easy. Making it easier to mail in the form, and thus reducing sludge, significantly increased people's willingness to act. The redemption rate rose to about 54 percent, which means that the disparity between belief and behavior was cut in half. This is concrete evidence of the potentially significant effect of sludge reduction on increasing people's welfare. But, of course, marketing firms are not likely to adopt this policy because that would defeat the entire purpose of the rebate, which is to take advantage of people's overly optimistic intentions, and even their belief in (a certain type of) redemption.

Shrouded Attributes as Sludge

King C. Gillette, the founder of the razor company bearing his name, is said to have invented the marketing strategy of giving away the razor and making the money on the blades. The idea is that if the razor is essentially free and you get customers into the habit of buying blades from Gillette, then the company will be able to charge a higher price for the blades. The model seems to have worked: Gillette still sells a substantial percentage of the razor blades in the United States, and its blades are found all around the world. We don't find anything especially troubling about the razor example (the cost of switching is pretty low), but the same model is used in several markets with higher stakes, such as inkjet printers. The strategy here: sell the printer cheap and make the money on the ink.

From the standpoint of consumers' welfare, the problem is that it can be hard for people to know the real cost of using a printer. If you go shopping online, it is easy to find models with all the latest features, such as wireless printing; they cost less than $100. But try to find out how much the ink costs and how often you have to replace the cartridges, and you will have more trouble. Furthermore, printers are often designed so that they will not accept ink cartridges from other suppliers (to make sure that your valuable printer is not damaged, of course).

The ink cartridges are an example of what behavioral economists Xavier Gabaix and David Laibson call "shrouded attributes."[5] The headline price of the good understates the true cost to the user because the shrouded attributes, and their costs, are hard to discover. Hotels are notorious for shrouding the prices of various services such as parking and wi-fi, and they sometimes hit guests with something called a "resort fee," which is not an optional extra. As anyone who has been unfortunate enough to have to get a suit cleaned at a hotel has learned, the cost is usually at least two or three times that of a local dry cleaner. Of course, an economy-minded hotel guest can find a local service provider and get the suit cleaned there, but whether traveling on business or for pleasure, it can be hard to find the time to run errands.

In our view, shrouded attributes should be seen as a source of sludge. To identify them, consumers, patients, investors, and others have to navigate their way through a viscous mixture. Shrouded attributes make shopping far more difficult. Of course, if comprehensive Smart Disclosure were incorporated into good travel choice engines, the problem would be greatly mitigated, at least for travel (until hotels think up new things to charge extra for, such as using the shower). But until that day comes, this is a market with a lot of sludge. As we will see in Chapter 11, the market for credit cards also includes a lot of shrouded attributes, and that is true more generally for many retail banking services. A checking account is free as long as you keep a certain balance, but what if you dip below that balance? Then what happens?

It is reasonable to ask why competition among hotel chains or banks doesn't eliminate this sludge, but it should be easy to see why it has not happened. (Recall the discussion of snake oil.) Suppose Cheap Bank advertises "Free Checking!" and makes all its money on sneaky fees. Let's suppose that the cost to the bank of maintaining a checking account is $100 per year, and a competitor comes in and offers "Checking account for just $100 and No Hidden Fees." Who is going to win this battle? No one opens a checking account intending to bounce checks, just as no one intends to scratch the entire back quarter of their car pulling into a parking garage. Somehow stuff happens.

There is a more general point linking the three examples—the subscription trap, rebates, and shrouded attributes—we have discussed here. All these strategies have at their core the goal of making pricing less transparent. That is obviously true for the latter two examples, but its relevance to the subscription trap may be less clear. One of the reasons why magazines, cable companies, and gyms make it hard for people to quit is that they want to price discriminate—that is, charge varying prices for the same product (one month of service). The way they can accomplish this is to make some prices available only to those who make a fuss, for example by threatening to quit!

Suppose that a customer service agent (on the phone or via an online chat) asks customers why they want to unsubscribe. If the answer is, "It costs too much," they are armed with a "special deal we can offer to loyal customers." In fact, just the opposite is true. This is a special deal that is available only to disloyal customers who threaten to leave. Some credit cards that charge an annual fee will waive it to anyone who threatens to cancel the card. This is price discrimination via sludge. As customers, we prefer to deal with businesses that post their prices and don't offer lower prices just to those who complain. That is also the way we would choose to run a business.

Private Sector Red Tape

Although government agencies have a well-deserved reputation for excessive bureaucratic rules and regulations even (or perhaps especially) for their own employees, private companies, hospitals, and certainly universities are often not much better. To be hired in the first place, employees often face a lot of sludge. In the workplace, daily life often contains a lot of sludge too. Just ask nurses and doctors in whose workplace documents are sometimes still required to be sent via fax. (One reason for the high costs of health care in the United States is simple: far too much sludge![6])

A good example is how business travel is monitored and reimbursed. In fact, in some ways the U.S. government offers its employees a better experience than private companies on this dimension. If a trip has been approved (and we won't go into what that entails), the government's travel office will often book the flights and hotel rooms directly and pay for them. They have even negotiated special prices. Now, should your flight get canceled, forcing you to take the train back home, we wish you the best of luck.

Our experience with travel rules and regulations within the private sector suggests that the process is excessively sludgy. Here is an example: You plan to attend a conference in another city that is two hours away by air. The conference is an important one, and getting approval to be reimbursed for the travel is no issue, but it is also up to you whether to go. Your employer does not require you to go but will pay for your travel if you do. Here is the rub: Something might come up that will make you want to skip the conference. It could be anything. Of course, there is always some chance that something comes up, but suppose that in this particular case, you know the risk is higher than normal.

When you look into flights, the airline offers two options. There is a cheap, nonrefundable round-trip ticket for $400, but if you don't go you lose the entire amount. Or there is an expensive, fully refundable ticket for $1,200. Which ticket should you buy? When this came up for one of us, he asked his university what would happen if he bought the cheaper ticket and did not attend the conference—and was told that he could not be reimbursed for a conference that he did not attend. So, he bought the expensive ticket, attended the conference, and the university paid for the ticket. Sludge!

Someone who shares our view on travel expenses is Reed Hastings, the cofounder and CEO of Netflix, who writes about this in his book, *No Rules Rules*.[7] You can see by the title that he is our kind of guy. Hastings tells the story of someone at his prior company who complained about a travel experience. The corporate travel policy was that if you went to some city, you could either rent a car or take cabs, but not both. The employee had rented a car because the client's office was a two-hour drive from the city where he was staying but took a cab to an evening event with clients that would involve drinking. When he submitted his expenses the cab fare was not reimbursed. He was furious, and he eventually quit because he did not want to work for the kind of company that would have such a dumb policy. When Hastings started Netflix, he vowed that it would be run differently.

He says that his primary message to employees is "Spend company money as if it were your own." In practice this means book the flights and hotels that you think are reasonable, and if you are in doubt ask your manager. Managers are told to do some monitoring of expenses, and if they find that someone is abusing the system, initially let the employee know but be prepared to fire anyone who is a repeat offender. Hastings summarizes his view, which applies to more than travel, in two bullets:

- Some expenses may increase with freedom. But the costs from overspending are not nearly as high as the gains that freedom provides.
- With expense freedom, employees will be able to make quick decisions to spend money in ways that help the business.[8]

We would be happy to work for a company like Netflix.

College Admissions

In the United States, the process of applying to colleges and universities is complicated, and that is especially so for students who qualify for financial aid. Sludge can be found at every step. That is unfortunate because students from lower-income families are severely underrepresented. There are currently more students from the top 1 percent of the income distribution attending top universities in the United States than from the bottom 50 percent! You might think this fact has a simple explanation, namely that the top schools are very expensive. But in fact, many of the best universities are eager to pay all the costs of attending the school to qualified low-income students. Furthermore, attending a top school can create many attractive career opportunities. So why don't more students from poor families apply? Sludge is an important factor, and getting rid of it can help a lot.

The potential power of aggressive sludge removal has been demonstrated in a large-scale field experiment conducted by the economist Susan Dynarski and her colleagues.[9] Their goal was to encourage high-achieving Michigan high school students from low-income families to apply to the University of Michigan (the flagship university in the state). To do so they approached four thousand such students at the beginning of their last year of high school. Half of them received a packet in the first week of September *guaranteeing* them financial aid at the university as long as they applied and were admitted. They did not have to complete the onerous financial aid forms. Instead the financial aid was offered on the basis of their eligibility for subsidized meals at their high school, which was observable to the researchers. The other students just received an information package from the university encouraging them to apply.

By offering the experimental group the financial aid up front, the researchers managed to flip the traditional college application timeline: a student typically receives financial aid grants from schools *after* she is already admitted, not before she even applies. So, not only could the students skip filling out the forms, the amount of uncertainty they faced was significantly reduced. The results were striking. Only 26 percent of the students who received no tuition guarantee applied to University of Michigan, while 68 percent of students with the guarantee applied. Enrollment more than doubled, and this cannot be attributed to any change in financial incentives. Students who did not receive the special treatment but nevertheless applied received the same financial aid. They just had to overcome more sludge to get that aid.

Schools can also attract more students by de-sludging other aspects of the admissions process, in addition to financial aid. For example, the University of Texas at Austin admits all students who are in the top 6 percent of their high school class.[10] The city of West Sacramento, California, goes even further. It partnered with Sacramento City College to ensure that each of its high school seniors received admission to that local, two-year college upon graduation.[11] By eliminating the forms, Sacramento's plan strives to make higher education the default option for graduating seniors who would otherwise just not go to the trouble.

Governments

One of the most important jobs of government is to write and enforce the rules that citizens are expected to obey. But it is a fact of life that rules have to be both implemented and enforced, and those activities can be costly. In thinking about the expense policy at Netflix, Hastings was trying to find a balance between "do anything you want" and "spend needless hours of your time and others' asking and getting permission." This balance is a type of cost-benefit analysis. Sludge should be included on the cost side of the ledger.

Here is an analogy: Suppose a government decides to build a new bridge over a river, but only if the revenues from the tolls would exceed the cost of the bridge (properly discounted, of course). A good analysis of this decision will recognize that collecting the toll is costly. At one time collecting tolls meant building toll booths and paying toll collectors. But there is another aspect of collecting the toll that can easily get lost: *How much time will people spend waiting in line to pay the toll?* Time spent waiting in line is a good example of sludge, and although the costs of sludge are not borne directly by the government, they do fall upon the citizens, and they are real costs.

When governments make decisions, they often give too little attention to these types of costs. To return to the bridge example, think of how long it took (decades!) for someone to realize that in many contexts there is no reason to collect a toll in both directions. You have to pay a toll to drive your car *into* New York City but (unlike the Hotel California) you can leave for free anytime. Over time, technology has significantly reduced the costs of collecting tolls, both in terms of labor costs and customer waiting times. The technological improvements allow tolls to be used in situations in which it would previously have been impossible, such as the congestion fees imposed when entering the central business district of London or Singapore. Entry is monitored by cameras.

We find this toll collection analogy useful in thinking about many governmental regulations, paperwork requirements, and administrative burdens. The evaluation of any rule must include all the costs and benefits that the rule creates, emphatically including time. Using technology to reduce or eliminate sludge can greatly expand the range of possible policy alternatives.

Governments both create and reduce sludge. In recent years, the United States government has imposed a whopping eleven billion hours in annual paperwork burdens on the American people. This number includes burdens imposed on hospitals, doctors, and nurses, who have to spend a lot of time satisfying government requirements; on poor people seeking to get benefits to which they are legally entitled; on truckers, who have to fill out a lot of forms; on students, colleges, and universities; on people who are seeking visas to study or work in the United States. The cost of those eleven billion hours is not merely time. In many cases, sludge operates as a wall, and people cannot find a way to get over it. As a result, they are blocked from getting permits, licenses, money, health care, or some other kind of right or assistance. A sludge-reduction effort would pay big dividends. Here we give just a few examples of what governments have done to increase or decrease sludge.

Sludge at the Airport

As anyone who has flown on a commercial airline since September 11, 2001, knows, the experience of flying has become much more sludge-ridden. In the United States, the federal government created the Transportation Security Administration (TSA) on November 19, 2001, to conduct the security checks that have now become so familiar around the world. Although the annual budget of the TSA is not particularly large by government standards (in the vicinity of $8 billion[12]), much of the true cost of this operation is the time passengers have to spend both waiting to get through the checkpoint and in planning arrival times to the airport. The TSA recommends that people get to the airport at least two hours before their flight. Two hours!

One successful innovation to reduce the amount of waiting-time sludge has been the introduction of the government's Global Entry and TSA PreCheck programs, which allow millions of regular airline passengers to go through the process more quickly.

This is a genuine sludge buster. The security steps are greatly reduced: passengers do not have to remove their shoes or take their laptops out of their carry-on bags. This has been estimated to save hundreds of millions of hours per year in passenger time. That is great. But we are confident that the worldwide costs of airline security checks are underestimated because they are not monetized, which is often the case for sludge. More generally, the costs governments impose on their citizens via sludge are often neglected in the design and evaluation of policies.

Sludge vs. Sludge: Online

As we all spend an increasing proportion of our time online, people have justifiably become concerned about issues of privacy. What personal information are the websites we so often use collecting about us? Some of this information is collected using what are called cookies. These are files that remain on your browser and that record data about your use on that browser, such as browsing activity, purchases and preferences, geographical location, and the like. Usually, this information is used for targeted marketing.

The European Union regulates cookies through the General Protection Regulation (GDPR) as well as through something called the ePrivacy Directive (or "Cookie Law"). These regulations include a bit of choice architecture: cookies can be installed only if the user has given active consent. Cookies that are "strictly necessary" to fulfill the services of a site are excluded from this requirement (for example, Amazon is allowed to use cookies for its shopping cart), but otherwise allowing cookies is an opt-in policy.

It is possible that this policy is a good idea, but if you have logged on to any website that is subject to this regulation, you have undoubtedly found yourself buried in sludge. The problem, as we see it, is that although you have to opt in to permit cookies, the alternatives are by no means clear. Based on our experiences, if you are using your phone or other mobile device and you log on to a new site, you are immediately shown a screen on which you can say yes or no to cookies. The problem comes when you say no. You are *not* then painlessly switched over to the article you were hoping to read. Instead, you are asked what appears to be an endless list of questions about cookies in a very small font. Neither of us has actually gotten through this process. We either give up and say yes to cookies or leave the site.

We do not appear to be the only ones acting this way. Researchers ran a study on how users react to the EU cookie consent notices in Germany. They found that websites use nudges to get users to consent (for example, highlighting the accept button or burying the non-accept button at the bottom of the page), and many do not even give users a choice.[13] In a subsequent experiment, the researchers found that the positioning, wording, and design of the consent notices "substantially affect people's consent behavior"—and that nudging had a strong effect on people's choices. The study also found that only 0.1 percent of users would freely consent to be tracked by third parties if websites offered them a genuine informed opt-in choice. This is sludge, not nudge. As we write this, the EU is considering reforms. We hope they are more sensitive to user experiences.

Taxes

The toll booth analogy applies directly to any way in which governments collect money, with taxes being the most obvious example. The design of tax systems is the subject of a vast economic literature that you will be relieved to learn we will not attempt to summarize. The factors economists emphasize most are: *incentives* (how taxes alter behavior), *equity* (how much each person should pay), *incidence* (who actually pays for a particular tax), and *compliance* (to what extent people pay what they legally owe). All of these are obviously important, but to that list we would like to add sludge: how much time and effort is spent either complying with or evading a given tax. Although this subject is not ignored by either academics or policymakers, we think it is often given too little weight.

We believe that the American tax code is among the world leaders in sludge production. To give one example, the most commonly used tax form in the United States, Form 1040, came with a whopping 108 pages of instructions in 2019, and this is already slimmed down from the more than 200 pages a few years earlier.[14] Simply following these instructions is so daunting that more than 94 percent of American filers pay a professional or use commercial software to help prepare their tax returns; on average Americans spend about 13 hours—and pay around $200—preparing their 1040s every year.[15] Meanwhile, in many other wealthy countries, filing your taxes is relatively painless.[16] In Sweden, 80 percent of taxpayers file their tax returns in a matter of minutes, free of charge, using only their cell phones.

The sludge in the tax system can come simply from the straightforward task of attempting to follow the law as written, but it can also extend to the legal efforts to minimize one's tax bill by taking advantage of myriad breaks to which the law says you are entitled. One of the problems is that whereas everyone is in favor of the *principle* of making the tax code simpler, groups organize to oppose getting rid of the particular tax breaks from which they benefit.

Even with the tax code monster that currently exists in America, it would be possible to eliminate vast amounts of sludge in one quick step suggested in 2006 by our friend, the economist Austan Goolsbee.[17] He suggests that the Internal Revenue Service (IRS)—which administers the income tax—should send as many people as possible a prefilled tax return, which taxpayers could easily file online by agreeing to the terms on a secure web page. This would be similar to the system used in Sweden. It turns out that nearly 90 percent of taxpayers would be able to use this service, because most Americans have very simple tax returns. Taxpayers have the choice between itemizing every deduction for which they are qualified (lots of sludge) or taking the standard deduction, which for a couple filing jointly in 2020 is $24,800. For any household whose income comes from their employers (that is, household members are not self-employed or business owners) and that chooses the standard deduction, the IRS has all the information it needs to calculate the tax bill. A recent increase in the standard deduction is the reason why so many taxpayers would be able to use this service.[18]

We should stress that preparing the prefilled tax returns would not create much new work for the IRS. Wage income is reported to the IRS by employers, and investment income is reported by banks and investment firms. The agency already knows how to compute tax bills because when you file your taxes, its computer programs check to see that your calculations match theirs. As we are writing, Canadian legislators have proposed a very similar plan.[19]

You may be wondering why such an obviously good idea has not already been adopted. Well, you can make a pretty good guess as to who would be opposed to such a bill: the companies that make money charging people for filing such a return! News bulletin: business lobbies can have a powerful effect on Congress. Rather than supporting a bill requiring the IRS to provide free returns, they convinced Congress to enact a bill forbidding it! In return, the tax preparation firms promised to do such returns for "free." Of course, having to visit a physical or online service is not as easy as clicking "Yes," and anyone who does so is quite likely to run into additional sludge, such as an offer for a tax refund loan, or a fee to do their state income tax return, which should also be done automatically.

There is another advantage of the auto-return model, which is that the government can make sure taxpayers apply for and receive any tax benefits to which they are entitled—but for which they are currently required to ask. The Earned Income Tax Credit is one example. This tax credit is intended to both encourage work and transfer income to the working poor. It has an assortment of short-term and long-term benefits for working people and their children. The IRS has all the information necessary to make these adjustments for any eligible taxpayer who files a return. But instead, many eligible taxpayers fail to fill in a required form to receive the payment, thus depriving themselves of the work subsidy that Congress intended they receive. The result is about 20 percent of people who are eligible for this very important benefit do not get anything at all.[20]

Short of auto-return, there is a lot that government can do to reduce the billions of hours now spent on complying with tax law. Simpler and shorter forms would help. In addition, anticipated sludge should be part of the analysis of any new tax proposals.

One example is the concept of a wealth tax, in which households are taxed on wealth they hold above some (high) threshold. For example, in the 2020 Democratic primary campaign, Senator Elizabeth Warren proposed the imposition of a wealth tax on households that have a net worth exceeding $50 million. Imposing the tax only on the very wealthy is sensible on the sludge front, since the vast majority of families would be exempt.

Don't worry, we do not feel either qualified or inclined to

analyze the overall merits of a wealth tax. We stipulate that the proportion of the wealth held by the highest 1 percent or 0.01 percent of households has risen greatly over time, and we understand and sympathize with the motivations for considering a tax on wealth to mitigate this rising inequality. But our concern here is sludge, and when it comes to a wealth tax, mountains of sludge would be unavoidable. The essential problem is that to impose a tax on wealth you have to know how much wealth someone has. This is not as easy as it may seem.

The simple cases are when most wealth is held in liquid market securities such as shares of publicly traded stock. The wealth that Jeff Bezos holds in shares of Amazon stock is easily measured. But what about the rest? Senator Warren was fond of saying on the campaign trail that she would tax the jewelry, art, and yachts owned by billionaires.[21] Let's take art as an example of how hard this would be to do. There are two critical problems: we don't know what art people have, and we don't know what it is worth. There is no national (much less international) registry of artworks. In order to tax wealth, the IRS would have to know each piece of art held by every rich family, and its current market value.* Now think about jewelry, or stamps, or sports memorabilia.

Our goal here is not to have you shed a tear for the accountants and art dealers of billionaires. Rather, just think of the staffing requirements that would be needed to administer such a tax. Now, you might think we could reduce the sludge by limiting the tax to wealth held in liquid assets, but of course that would encourage the rich to put even more of their money into other forms of wealth, and might also induce more large companies to become privately

---

* Here is another source of sludge in the wealth tax: If the tax applies only to wealth above $50 million, at what wealth level does a family have to file a return? If someone has a mere $30 million, does she have to prove to the IRS that she doesn't have $60 million? Suffice it to say we have a lot of questions.

held like Cargill or Fidelity Investments. They would be encouraged to do so because it is difficult to determine the value of a privately held business whose shares do not trade.

Our message is clear: every part of the tax system should be designed with a careful eye on the sludge burden. If the goal is to raise taxes on the ultrarich, we think taxing large inheritances as ordinary income is a more promising path. The estate tax offers another possibility, but it would need substantial reform because the current estate tax is written and enforced in a way that generates a high ratio of sludge to revenue.

Reducing Sludge: One Step at a Time

Let's return to the toll bridge example. By enlisting just a bit of technology, such as cameras, officials have spared people countless hours of waiting in line. Time is money, as they say, and time is also time; officials should be working very hard to give people more of it. Unfortunately, governments can find such changes to be challenging. The jobs of toll booth collectors are reduced or eliminated, and their unions can be expected to oppose the change. Privacy advocates worry about those cameras. More generally, especially when compared to the private sector, governments are not well suited to disruption.

Earlier in the chapter we mentioned Reed Hastings, the CEO of Netflix. Netflix is a repeat disrupter. When the company introduced the not-so-high-tech model of mailing physical DVDs to customers via the post office, they faced an entrenched market leader in Blockbuster video, which itself had disrupted the relatively new video rental industry that had begun mostly as one-off small businesses. Hastings and his cofounder tried to sell their start-up to Blockbuster for $50 million, but their offer was de-clined. There is now only one Blockbuster video store left.[22] Net-flix disrupted the industry twice more, first by offering a streaming service and then by creating its own content. More generally, many of the largest companies in the world, such as Amazon, Apple, Google, Facebook, Microsoft, and Tesla, are relatively new.

The only way something similar can happen in governments is by fighting and winning wars. Yes, the Cold War was "fought" mostly peaceably, and capitalism "defeated" communism. But within countries, even in the rare cases when new parties emerge and win, such as Emmanuel Macron's En Marche! in France, they inherit the entire governmental bureaucracy, and when it comes to sludge, even modest changes can be met with skepticism and resistance (especially, as Sunstein can attest, among lawyers, who sometimes insist that the law requires sludge). For people who are unwilling or unable to move to another country, the closest one can get to choosing one's government is by picking the city or town in which one lives, but that town is just a part of the multi-layer system above it. If the British or Italians or Dutch would rather have the government of Canada, New Zealand, or Switzer-land they are out of luck. You cannot easily move from a sludge-pervaded country to one that is winning heroic battles against sludge.

All this means that progress on reducing sludge in government will likely be incremental. Sunstein held a position in the Obama administration in which he could take steps to reduce sludge. He did what he could; he wishes he had done much more. In the United States and elsewhere, too much sludge remains, and a lot can be done to reduce it. Shouldn't we all get to work? Start with the sludge you create, for yourself and others?

 PART III

MONEY

We hope that by now we have convinced you that libertarian paternalism is not as crazy as it sounds, and that the tools of choice architecture can be powerful ways to influence decisions, for good and for bad. But, you may ask, why should I care about any of this? This reminds us of a famous scene from the movie *Jerry Maguire*, when Tom Cruise's character (a sports agent) asks his client, played by Cuba Gooding Jr., what he can do for him. After a big warm-up, Gooding replies quite succinctly: SHOW ME THE MONEY!

In the next four chapters we try to show you the money. How can we use choice architecture to improve people's financial well-being? Read on. And keep the change.

9

Save More Tomorrow

When Sunstein was a young law student, he interviewed for summer jobs at Washington law firms. During one of those interviews, he met with a senior partner, one of the most important people at the firm, who posed the classic interview question: "What would you most like to ask me?" A bit terrified, Sunstein shyly responded, "What's the best thing about your firm?" The senior partner's answer: "We have a really terrific pension plan!"

Sunstein was not sure what a pension plan was. He thought it might be something for old people? Maybe it had something to do with retirement? Does anyone really need a pension plan? In any case, he would have rather heard about the lunches. But now he knows, and not just because he is older, that helping people plan for retirement is really important.

Saving for retirement is one of the hardest tasks Humans face. Just doing the computations is hard enough, even with some good software, but then implementing the plan involves a lot of self-discipline. Also, it is a task that is relatively new for our species, so we are still figuring out how best to do it. It is new because for most of our time on earth, we Humans did not have to worry much about saving for retirement; most people died before the problem arose. Those who were lucky enough to make it to old age were generally cared for by their extended families.

Only recently did the combination of rising life expectancy and geographical dispersion of families make it necessary for people to think about providing for their own retirement income rather than depending on their children. In the span of human history, this is a very short period of time. Humans have been cooking for thousands of years and many people still can't make scrambled eggs, so it is not surprising that we need help with this more complex task. Gradually both employers and governments began to take steps to deal with this problem, with Otto von Bismarck's early social security program in Germany leading the way in 1889.[1]

Early private pension plans tended to be what are called "defined-benefit" plans, so named because the promises made to workers are about the payments, or benefits, they will receive when they retire. In such plans, participants are usually entitled to a lifetime payment stream that starts when they retire. In a typical private plan, a worker is entitled to receive a benefit that is a proportion of the salary paid over the last few years of work, the proportion depending on years of service. Most public social security systems, including that of the United States, are also defined-benefit plans.

From the perspective of choice architecture, defined-benefit plans have an important virtue: they are forgiving to even the most mindless of Humans. In the American Social Security system, for example, the only decisions workers have to make are when to start receiving benefits and how to coordinate them with a spouse. There is very little sludge. For most people, the only form to be filled out is when they apply for a Social Security number, often filled in by parents. Then they just have to provide that number to their employer when starting work, which they need to do anyway if they want to get paid! In the private sector, defined-benefit plans are also easy and forgiving to the employees, as long as the worker keeps working for the same employer and that employer stays in business (two important provisos).

While a defined-benefit world can be an easy one for someone who stays in one job his entire life, employees who change jobs frequently can end up with virtually no retirement benefits, because there is often a minimum employment period (such as five years) before any benefits are vested (that is, owned by the employee). Defined-benefit plans are also expensive for employers to administer. So, in the United States, when a new type of employer-based retirement plan was created in 1980 (oddly called 401(k) plans after the section of the law that made them possible), existing firms began to switch over to what are called defined-contribution plans, which have become the norm.

The term *defined contribution* comes from the fact that the plans stipulate only how much employers and their employees contribute (invest) into a tax-sheltered account in the employee's name. Although the contributions are well defined, the benefits received by employees in retirement depend on the decisions they make about how much to save and how to invest, and the performance of the investments they choose to make. The defined-contribution structure is also being adopted around the world either to replace or to supplement the traditional defined-benefit government-sponsored retirement savings programs. We discuss one example of this type in the next chapter.

For modern workers, defined-contribution plans have many desirable features. The plans are completely portable, so a worker is free to move from one job to another. They are also customizable, giving employees the opportunity to adjust their savings and investment decisions to reflect their own financial situation and risk preferences. However, that ability to control one's own destiny comes with the responsibility to make good choices. Driving your own car gives you more options than does taking public transportation, but if you don't pay attention (or are a terrible driver), you might well crash. Employees have to make sure they enroll in the plan, figure out how much to save, manage their portfolio over a period of decades, and then decide what to do with the proceeds when they finally retire. People can find the whole process frightening, and many seem to be making a mess of it.

Are People Saving Enough?

Sometimes good choice architecture is simply making life more navigable, making decision tasks as easy as following the directions on Google Maps. In such cases, the choice architect is not encouraging or discouraging any particular choice, but instead is just making the process of deciding and implementing as easy as possible. This approach often yields good outcomes. But other times the choice architect drops this goal of neutrality (which we know is impossible to achieve completely in any case) and decides to nudge directionally—that is, to gently encourage some choices and to discourage others. When is this sort of nudging warranted? There is no simple answer to this question, but recall: whenever we engage in directional nudging, we should be confident that we are likely to make people better off, as judged by them. Some of this chapter is devoted to the goal of helping people increase their retirement savings. Is that a legitimate goal?

A basic question one can ask about any retirement savings system (including both public and private components) is whether people are achieving the ultimate goal of having enough money to live comfortably after they stop working. This turns out to be a complex and controversial question, and the answers differ from one country to another. It is a hard question in part because economists do not agree about how much saving is appropriate—that is, what is the right level of postretirement income? Some economists argue that people should aim to have retirement income that is at least as high as the income enjoyed when working, because retirement years often offer the opportunity for time-intensive, expensive activities such as travel. In many countries, retired people also have to worry about growing health care costs. Other economists stress that retirees can use their greater leisure time to live a more economical lifestyle: saving the money once spent on business clothes, taking the time to shop carefully and prepare meals at home, and taking advantage of senior discounts. On the basis of these considerations, they would set a more modest savings goal.

We do not take a strong position on this debate, but consider a few points. First, it seems clear the costs of saving too little are usually greater than the costs of saving too much. There are many ways to cope with having saved too much—from retiring earlier than expected to taking up golf to traveling to exotic locations to spoiling the grandchildren. Coping in the opposite direction, meaning continuing to work or accepting a reduced lifestyle, is less pleasant. Second, some people are definitely saving too little—namely, those employees who are not participating at all in their retirement plan (or don't even have such a plan available to join). We also worry about those who have reached middle age and have not managed to begin to establish a retirement nest egg, and may even have more debt than savings. These folks could clearly use a nudge.

For what it is worth, many employees themselves think that they should be saving more. In one study, 68 percent of the participants in a defined-contribution savings plan said that they consider their savings rate to be "too low," 31 percent said that their savings rate is "about right," and only 1 percent said their savings rate is "too high."[2] Economists tend to belittle such statements, and partly for good reason. It is easy to say that you "should" be doing many good things—dieting, exercising, spending more time with your children—but people's actions may tell us more than their words. When people say they should be saving more, they might not be thinking that they should be spending less; they might just mean it would be nice to have more money in the bank.

Indeed, few of the participants who said they should be saving more actually did make changes in their behavior. But such statements are not meaningless or random. Many people announce an intention to eat less and exercise more next year, but few say they hope to smoke more next year or eat more potato chips. We interpret the statement "I should be saving [or dieting, or exercising] more" to imply that people would be favorably disposed to strategies that offer to help them achieve these goals. In other words, they are open to being nudged. They might even be grateful.

Early experiences with defined-contribution savings plans revealed that Humans could use some help on three fronts: enrolling in the plans, increasing their contribution rates, and improving their investment returns. Nudges have proven to be helpful on all three fronts.

Enrollment Decisions: Nudging People to Join

The first step in participating in a defined-contribution plan is enrollment. Most workers should find joining the plan very attractive. In the United States and many other countries, contributions are tax deductible, accumulation is tax deferred, and in many plans the employer matches at least part of the contributions of the employee. For example, a common plan feature is that the employer will match 50 percent of the employee's contributions up to some threshold, such as 6 percent of salary.

This match is virtually free money! It is offering an immediate 50 percent return on contributions. Taking full advantage of the match should be a no-brainer for all but the most impatient or cash-strapped households. Nevertheless, enrollment rates in such plans are far from 100 percent. Typically, younger, less-educated, and lower-income employees are less likely to join, but even high-paid workers sometimes fail to sign up.

To be sure, there are situations, say, for young workers with other pressing financial needs, in which it could be sensible not to join the retirement plan immediately even with an employer match. But in most cases, especially for anyone over thirty, the failure to join is usually a blunder, and a directional nudge (with an easy opt-out, of course) seems justified. How can we nudge these people to join sooner?

The solution to solving the enrollment problem is obvious, at least in hindsight. Make it easy! Make joining the default. The way plans were originally designed, when workers were first eligible to join (sometimes immediately upon employment) they would receive some forms to fill out. Employees who wanted to join would have to decide how much to put aside and how to allocate their investments among the funds offered in the plan. Forms can be a headache, and many employees just put them aside, treating them as sludge.

The alternative is to adopt what has become known as automatic enrollment. Here's how it works. When an employee first becomes eligible, she receives a form indicating that she will be enrolled in the plan (at a specified savings rate and asset allocation), *unless* she actively fills out a form asking to opt out. It didn't take a genius to realize this would work. In fact, one of us, a certifiable non-genius, suggested the idea in an article published in 1994.[3] No one seemed to notice. A few firms, including the fast-food giant McDonald's, did try the idea, but the policy was given a less-than-beautiful name: "negative election."[4] Even a good idea can be killed by a bad label.

In addition to the bad name, some firms worried that automatic enrollment might not be legal, since the firm would be taking an action without the explicit (active) permission of the employee. To help assuage this fear, the federal government issued a series of rulings and pronouncements that defined, approved, and promoted the use of automatic enrollment.[5] That helped reassure cautious employers, though it inadvertently created a problem, to which we will return shortly.

An important milestone was the publication of an academic paper on automatic enrollment by Brigitte Madrian and Dennis Shea.[6] Shea had worked at a firm that tried the idea, and he recruited Madrian, at that time an economics professor at the University of Chicago, to help him evaluate what happened. The firm had tried automatic enrollment because it was having trouble getting employees to join the plan using the usual opt-in design, even with a generous 50 percent match of contributions up to 6 percent of salary after one year of employment. To evaluate the effect of automatic enrollment, Madrian and Shea compared the enrollment rates of workers newly eligible for the plan in the year before the policy was changed with the enrollment rate in the plan with the improved default. The results were striking. In the opt-in system, only 49 percent of employees joined within a year of joining the firm, but once automatic enrollment was introduced, enrollment jumped to 86 percent. Only 14 percent opted out!

With the help of some supportive legislation in 2006, automatic enrollment took off and has now become quite common in the United States and around the world. Its success at getting people into the plan is now well established. A report by Vanguard in 2018, based on the 473 plans for which they serve as the record keeper, found that fully 59 percent of the employers in their sample use automatic enrollment, and those firms have an average participation rate of 93 percent.[7] In contrast, the firms that still require employees to opt in obtain only a 47 percent participation rate. Hurray!

However, it is premature to declare victory. To stress what may seem like an obvious point, the benefits from making a policy the default option depend on the merits of that policy. If people are defaulted into a terrible pension plan, they can end up worse off. Even if they can easily opt out, inertia and procrastination might mean that they will not do so. A bad default can be sticky, especially if its bad aspects (such as the fees charged by the funds) are not very salient. *The point is that high take-up of the default option cannot be viewed as a success in and of itself.* We will reiterate this general point occasionally throughout the book, because it can be tempting to observe high take-up of a default option and declare victory. Please don't!

The experience at the firm originally studied by Madrian and Shea illustrates this point. Note that when a firm uses automatic enrollment, it has to select a specific default investment rate and an investment strategy. In their case, the default was a 3 percent savings rate that was invested in a money market account (the least risky option). Unsurprisingly, if workers are saying "yeah, whatever" to joining the retirement plan, they are likely to accept these default details, which is unfortunate. That savings rate is too low, and the investment strategy is too conservative. Certainly, young workers should be investing some of their portfolio in stocks.

Of course, making a particular savings rate and investment option the default does not mean that everyone will accept those options. Some will actively choose something else, at least eventually. Nevertheless, many of the employees passively accepted the specific default options, even some who would have actively chosen to join in the previous regime. This group was nudged to their detriment, in terms of both how much they saved and how they invested.

We know this by looking at the behavior of people who joined under the previous regime. Before the introduction of automatic enrollment, the savings rates of those who actively chose to join were strongly influenced by the match formula. Recall that contributions were matched at a 50 percent rate up to a limit of 6 percent of salary. Unsurprisingly, about two-thirds of those enrolling chose a savings rate of exactly 6 percent. In contrast, when employees were enrolled automatically, the most common savings rate was the default: 3 percent. In other words, some of those who were automatically enrolled would have chosen a higher savings rate if they had been left to their own devices. Making matters worse, the default investment choice of the low-risk money market account meant that low contributions would earn tiny returns. Let's underline what happened: more people were participating, which is good, but their savings rates were far too low and their investments were far too conservative. Automatically enrolling people in a bad or mediocre option has serious pitfalls. But both of these problems can be addressed by better choice architecture.

Increasing Savings Rates

The 3 percent savings rate used in the plan studied by Madrian and Shea was not quite selected at random, but it might as well have been. Recall the advisory rulings we mentioned earlier that helped clarify the legality of automatic enrollment. Such rulings usually include specific examples, and one of them had this phrase: "Suppose a firm automatically enrolls employees into a retirement plan at a three percent savings rate . . ." Oops! The official who wrote this never had any intention of suggesting that the number three was a particularly good one to use as a suggested savings rate. It was just a numerical example. However, we know that anchors can be highly influential, and for many years, nearly every firm that employed automatic enrollment used 3 percent as the default. What to do?

One answer would be: just use a higher rate, based on a judgment about what would serve the needs of most workers. (We will get to that, and similar approaches, before long.) As an alternative, Thaler and his frequent collaborator Shlomo Benartzi came up with a potential solution that they called Save More Tomorrow.[8] Their goal was to devise a choice-architecture system that would be conscious of five important psychological principles that are relevant in this context:

- Many participants say that they think they should be saving more and plan to save more, but never follow through.
- Self-control restrictions are easier to adopt if they take place sometime in the future. (Many of us are planning to start diets soon, but not today. In the words of Saint Augustine: "God, give me chastity. . . . But not yet.")
- Loss aversion: people hate to see their paychecks go down.
- Money illusion: losses are felt in nominal dollars (that is, not adjusted for inflation). A 3 percent raise is viewed as a gain, even if inflation is running at 4 percent. But actual cuts in take-home pay are strongly resisted, at least if they are noticed.
- Inertia plays a powerful role. For many employees, the day they join the plan is the last time they look at their choices for a decade or more.

The Save More Tomorrow plan invites participants to commit themselves, in advance, to a series of contribution increases timed to coincide with pay raises. By synchronizing pay raises and savings increases, participants never see their take-home amounts go down, so they don't view their increased retirement contributions as losses. Once someone joins the program, the savings increases are automatic, using inertia to increase savings rather than prevent them. When combined with automatic enrollment, this design can achieve both high participation rates and increased savings rates.

The first implementation of Save More Tomorrow occurred in 1998, at a midsize manufacturing firm. Employees were given the opportunity to meet one-on-one with a financial consultant, who had a laptop with software designed to compute suggested savings rates based on relevant information provided by each employee (such as past savings and the retirement plan of a spouse). About 90 percent of the employees accepted the offer to meet with the financial consultant. When they had that meeting, many were a bit surprised by what they heard. Because most employees were saving at very low rates, the adviser told almost all of them that they needed to save a lot more. Often the software suggested a savings rate equal to the maximum allowed in the plan: 15 percent of pay. But the consultant realized that such suggestions would be immediately rejected as infeasible, so he generally suggested increasing the savings rate by five percentage points of pay.

About 25 percent of the participants accepted this advice and immediately increased their savings rates by the recommended five percent. The rest said that they could not afford the cut in pay; these reluctant savers were offered the Save More Tomorrow program. Specifically, they were offered a plan in which their savings rates would go up by 3 percent every time they got a pay raise. (A typical pay raise was about 3.25 to 3.5 percent.) Of this group of employees who were unwilling to increase their savings rate immediately, 78 percent joined the program to increase their contribution with every pay raise.

The results illustrate the potential power of choice architecture. Compare the behavior of three groups of employees. The first group consists of those who chose not to meet with the consultant. This group was saving about 6 percent of their income when the program started, and that percentage did not budge over the next three years. The second group consists of the employees who accepted the advice to increase their savings rates by five percentage points. Their average savings rate jumped from just over 4 percent to just over 9 percent after the first raise occurred. This rate was then essentially constant over the next few years. The third group includes those who joined the Save More Tomorrow plan. That group started with the lowest savings rate of the three groups, around 3.5 percent of income. Under the program, however, their savings rates steadily rose, and three and a half years and four pay increases later, their savings rate had almost quadrupled, to 13.6 percent—considerably higher than the 9 percent savings rate for those who accepted the consultant's initial recommendation to raise savings by 5 percentage points.

Most of the people who enrolled in the Save More Tomorrow program stuck with it for the full four raises, whereupon the increases were halted because the employees had reached the maximum they were allowed to contribute to the plan. The few employees who did leave the program did not ask that their savings rates be dropped back to their earlier low levels. Instead, they just stopped increasing their contribution rates.

In designing the Save More Tomorrow program, Thaler and Benartzi had used the "kitchen sink" strategy of incorporating as many favorable features as possible. Over the years we have learned that two of the ingredients are attractive but not essential. It is not necessary to tie savings increases to pay increases (which many firms find difficult to implement), and letting people decide now to join later is also not crucial.

In light of these findings, the Save More Tomorrow program has been simplified and has become known as *automatic escalation*: savings rates are automatically increased annually, usually by 1 percent per year. Some firms make automatic escalation part of the default enrollment plan, in which employees start at 3 percent and increase by 1 percent per year up to some maximum, such as 10 percent. Others simply make it an option that employees can elect. The Vanguard study mentioned earlier reports that about 70 percent of firms that use automatic enrollment now include (opt-out) automatic escalation as part of the plan. Nearly all the rest offer automatic escalation as an option.

Generally, automatic escalation does help to increase savings rates, though not as dramatically as in the original experiment, in which the increases were three percentage points a year. In the Vanguard sample, of the participants who are still working in the firm after three years, about half have stuck with the scheduled increases of 1 percent a year, while most of the others have taken some action to increase savings rates even more. They are inclined to do so because, in spite of the accidental creation of the 3 percent starting savings rate in automatic enrollment plans, that norm stubbornly remains. However, we are happy to see that there appears to be a gradual shift toward a higher starting savings rate, of either 4 or 6 percent.

Default Investment Options

Recall that the other drawback of the plan studied by Madrian and Shea was that the default investment plan was a low-risk money market account. The firm chose this because it was the only option then blessed by the U.S. Department of Labor, the regulator of retirement plans in the United States. Fortunately, after much nudging (bordering on noodging), the Labor Department issued new regulations creating a set of what they called Qualified Default Investment Alternatives.[9] Most companies now pick a so-called balanced fund, which means a mixture of stocks and bonds.

The most popular version of this is called a "target-date fund" because participants choose a date at which they plan to retire and the fund adjusts the portfolio over time with this goal in mind. The idea is that as investors get closer to retirement they become more conservative about their investments, so the fund gradually reduces the proportion invested in stocks over time. Although the specifics of how these funds are constructed varies considerably, the general concept is sensible and practical as long as the fees are kept low. It is sensible because such funds offer customization based on a known attribute of the investor: his or her age. If the investor does not choose to actively change the fund, the target date will be based on a good guess of when someone that age plans to retire. Target-date funds also protect many investors from their instinct, which is to panic when stock prices fall. (Sunstein invariably panics when that happens, and immediately calls Thaler, who usually, but not always, calms him down.)

Sunstein is not the only Human investor who gets spooked when markets get volatile. Throughout the history of defined-contribution retirement plans, investors have shown an uncanny ability to mistime their investment decisions. They end up seeming to be following a policy of buying high and selling low—not a good pattern. There is growing evidence that most people would be better off not paying attention to the ebbs and flows of the stock market. In 2019, the financial research firm Morningstar estimated that the average fund investor lost about half a percent per year from badly timed trades.

The market timing trap is not just a danger for people inexperienced with financial markets—in fact, some data suggests the opposite is true. Some retirement plans offer "brokerage windows," which allow investors to access investment options outside their own plan's menu and often lead to more frequent trading. While individuals who enroll in brokerage windows have significantly higher incomes and account balances, an Aon Hewitt study found that in 2015 the average brokerage-window participant return trailed other 401(k) investors by more than 3 percent per year. People's instincts to sell or buy at the "right time" once again ended up in worse outcomes.

As readers would now guess, the vast majority of workers who are automatically enrolled invest exclusively in the default fund, at least for a while. Over time, as assets begin to accumulate and workers take a greater interest in investing, a growing number choose to modify their investment portfolio, for better or for worse.

But Where Does the Money Come From?

An important question to ask is whether nudging people to increase their contributions to a retirement savings account produces an actual increase in net savings or just shifts money around from other (taxable) accounts or, worse, makes people incur debt (by, for example, taking out more loans).

The first worry is quite legitimate, but it has little to do with nudging per se. Compare two hypothetical government policies:

1. Require firms to adopt automatic enrollment.

2. Increase the limit on how much people can contribute to their retirement account.

We can be confident that the contributions to retirement savings that are induced by the automatic enrollment policy are almost entirely new savings, because those who are nudged to join were, as a group, doing almost no saving elsewhere. The workers who do not opt in to a 401(k) plan are predominantly lower-paid employees without a college degree. In contrast, increasing the savings *limit* will produce very little new savings because only a small percentage of workers are at the maximum, and those who are maxed out did not need any nudges to get them there. If they weren't figuring that out for themselves, their financial advisers would have helped them!

But if nudging people to join the plan or increase their savings rate is mostly influencing the bottom half of the income distribution, we should be concerned whether those encouraged to enroll or save more will end up having more debt sometime down the road. After all, the money has to come from somewhere. It has long been hard to assess this issue because researchers do not have access to the financial records of the participants in the plan. However, two recent studies have overcome this problem, and provide reassuring results.

The first study took place in Denmark and was possible because the Danes keep meticulous records on household wealth as well as income.[10] The research team examined what happened when workers switched jobs, say, to a company with a more generous retirement savings plan. They concluded that these plan features produced almost entirely new savings with no noticeable increase in debt. A second study evaluated the effect of introducing automatic enrollment in 2010 to a group of civilian employees of the military.[11] They found that after four years there was no significant change in credit scores or debt balances. They did find some statistically weak evidence of increases in mortgage debt, but we do not find that worrying. If Joe and Harry are identical in every way except that Harry has taken out a mortgage to buy a home, who would you guess is better off financially? We would bet on Harry, except perhaps in the years just before the financial crisis, when many people were induced to take on ill-advised mortgages.

Best Practices

In the past decade, defined-contribution plans have continued to grow in importance, and we are pleased with the directions in which they have evolved. The growing use of automatic enroll-ment, automatic escalation, and sensible default funds has created an environment that is a big improvement on what had existed. And we like the trends we are seeing. The ubiquitous and too-low default savings rate of 3 percent is less universal than it was be-fore. A significant number of firms are starting employees off at 6 percent without seeing a significant increase in opt-out rates. And firms are no longer applying these policies just to new employees. Best practices now include "sweeping" seasoned employees into the enrollment process periodically. Someone who opted out at age twenty-two may have a different view at age twenty-seven or thirty-two.

Although the way defined-contribution plans are being run has improved a lot over the past decade, the biggest problem in the United States and many other countries is that many workers (perhaps half) do not have a retirement plan offered by their em-ployer.[12] This is a problem because the most effective way for peo-ple to save is to have the money withdrawn from their paycheck before they have a chance to spend it. It is just like moving that cashew bowl away. Among those who lack this basic benefit are the self-employed, those who work for small businesses, gig workers, and everyone in the informal economy. In many countries, that last segment can be very large indeed.

The Obama administration tried to introduce a nationwide system to alleviate this problem, but no bill was ever enacted by Congress. Aware of the issue, some states, including California, Oregon, Illinois, and others, have initiated programs at the state level. For other states or nations facing this problem, the basic outline of what is needed is illustrated by the National Employment Savings Trust (NEST) system that was created in the UK in 2008. The law required that all employers that do not offer a retirement plan automatically enroll their workers into NEST, with an opt-out option, of course. Both employees and employers make contributions, and the government administers the plan. The plan started out gently, with initial savings rates at just 2 percent of income. Much to the surprise of skeptics, less than 10 percent of workers opted out.[13] After the initial rollout, the savings rate was increased in steps, first to 5 percent and then to 8 percent, and opt-out rates continued to be less than 10 percent. A small number of investment options are offered, the default being a target-date fund. Fees are reasonable.

The UK option is just one design among many. The next chapter discusses the Swedish system in some detail. No one design is perfect for every country. But every country should be thinking hard about how to identify one that suits the needs of its citizens. A national plan can also help solve a serious leakage problem in the employer plans. When employees leave, they often cash out their pension benefits, especially if the account balance is small. Since turnover is high in low-paying jobs, this is a pernicious problem, but one that we can solve.

Do Nudges Last Forever?
Perhaps in Sweden

In all forms of design or architecture, including the choice variety, every detail can matter. The previous chapter highlighted the strategies used to increase participation and savings rates, showing that seemingly small interventions can have big effects. We now turn to Sweden, which two decades ago created a unique retirement savings plan that provides fascinating insights into the impact of design details, and a chance to see what happens over time. We cannot yet say whether and when nudges last forever, but as we will see, some of them do persist for quite a while. We are going to get a bit into the weeds here, not because we are obsessed with Swedish savings plans, but because the details offer some larger lessons about the problems with maximizing choices, the possibility of weakening the effects of defaults, and the power of inertia.

As the UK NEST plan illustrates, the spread of defined-contribution retirement savings plans has reached the public sector as well as the private sector. One reason is that the traditional safety net plans such as Social Security are usually funded on a "pay as you go" basis, meaning that the taxes paid by people working now support the benefits to those retired. That system is being threatened by two demographic trends. The first is that people are living longer, which means they collect benefits for more years. The second is that people are having fewer children, so the ratio of workers to retirees is falling, threatening the viability of the system.

A pioneer in this space was Sweden, which (after a long period of planning) launched its plan in 2000. Because of its unique approach, it offers some unique insights into choice architecture. First, a bit of context. As one might guess, Sweden has a very generous social safety net, and retirement savings are no exception. The social security tax rate is 16 percent of income. Participation is mandatory and it is mostly a defined-benefit plan. The reform we are discussing here was to carve out a portion of that tax to create individual defined-contribution accounts in what they called the Swedish Premium Pension Plan. Here we will just call it the Swedish plan for short.

Because participation is mandatory, neither automatic enrollment nor escalation is relevant in this context. Rather, our focus will be on other features of the choice architecture, specifically the number of options offered in the plan and the design and treatment of the default fund that was created. Because the plan has now been around for two decades, we can also examine how participant behavior varied over time. In particular, we can examine a question that is often difficult to answer: How long do nudges last? At least in this particular context, some nudges seem to be like diamonds: they last forever.

If we were to pick a single phrase to characterize the design of the Swedish plan, it would be "pro-choice." In fact, the plan is a good example of the Just Maximize Choices strategy. Give people as many options as possible, and then let them do whatever they want. At almost every stage, the designers opted for a laissez-faire approach. In particular, the plan had the following key features:

+ Participants were allowed to create their own portfolios by selecting up to five funds from an approved list.

- One fund was chosen (with some care) to be a default fund for anyone who, for whatever reason, did not make an active choice.
- Participants were encouraged (via a massive advertising campaign) to choose their own portfolios rather than rely on the default fund.
- Any fund meeting certain fiduciary standards was allowed to enter the system. Thus, market entry determined the mix of funds from which participants could choose. As a result of this process, there were initially 456 (!) available funds.
- Information about the funds, including fees, past performance, and risk, was provided in a booklet to all participants.
- Funds (except for the default) were permitted to advertise to attract money.

You may be asking yourself, are we sure this happened in Sweden? The plan is one that would make Milton Friedman happy. From his point of view, the combination of free entry, unfettered competition, and lots of choices would seem great. But knowledgeable choice architects might worry that presenting Humans with so many choices might create problems. As we shall see, such worries would be well-founded.

The Default Fund

We mentioned that there was a designated default fund. This is called AP7, the makeup of which we will discuss shortly, and its creation requires that other choice architecture decisions be made. Specifically, what status should it get from the government? Does the government want to encourage people to take up the fund, discourage them from doing so, or what? Here are a few of the many possible options that the designers of the plan might have selected:

A. Participants are given no choice: the default fund is the only fund offered.

B. A default is picked, but its selection is discouraged.

C. A default is picked, and its selection is encouraged.

D. A default is picked, and its selection is neither encouraged nor discouraged.

E. Required choosing. There is no default option; participants must make an active choice or they forfeit their contributions.

Which of these would a good choice architect select? That depends on the architect's level of confidence in the ability and willingness of the participants to do a good job of choosing portfolios on their own. Option A is hardly a nudge. It eliminates all choice, and would obviously be in direct opposition to the overall philosophy of the plan, so we are confident that it was not seriously considered.

At the other extreme, plan designers could avoid picking a default fund entirely by forcing everyone to choose a portfolio for themselves—option E, required choosing. If the designers are confident that people will do a good job picking portfolios for themselves, then they might consider this policy. Although required choosing can be attractive in some domains, we think that the Swedish government was right not to insist on it in this particular setting.[1] Inevitably some participants will fail to respond to attempts to reach them (maybe because they are out of the country, ill, preoccupied, unable to communicate, or just clueless). Cutting such people off from all benefits would be harsh, and it is probably unacceptable as a matter of politics or principle. In any case it isn't easy to choose among more than four hundred funds; why should a government force its citizens to make that choice when some would prefer to rely on what experts say, as captured in the default?

So, we are left with the three middle options. If we are to have a default option as well as other choices, should we encourage or discourage its use? Clearly there is a wide variety of choices along the continuum from strongly discouraging the default to strongly encouraging it. What's best? Option D has obvious appeal: simply designate a default but neither encourage nor discourage it. But it is an illusion to think this alternative fully solves the problem. What does it mean to be neutral? If we notify people that the plan was designed by experts and has low fees (both true about the actual default chosen), does this constitute encouragement? We don't mean to split hairs here. Our point is simply that designers have to make decisions about how to describe the default plan, and these decisions will help determine the market share it attracts.

In analyzing the middle options, we also would want to know something about the competence of those who design and manage the default fund, and the competence and diversity of those citizens who might decline it. If the default fund is terrific and can work well for most participants, or if the choosers are likely to blunder, then it might make sense to encourage people to select the default. If the creators of the default fund are not really experts, if the choosers know a lot, and if the situations of different choosers are relevantly different, then it might be best to err on the side of official neutrality. These are the types of decisions that good choice architects need to ponder.

In any case, the Swedish plan adopted a version of Option B. Participants were actively encouraged to choose their own portfolios, via an extensive advertising campaign. This created what amounts to a battle of the nudges. On the one hand, we know that selecting one of the funds to be a default is often a quite powerful nudge. The vast majority of participants in the American 401(k) plans we discussed in the previous chapter are invested in the default fund. On the other hand, both the government and the fund companies were nudging in the opposite direction: choose for yourself! Which nudge won?

And the winner is . . . advertising! The combined efforts of the government campaign and the fund company ads induced two-thirds of participants to select portfolios on their own. We will call these people *Active Choosers*. Participants were more likely to be Active Choosers if they had more money at stake, and, controlling for how much money they had to invest, women and younger participants were more likely to make active choices. (We have a theory about why women were more likely to make active choices: We think they were less likely to lose the enrollment forms and more likely to remember to mail them in. We admit to having no data to support this theory and plead guilty to the possibility that we are being overly influenced—via the availability bias—by the fact that our spouses are considerably more organized than we are.)

The other one-third of the participants ended up with the default fund. We will call these folks *Delegators* since they left the portfolio management to others. The Delegators gave the default fund the largest market share of any fund.

Did Active Choosers Make Good Choices?

How did people do at choosing their own portfolios? Of course, we do not have any way of knowing the preferences of individual participants, and we also do not know what assets they may be holding outside the social security system, so it is not possible for us to say anything definitive about how good a job they did picking a portfolio. But we can nonetheless compare the portfolios people actively constructed with the default fund on dimensions that sensible investors should value, such as fees, risk, and performance.

The initial default fund was chosen with some care, though also with some eccentricities. The asset allocation was 65 percent foreign (that is, non-Swedish) stocks, 17 percent Swedish stocks, 10 percent fixed-income securities (bonds), 4 percent hedge funds, and 4 percent private equity. Across all asset classes, 60 percent of the funds were managed passively, meaning the portfolio managers were simply buying an index of stocks and not trying to beat the market. That helped keep fees low, namely 0.17 percent per year. (This means that for every $100 invested, the investor is charged 17 cents per year.) That was a very low rate, especially at that time. Overall, though many would quibble with some of the choices made, most experts would consider this fund to be a reasonable and inexpensive option. We know several prominent Swedish economists who actively chose to invest in the default fund.

To see how the Active Choosers did as a group, we can examine the comparable figures for their aggregate portfolio. There are three points of interest in this comparison. First, although the allocation to stocks in the default plan was quite high, it is even higher in the portfolios actively chosen: 96.2 percent. People probably chose to invest so heavily in stocks partly because the stock market had been booming for the previous few years.

Second, the Active Choosers elected to invest nearly half their money (48.2 percent) in the stocks of Swedish companies. This reflects the well-known tendency of investors to buy stocks from their home country, something that economists refer to as the home bias.[2] Of course, you might think that investing at home makes sense: "Buy what you know!" But when it comes to investing, buying what you think you know does not necessarily make sense. Just because you have heard about a company does not mean that you can predict its future returns.[*3]

Consider the following fact: Sweden accounts for about 1 percent of the world economy. An investor in Germany or Japan looking for a globally diversified portfolio would invest about 1 percent of his assets in Swedish stocks. Can it make sense for Swedish investors to invest 48 times more? No.[†]

Third, the fees paid by the Active Choosers were much higher: 0.77 percent compared with the 0.17 percent charged by the default fund. This means that if two people invest $10,000 each, the active investor is paying $60 a year more in fees than the one who took the default portfolio. Over time, these fees add up.[‡] In summary, those who selected portfolios for themselves selected a higher equity exposure, less investment in index funds, much more local concentration, and higher fees.

At the time these investments were made, it would have been

---

* For the same reason, it is not wise to invest a large proportion of your retirement wealth in the company where you work. Employees at companies such as Enron and Bear Stearns learned this lesson the hard way when their employer suddenly disappeared and so did much of their retirement savings. In both cases, the employer had encouraged these investments in the company stock.

† If you are worried about currency risk, that is a problem easily solved, and in fact the default fund did solve it, by hedging the currency markets (essentially a type of insurance).

‡ The fees we report here are the ones that were advertised. Later some funds offered discounts, so fees fell.

hard to make the case that the portfolios selected by the Active Choosers were better investments than the default fund. An interesting feature of the Swedish experience is that the launch of the fund occurred just as the bull market in stocks (and the bubble in technology stocks) was ending. Although it is impossible to specify the precise effect of this accident of timing on people's choices (or even on the decision to launch the privatization program), the data provide some strong hints. We have already noted that the actively chosen portfolios had more than 96 percent of their money in stocks. Had the launch occurred just two years later, the proportion invested in stocks would almost certainly have been lower. As we saw earlier, individual investors tend to be trend followers, rather than good forecasters, in their asset-allocation decisions.

In a period in which technology stocks had been soaring, it is not surprising that the investments were also tilted toward those stocks. To give one illustrative example, the fund that attracted the largest market share (aside from the default fund) was Robur Aktiefond Contura, which received 4.2 percent of the investment pool. (This is a huge market share: keep in mind that there were 456 funds, and one-third of the money went into the default fund.) Robur Aktiefond Contura invested primarily in technology and health care stocks in Sweden and elsewhere. Over the five-year period leading up to the choice, its value increased by 534.2 percent, the highest of all the funds in the pool. In the first three years after the launch of the program, it lost 69.5 percent of its value. In the subsequent three years, the returns have continued to be volatile.

In retrospect, it cannot be a surprise that a fund like Robur Aktiefond Contura would get a large percentage of the investments in the pool. Think about what people are being asked to do. They receive a book that lists the returns for 456 funds over various time horizons, along with a lot of other important information, involving fees and risk, that they are not well equipped to understand. The one thing they are probably sure of is that high returns are good. Of course, these are past returns, but investors have traditionally had trouble distinguishing between past returns and forecasts of future returns. We can't help but imagine the following conversation going on over a kitchen table somewhere in Sweden between Mr. and Ms. Svenson.

Mr. Svenson (sipping his coffee): Wilma, what are you doing with that book?

Ms. Svenson: I am looking for the best fund in which to invest, Bjorn. And I think I just found it. Robur Aktiefond Contura is the winner. It is up 534 percent over the past five years. If we invest in this we can retire in Majorca!

Mr. Svenson: Yeah, whatever. Can you pass the gravlax?

Advertising

The decision to allow funds to advertise does not seem particularly controversial. In fact, given the rest of the design of this system, it is hard to imagine an advertising ban. If funds are free to enter this market, then presumably they should be free to court customers by all legal means, which naturally include (truthful) advertising. Still, it is interesting to see what effect advertising had on this market. What should we expect?

Consider two extreme "dream" scenarios. In the first dream, one being dreamt by a free-market economist with a peaceful smile on his face, advertisers are helping to educate consumers by explaining the benefits of lower costs, diversification, and long-run investing, as well as the folly of extrapolating recent returns into the future. In this dream, ads help each consumer discover his own ideal location on what economists call the "efficient frontier"— the place all rational investors want to find. In other words, the advertising helps consumers make better, smarter choices.

The other dream is more of a nightmare, one that keeps psychologists and behavioral economists tossing and turning. In this dream, advertisers are encouraging participants to think big, not to settle for average (by indexing), and to think of investing as a way to get rich. In this nightmare, ads almost never mention fees. But they do talk a lot about past performance, even though there is essentially no evidence that past performance predicts future performance. (People who like to bet on sporting events will recognize a parallel in advertisements telling people about "locks" on upcoming games and about the amazing and nearly infallible forecasts over, say, the past three weeks.)

How did reality turn out? A typical ad showed the actor Harrison Ford, of Star Wars and Indiana Jones fame, plugging a Swedish fund company's products. According to the ad copy, "Harrison Ford can give you a better pension." We are not sure which of Ford's roles qualifies him to provide this advice. (We do know that Indiana Jones is depicted as a professor from the University of Chicago, but so far as we are aware, he was not thought to have much training in finance.)

More generally, a study by financial economist Henrik Cronqvist shows that the ads resembled the nightmare more than the happy dream.[4] Only a small proportion of fund advertising could be construed as directly informative about characteristics relevant for rational investors, such as funds' fees. And while funds with good past track records heavily advertised past returns, such ads were useless in predicting future returns. Nevertheless, fund advertising did strongly affect investors' portfolio choices. It steered people into portfolios with lower expected returns (because of higher fees) and higher risk (through a higher exposure to equities, more active management, more "hot" sectors, and more home bias).

How Long Do Nudges Last?

> VLADIMIR: Well? Shall we go?
> ESTRAGON: Yes, let's go.
> *They do not move.*
>
> —Samuel Beckett, *Waiting for Godot*

One question that we have not discussed is whether nudges are long lasting.[5] One possibility is that people initially exhibit default behavior for reasons such as status quo bias,[6] laziness, procrastination, and so forth, but over time get their act together and make sensible changes to their initial choices. In such a world, the specific design by the choice architect has only a transitory effect. But if the effects of nudges are persistent, then the choice architecture design can be critical, with effects lasting decades. This Swedish experience offers a unique opportunity to provide some insight on this issue because it is possible to track what has happened from the launch up until the end of 2016.

First, some background. After the initial launch of the pension system with all its fanfare, the pension plan became less salient to everyone. The government reduced its advertising significantly, and so did the individual funds, because most of the citizens had already been onboarded. Whereas the initial cohort in 2000, when the plan was launched, included all 4.4 million people who were in the workforce at the time, subsequent cohorts only consist of new entrants into the system; that is, mostly younger people when they start to earn an income, plus new immigrants. For example, the 2016 cohort had only 183,870 people, not enough to make advertising an economically attractive option for fund managers.

In the absence of public and private advertising, over time the public gradually disengaged, and the default had its more typical effect. By 2003, only three years after the new system had launched, fewer than one out of ten (9.4 percent) of the new participants elected to be Active Choosers, a share that declined to only 3 percent in 2010 and was below 1 percent in the most recent years.

Moreover, participants seem to have adopted a "set it and forget it" mindset. When first confronted with a choice, they made a decision, but most failed to revisit it. We can see this by looking at how individuals' portfolio choices varied depending on when they joined the system. To see how we can study this issue consider two hypothetical retirement savers, Madeleine and Per, who were born on January 1, 1982, and were thus eighteen when the Premium Pension Plan was launched. They were both attending university at the time, but Madeleine had a part-time job when she started school, making her eligible to join the pension system, whereas Per did not begin working until 2002. Both experienced all the advertising accompanying the launch of the system, but only Madeleine was nudged to think about making a choice at that time. Per never gave it a thought. To estimate the differential effect of being exposed to the ads depending on whether they were relevant, we can compare people in Madeleine's situation to that of Per's, by comparing the choices of young people who joined in 2000 to those who joined in the next couple of years.

Statistical analyses show that after controlling for other observable characteristics, the odds of becoming an Active Chooser were about six times higher for people in the 2000 cohort compared with those in the two years just following the launch, 2001 and 2002. Thus, the ads mostly affected the people who were in a "deciding" mindset when those ads ran.

Another question of interest is what happens over time. Do people stick with their initial choices or do they reconsider over time as they see how things are working out? One way of looking at that question is to ask what proportion of people changed their mind and switched from being a Delegator to an Active Chooser, and vice versa. It is possible to study the choices of the 4.4 million Swedish retirement savers who joined the system in 2000 and then follow them from the launch until 2016.*

Just over a quarter (27.4 percent) of the initial Delegators changed their minds and decided to become Active Choosers.[7] The bulk of these switches occurred during the first decade after the initial choices. What prompted them to become active? Some of these switches were, uh, "helped" by third parties who offered to give participants investment advice. This was particularly common in the early years, when advisers could make changes on behalf of clients easily if they were given a PIN number. (Sensibly, these rules were later changed.) Thus, the 27 percent represents an upper bound on the number of Delegators who independently decided to start managing their own portfolio. Everyone else just stuck with the default for at least the sixteen years we've observed.

Perhaps surprisingly, the impact of the advertising to encourage Active Choosing was even more persistent. Only a tiny percentage

---

* One proviso: Those who chose the default fund (the Delegators) could switch to being Active Choosers at any time, but when the system started, if you did not choose the default fund initially, you could not switch into it later. This rule was changed in 2009, at which point switches in either direction were permitted and costless.

(2.9 percent) of the initial wave of Active Choosers ever switched to becoming a Delegator. Once an Active Chooser, always an Active Chooser!

We have seen so far that switching between being an Active Chooser and a Delegator was uncommon. Most people chose one strategy or the other and stuck with it. Additionally, the group we are calling Active Choosers was not very active. Recall that we gave them that label on the basis of a single decision (under the influence of big ad campaigns) to pick funds for themselves. That was pretty much the end of their "activity." For the group, the median number of trades over the entire sixteen-year period was just one. This is a similar level of activity that is observed by American investors in 401(k) plans.

A natural follow-up question is what it would take to capture the attention of the vast majority of investors who were behaving quite passively. Could anything awaken them from their stupor? Two events give us a chance to examine this issue: one that affected the default fund and another that concerned one of the individual funds in the pension system.

The default fund has undergone some changes over time. While it has always been a low-fee fund with global diversification, we mentioned that when it was first launched it had some quirky features such as the home bias toward Swedish stocks and some small investments in hedge funds and venture capital. In 2010, the fund switched to become essentially a global index fund (investing all over the world) and fees were reduced further to 0.11 percent.*

---

* The fund also has an age-related rebalancing feature that reduces equity exposure for the elderly. The reasoning for why the default fund should be (at least) 100 percent equities is that this is a small portion of the social security system (2.5 percent payroll tax from a total tax of 16 percent). The remaining part is considered to be more like a fixed income investment.

In 2010, the Swedish government approved a much more radical change: It decided to permit the default fund to employ financial leverage at the discretion of the fund's management. The statute allowed for up to 50 percent leverage. What this means is that the fund managers were allowed to essentially borrow money to buy even more stocks, and they took advantage of the new discretion. Fifty percent leverage means that if the market went up by 10 percent, the fund would grow by 15 percent, but conversely, if prices fell, the fund would fall by 50 percent more. That is pretty risky!

Any investor who was worried about this massive increase in the riskiness of their portfolio had a great alternative: they could switch at no cost to another fund that was identical to the default fund, but without the leverage. But almost no one did. This is particularly surprising because a study of Swedish investors reported that users of the default fund considered themselves relatively more risk-averse than average and said they wanted a safe investment.[8] It seems likely that they just didn't notice (or understand) the change in the fund.

The other event that tested the limits of investor inertia came in January 2017 when a leading Swedish business magazine reported that the CEO of Allra, one of the fund companies in the pension system, had purchased the most expensive house in Sweden the previous year. Oh, and he bought a helicopter. Pro tip: if you plan to steal money from your investors, it is probably not a good idea to flaunt your wealth. Less than a month later, one of the leading Swedish newspapers launched a series of articles pointing to possibly fraudulent practices by Allra. After a few weeks, the Swedish Pensions Agency decided to prohibit people from switching *into* Allra's funds, pending a fraud investigation. It is important to emphasize that people were still permitted to shift contributions *out of* Allra to other funds at any time and at no cost.*

Before the fraud allegations, Allra participated in the pension system with four different funds. A total of 123,217 investors had picked these funds, with about $2 billion of assets invested. One might expect a significant portion of these so-called Active Choosers to dump their Allra investments based on the credible news of possible fraud. In fact, a sudden run on the fund might well have been expected. Yet nothing of the kind occurred. In the week after the revelation of the fraud allegations, only 1.4 percent of the Allra investors sold their shares. And even after the accounting firm Deloitte, which thereafter resigned as auditor, reported Allra to the authorities, only 16.5 percent of the start-of-the-year investors had elected to move their money into some other fund.

What do we conclude from this episode? At the time of the scandal, in early 2017, the number of funds in the system had grown to almost nine hundred, which is obviously too high. In fact, Sweden was quickly approaching the absurd situation in which there would be more funds offered than there were new participants becoming Active Choosers. We think most would agree that one fund per investor seems more than necessary. Furthermore, it is clearly impossible for a small country like Sweden to adequately monitor such a large number of funds. Reporters, not regulators, discovered the scandal involving Allra.

---

* Adding to the attention was the fact that a prominent attorney, and Sweden's previous minister for justice, served as the chairman of Allra's board of directors.

Lessons

The Swedish experience illustrates the power of inertia at several levels. Citizens who were nudged by the government and advertisements to become their own portfolio managers steadfastly stuck with that approach, but then they became highly passive. Even a major scandal involving a fund manager did not set off alarm bells. Perhaps not surprisingly, those in the default fund were also oblivious to a massive change in the makeup of the fund. Maybe just as interestingly, the policymakers have not been willing to rethink the design of the system in light of what happened. The designers of the plan did not set out to offer nine hundred funds to choose from, and clearly no one would think that a good idea if nearly all new investors are choosing the default fund. Of course, these facts have not gone unnoticed by the government. The number of funds has now been trimmed back to just under five hundred, and the Swedish parliament is currently considering additional reforms but not a radical rethink of the entire structure. The design features of even new government programs can be surprisingly sticky. (And when it comes to older traditions, have we mentioned that ultramodern Sweden still has a monarchy, which they seem to treasure? Humans are endlessly interesting.)

In this context, we much like the idea of relying on a sensible default. But if it were up to us, we would make some changes to the Swedish plan, including a drastic reduction in the number of funds and elimination of leverage in the default fund. (Call us cautious, but we think that if a leveraged fund is included in the mix, investors should have to actively select it.) We would also urge something that we think should be common practice in all participant-directed investment plans: a restart. Just as you should regularly reboot your computer, we think it is healthy for investors to be encouraged occasionally (once every twenty years does not seem too often) just to start over. Ideally, they would do so without being reminded of what they currently own. (There are no taxes or transaction costs involved in switching.) If the best explanation for why someone is doing something is that long ago, they made an ill-informed investment choice possibly based on advice from Harrison Ford, it might be time to reconsider.

Importantly, doing so would require picking a default for the many people who are likely not to respond to the request to reboot. There is no escaping that one.

As to the more general question about the stickiness of nudges, we think that the results here are highly instructive, but we urge caution in extrapolating from them to nudges in general. The longevity of nudges is inevitably an empirical question, and we should expect variability across populations and contexts. Nudges vary from default rules to text reminders to graphic warnings to the size and color of a font. And environments vary greatly in how much attention people are devoting to the task at hand. Are participants like *Godot*'s Vladimir and Estragon, or do they behave like drivers who are constantly changing lanes? Having been nudged, some demographic groups might behave differently than others, because they are more likely to be paying attention, because they have more time on their hands, because they are more or less educated, or simply because they care more.

Graphic warnings may or may not have a long-term effect; people might get used to them and their impact might wear off. If so, choice architects might want to rotate them, changing them every few months (as indeed the U.S. Food and Drug Administration is planning to do with graphic warnings for cigarettes). If people are sent a text reminder every month that a bill is due, the reminder might work every time—unless people stop paying attention because they are getting too many notifications. It seems a good bet that nudges will have the longest life when people are on auto-pilot, in which case default rules are likely to be sticky. In outer space, an object that has been nudged will keep going in that direction until it is nudged again. Swedish retirement savers appear to resemble such objects.

II

Borrow More Today:
Mortgages and Credit Cards

We have seen that Humans can suffer from self-control problems, causing them to be present-biased, meaning that they put undue weight on things they can have now versus things they can only get later. This is the inherent problem to overcome in helping people save for retirement. When a family invests in a retirement savings plan, it is deferring consumption today for a better life later, perhaps many decades later. To be able to retire, members of the household have to figure out how to keep their current spending less than their income. Unfortunately, many families struggle with a more basic problem: spending more each month than they make. They borrow money to spend more today, something that is easier to do now than it has ever been.

Although money lenders have a long history (even before Shakespeare's *The Merchant of Venice*), widespread access to consumer credit began in the 1920s, when it became common for merchants to offer consumers the opportunity to buy appliances, automobiles, and other big-ticket items on an installment plan. Interest rates were high and the sellers retained ownership of the goods as collateral, backing the loan until the payments were complete. Making credit available for fancy new appliances was like placing bowls of cashews all around the house, and many households could not resist the temptation to spend. The Great Depression of the 1930s came as a shock to those who lost their jobs and then had their appliances removed from their homes.

Automobile sales continue to be financed in much the same way as the old installment plans, since the lenders retain a lien on the car until the loan is paid off, but the advent of credit cards gave consumers a new way to satisfy their urges for immediate gratification. It is now almost essential to have some kind of credit or debit card to function in the modern economy, as cards are required to buy airline tickets, check into hotels, and use many other kinds of services. And in something of a vicious circle, a record of responsibly using a credit card is one of the most important determinants of a household's credit score, which determines whether one can get a mortgage, and the interest rate paid. In the fullness of time, and maybe sooner rather than later, physical currencies will be gone, or nearly so, and everyone will be using cards or some other electronic payment mechanism. Of course, one can use credit and debit cards just for the convenience they offer and avoid all interest payments by paying off the bill in full each month, but this requires considerable self-control. Americans now owe more than $1 trillion in credit card debt, and the United States is hardly unique in seeing growth in this type of lending. In fact, China now surpasses the United States in total credit card debt.

For someone who wants to own a home, paying the full amount in cash is usually not an option because many families pay more than several years of household income to buy a home. To do this, they get a mortgage. Homeowner mortgage debt in the United States now exceeds $15 trillion.[1] The existence of so much mortgage debt is not necessarily alarming because borrowers also have the equity in their home as an asset, but many borrowers obtain loans having put up less than 5 percent of the purchase price. That means that if real estate prices fall, they can find themselves "underwater"; the amount they owe is greater than the value of their home.

Although there are numerous ways that people can borrow money, from pawnshops, loan sharks, and payday lenders to student loans, in this chapter we focus on mortgages and credit cards because they are common around the world and offer interesting ways to apply the tools of choice architecture. In discussing these markets, we make a distinction we find useful in thinking about consumer decision-making in general, namely whether the most important aspect of the consumer experience depends on the process of *choosing* or *using*. An example can help explain what we mean. Consider first the purchase of a new television or computer monitor. This is a product for which the user experience depends almost entirely on whether the purchase was a good choice. Such things as the size, resolution, and brightness of the monitor will determine satisfaction, but once you get the thing set up and adjusted, there is really almost nothing else to do. Even the two of us have mastered the use of the power button on the remote control.

Compare that with a tennis racket. Sunstein, a pretty good club tennis player, has preferences about which racket to use, but no racket is yet available that will allow Thaler to beat Sunstein in tennis. In fact, back when they used to play together in Chicago, Sunstein managed to win (easily) after the strings on his racket broke. And give Rafael Nadal or Roger Federer an old wood racket with thirty-year-old strings and either could still beat Sunstein without breaking a sweat (alas, 6-0, 6-0, 6-0). When it comes to playing tennis, the way the racket is used is more important than the choice of the racket.

Although the contrast is not quite as stark, mortgages are more like monitors and credit cards are more like tennis rackets. If you choose a good mortgage and (importantly) pay the bills on time, you will generally do just fine.* Much the same would be true for credit cards if people paid off their full balance every month. You can even pick a card because it allows you to put a picture of your dog on the front, and you won't suffer too badly if you pay the entire bill every month. Unfortunately, many credit card users carry over outstanding debts on several cards, amounting to thousands of dollars. In these circumstances, the way the consumer uses the card is more important than the choice of the card. With this distinction in mind, our discussion of mortgages will focus on how we can help people make better selections, whereas with credit cards we will concentrate on helping people become smarter users.

Mortgages

Once upon a time, shopping for a mortgage was pretty easy. Most mortgages had a fixed rate for the life of the loan, which in the United States was typically thirty years. Most borrowers provided at least a 20 percent down payment. In this regime, comparing loans was a snap—just pick the one with the lowest interest rate, a task made easier by the fact that all lenders are required to report interest rates the same way, using the annual percentage rate (APR).

Mortgage shopping has now become much more complicated. Borrowers can choose from a variety of fixed-rate loans (for which the interest rate does not change over the life of the loan), as well

---

* There is one important exception to this statement about mortgages. There are opportunities to refinance a mortgage when interest rates fall. Sharp homeowners take advantage of these opportunities and could make use of the kind of advice we advocate for credit cards. However, Thaler wants Sunstein to finish reading the chapter, so this complexity will be ignored.

as numerous variable-rate loans, in which the interest rate can vary according to a formula tied to specific bond markets. Borrowers can also consider such exotic products as interest-only loans, under which the borrower makes no payments toward the principal on the loan, meaning it is never paid off unless the house is sold (with luck, at a profit) or the borrower either wins the lottery, refinances the loan, or sells the house and pays off the loan. Many variable-rate mortgages are further complicated by so-called teaser rates—a low interest rate that applies for a period of a year or two, after which the rate (and payments) go up, sometimes dramatically. (Teaser rates exploit present bias.) Then there is the matter of fees, which can vary greatly and include points (fixed payments the borrower makes in order to receive a lower interest rate), and prepayment penalties that must be paid if the loan is repaid early. There's much more. With this amount of complexity, choosing a mortgage can make picking a retirement portfolio look easy.

One factor that might seem comforting is that the market for mortgage lending is highly decentralized and competitive. Some economists argue that such highly competitive markets will protect consumers from making poor choices. However, this argument is flawed, both logically and empirically. One reason involves the pervasiveness of various forms of sludge that make shopping more difficult. For example, if some of the features of a mortgage are "shrouded,"[2] as we discussed in the chapter on sludge, consumers may not realize how much they are actually paying. In such circumstances, competition does not assure that the best or cheapest products win the race for customers. In fact, providers might have a lot of freedom to exploit people's limited attention, and those who play it straight may lose out to less-scrupulous competition. Exploitation of behavioral biases can be a winning strategy.

For some products, what you see is what you get, and competition often works well. If there are gas stations on each of four corners of an intersection, and prices are visibly posted, then the prices will not differ much among the stations. But if at another intersection there are four banks that issue mortgages, there is little reason to believe that the costs of borrowing will converge. Even if the banks advertised the interest rate for one particular mortgage on large signs, the shrouded costs will not be apparent to consumers. It is easier to compare fuel prices than mortgage costs.

One possible solution to the complexity problem is to have expert advisers provide help. Indeed, in many complex markets, careers emerge to provide specialized help such as that offered by financial planners and real estate brokers. In the mortgage market, these experts are mortgage brokers. The problem in all such settings is that the advisers can have conflicts of interest that can make good advice hard to obtain. Real estate agents get paid only if houses sell, which means they have a strong incentive to encourage transactions. Even those who represent buyers actually get paid a percentage of the sales price, so it is no surprise that they tend to show their clients houses in the top end of their stated price range. We are not saying that all such experts are crooks! (Sunstein's sister is a real estate agent, and she is honest. Really and truly.) We are just stating the obvious fact that a market for advice does not guarantee that the advice will be good. Fortune-tellers remain in business. So, yes, there are honest and knowledgeable experts in most complex domains, but for unsophisticated buyers, the very opacity of a market that creates a demand for expertise makes it difficult to evaluate the value of the advice they offer.

In the case of mortgage brokers, there is considerable evidence that at least some do not act in the best interest of their clients. To understand why, keep in mind that mortgage brokers get paid a fee that depends on the loan amount and the profitability of the loan to the lender, so the better the deal for the borrower, the less the broker makes. The 2008 financial crisis was caused by many factors, but one of them was a pervasive practice by which borrowers took out loans with tiny down payments and low teaser rates that were scheduled to rise substantially in a year or two. Often those borrowers would not be able to afford the higher payments, so they were counting on the possibility of refinancing the loan when the initial low rate jumped, creating another windfall to the broker. When real estate prices fell, they owed more money than the house was worth, and often defaulted.

The economist Susan Woodward has found numerous other troubling aspects of this market.[3] She studied which kinds of borrowers got the best deals, and under what circumstances, after controlling for risk and other factors. Here are some of her key findings:

- African American and Latino borrowers pay more for their loans after adjusting for risk.
- Borrowers who live in neighborhoods where adults have only a high school education pay more for their loans than those who live in neighborhoods where adults have a college education.
- There can be a big return to shopping. Calling two more mortgage brokers saves shoppers an average of nearly $1,400 in fees.
- Loans made by mortgage brokers are more expensive than those made by direct lenders.
- Sources of loan complexity such as points and seller contribution to closing costs (which can make comparing loans more difficult) are expensive for borrowers, and the additional cost is greater on brokered loans than on direct loans.

We can take some general lessons from this analysis. When markets get more complicated, unsophisticated and less-educated shoppers will be especially disadvantaged by the complexity. The unsophisticated shoppers are also more likely to be given bad or self-interested advice by people serving in roles that appear to be helpful and purely advisory. In this market, mortgage brokers who cater to rich clients probably have a greater incentive to establish a reputation for fair dealing in order to create future business. By contrast, mortgage brokers who cater to the poor are often more interested in making a quick buck. So, the problem we are describing is partly one of inequality.

What can be done to help? We have three sets of choice architecture suggestions for consideration. The first is to draw back the curtain on shrouded attributes—to make sure that fees and costs are not hidden. For example, mortgage providers might be required to fill out, on a single page (or maybe half a page), a list of "major costs," including everything that counts as more than trivial. And these costs should be added up and ideally incorporated into the quoted interest rate, to make comparisons easier!

Our second, more ambitious proposal would eliminate the need for the first one. It builds on the concept of the standard form lease to create more standardization. Going back to our comparison of competing gas stations and mortgage lenders, the idea would be to make comparison shopping easier. To do so, regulators might designate a relatively small number of mortgage types that every lender would have to include in their menu of options. Perhaps there would be two varieties, a fixed rate and variable rate, each offered in fifteen- and thirty-year durations, so four options in all. Let's call these EZ mortgages. All the fine print in such mortgages would be the same and would be created by the regulator in consultation with industry and consumer experts. Ideally there would be no fees other than the reported interest rate, and the formulas used in the adjustable-rate mortgages would be identical. This would include what interest rate the loans would be pegged to, by how much rates could change, and how often.[4]

In this setup, borrowers who are shopping for a loan and are willing to restrict their choices to EZ loans would just have to decide whether they wanted a fixed- or variable-rate mortgage, and whether they want a fifteen- or thirty-year term. Within any category, they could simply pick the mortgage with the lowest APR and be confident they were getting the best deal. Even if interest rates vary according to credit rating or down payment, borrowers could still search within their appropriate category and quickly find the best offer.

Because we are libertarian paternalists, we would have a presumption against banning other types of mortgages, including those with possible traps such as teaser rates. (The presumption could be rebutted if certain traps could be shown to be likely to harm consumers, and if nudges would not do enough to help.) At the same time, such loans would come with a warning that the loans are not EZ compliant, and that buyers should be wary. We can understand why some would go further and forbid some such products as "dangerous to your financial health," but we can also understand that such mortgages might be good choices for some borrowers. As in all regulatory domains, one has to make choices about how much to interfere with the choices of buyers and sellers. Our model creates at least a ring-fenced portion of the market in which shopping is easy. These would be the equivalent of the beginner slopes at a ski resort.

Our third proposal might not be necessary if the first and second are adopted, but governments have not always followed our suggestions, so let's be generous and give them another policy alternative. Here we would use the tool of Smart Disclosure. The terms of a (non-EZ) mortgage are so complicated that not even experts can be sure of all the provisions. Regulators have tried repeatedly to create simpler disclosure forms and, as noted, we like the general idea. But even these can be hard to digest, and even if our first proposal is adopted, important details might somehow be buried in that dreaded fine print. The solution is to make *all* the details available in a structured electronic format, continually updated in an online database we will call the Mortgage File.

A task that is hard even for an expert can be easy for a computer using modern tools such as machine learning. This means that if the Mortgage File existed, there could be a robust market for mortgage choice engines similar to travel websites. Borrowers would plug in their information, including down payment and credit score, and the choice engine would search for the best options available. Sophisticated choice engines could also help with the choice of fixed versus variable and duration. Of course, converting experts into robots does not guarantee that the advice will be unbiased. Robots can be programmed to suggest mortgages from lenders offering side payments to the company providing the choice engine. But we think that choice engines have a significant advantage over human advisers: they are much easier to audit.

Sensible regulations would require choice engines to keep track of their recommendations (in a way that keeps personal data private) and make them available to regulators upon request. It is also possible that choice engine aggregators like Kayak would emerge as they have in the travel sector. That would allow consumers to do their own audit pretty easily, especially for the EZ products. One final advantage of the online shopping we are trying to encourage: it is especially likely to help women and minority groups. A study of automobile shopping found that women and African Americans pay about the same amount as white males when they buy a car online, but at the dealership they pay more, even after accounting for other factors, such as income.[5]

Credit Cards

Credit cards serve two functions. First, they provide a mode of payment in lieu of cash. The second purpose of a credit card is to provide a ready source of liquidity if you want to spend more than you currently have in cash. Debit cards, which look just like credit cards, serve only the first function, because they are linked to a bank account and do not allow for borrowing unless linked also to a line of credit. (Warning: Some debit cards offer lines of credit at high fees. If you use a debit card to borrow, you should make sure that the fees you pay are lower than they would be with a credit card.)

Credit cards are blessedly convenient. Paying with a credit card is often faster than paying with cash and lets you avoid struggling with change; digging into your pocket to find the correct change and managing the large jar of pennies at home are vexations from which you are liberated. Not to mention the frequent-flier miles! These facts have not been lost on American consumers. In 2018, the average card user had four different cards.[6] But if you are not careful, credit cards can be addictive, and Humans often misuse them. Consider some numbers from the United States:

- Forty-three percent of balances are not fully paid off each month (revolvers), while 31 percent are entirely paid off (the rest have no balance or are inactive).
- Total credit card debt was $1.1 trillion in February 2020.

♦ The average outstanding debt balance of a U.S. household was around $6,000 in 2019 across 3.1 credit cards. Total interest payments were $121 billion with most interest rates hovering between 14 and 18 percent.

♦ By 2018, around 9 percent of general-purpose cardholders and about 4.5 percent of private-label cardholders had at least one severe delinquency in the preceding 12 months.

♦ On top of interest, users spend a lot of money on fees of some kind. Fees are about 5.5 percent of cycle-ending balances for the year, with just under half of that being late fees.

Comparable figures can be found in many other nations, and in some ways, the situation seems to be getting worse over time. Looking back at the problems of self-control discussed in Chapter 2, we can see how credit cards create serious problems for some people. In the pre–credit card era, households were pretty much forced to use a pay-as-you-go accounting system. That is why people used Christmas clubs and jars of money labeled according to purpose or payee. Now if you don't have the cash to fill your car up with gas, there is always your credit card. Credit cards inhibit self-control in other ways. One study by marketing professors Drazen Prelec and Duncan Simester found that people were willing to pay twice as much to bid on tickets to a basketball game if they could pay with their credit card rather than cash.[7] And there is no telling how much money people pay with the cards in order to get those precious frequent-flier miles. When the spending limit on one card is reached, there is always another card to use, or a new account can be opened using one of the solicitations that arrive announcing that you have been "preapproved."

The traditional approach to dealing with issues like this is thorough regulation. For example, in 2009, the U.S. Congress enacted the Credit Card Accountability Responsibility and Disclosure (CARD) Act, which was designed to protect Humans from various risks and costs, including over-the-limit fees and late fees. Informed by behavioral science, the law included several nudges in the form of disclosure requirements, intended to ensure that shrouded attributes were no longer so shrouded; for example, credit card statements have to offer clear information about the consequences of making only minimum payments for lengthy periods. Certain kinds of fees were also forbidden, and in that sense, the law goes far beyond nudging. Even when it does, it is designed to protect Humans from their mistakes, on the theory that financial institutions have been exploiting behavioral biases (above all, limited attention and unrealistic optimism). The good news is that the law has been found to save consumers about $11.9 billion annually.[8] Again, the distributional effects appear to be good: the savings are concentrated among people with poor credit ratings.

However, as with any regulation of complex products, sellers can always think of new ways to deceive buyers. We can and should use the tools of libertarian paternalism to offer consumers more help in making good decisions. Serious consideration should be given to more and better disclosure requirements, focused on protecting those at the bottom of the economic ladder. For debit cards, further steps might be taken to protect consumers from overdraft protection programs, through which they take out high-interest loans. Behaviorally informed regulations from the Federal Reserve Board prohibit banks from making overdraft protection the default option when opening a new account. That is a reasonable initiative, but as we have seen, default options are not always sticky.[9] When opening their accounts, customers are asked whether they would like the exciting option of being able to borrow money if they run short of cash. Few will inquire about the details of this seemingly generous offer—from which banks stand to make a lot of money.

At the same time, overdraft protection can be useful for some consumers. It's convenient not to be turned away at the ATM, and the fees for bouncing checks are high. There is a hard balance to be struck here. At the very least, the Federal Reserve Board ought to consider further nudges to protect customers from being lured into enrolling in supposedly protective programs from which they lose on balance.

As with mortgages, we think credit cards are a good domain in which to use Smart Disclosure. We suggest that credit card companies be required to post all their rules and fees in an online database much like the Mortgage File. As with mortgages, this would allow choice engines to help people make better decisions about which card(s) to use.

Here is an example: One way credit card companies have slyly raised prices is by reducing the number of days you have between the time you get your bill and the day your payment is due. If you miss that payment, you pay not only a penalty but also interest on all the purchases you make the next month, even if you normally pay off your bill in full. For a heavy credit card user, such as a frequent business traveler, missing a single large payment by just one day can result in an extra payment of hundreds of dollars.

The bigger advantage from Smart Disclosure, however, would come from helping to change behavior. Recall the difference between televisions and tennis rackets: the way a consumer uses the credit card is more important than the card chosen. As we have noted, the average American household that uses credit cards has four cards and more than $6,000 in outstanding balances. That means they are paying a *lot* of money on both interest and fees—in many cases, much more than they need to be paying.

One illustration of the suboptimal way in which families deal with their credit card debt is how they choose to allocate the money they pay off across the various cards they have. Take the following simple example. Dan owes $2,000 on Credit Card A, which charges 18 percent interest, and $1,000 on Credit Card B, which charges 23 percent interest. He has decided that he can afford to pay $600 this month to reduce his credit card debt. The minimum payments required by the two cards are $40 and $20. For consumers facing a problem like Dan's, how much do they pay to each card?

A team of economists has studied this question using data from the United Kingdom and later replicated the results using American data.[10] Before we get to what most people do, let's first ask what Dan *should* do? For sure he should pay at least the minimum on each card, since penalties for failing to pay that tiny amount are high. After allocating amounts for those minimum payments, the best strategy for Dan is to pay all the rest of the money to the high-interest-rate card. That is a simple enough rule: *pay the minimum on each card, then pay down the card with the highest interest rate.* Yet the researchers find that only about 10 percent of their sample follow something approximating this rule.

What do they do instead? There are many possible heuristics people might follow, including pay the same amount on each card, but the strategy that is most common is one the researchers call "balance matching." In our example, Dan would pay $400 to Card A and $200 to Card B. People appear to be nearly unresponsive to the differences in interest rates, which can be 6 percentage points or more. The more cards a household has, the more this mistake costs. Of course, it is also the case that the larger the balances, the greater the costs.

We should emphasize that this particular mistake is just the tip of the iceberg. There are many other forms of arbitrage families could use, the most obvious being not to run up so much debt. Other money-saving possibilities include drawing down savings to pay off more. It is not uncommon for households to have money in a checking or savings account earning essentially nothing and have large credit card debts.[11] Whether or not this is a poor choice depends on complicated mental accounting and self-control questions. Having a rainy-day mental account can be sensible, and some households use the balance limits on their cards as a self-control device to limit spending. The same kinds of issues arise in the case of borrowing elsewhere at a lower rate, such as with a home equity loan or against 401(k) assets.

Let's just concede that if people can't solve the easy problem of allocating their payments optimally across their various cards, they are unlikely to be getting the other stuff right, the most important of which is paying at least the minimum payment on time. This problem can be solved by setting up an auto-pay from your bank to the credit card, but only about 15 percent of cardholders use this service to pay their bills.[12] Of course, given the high fees that checking accounts charge for writing checks with insufficient funds, an auto-pay setup may not be smart for consumers who do not keep much money in their bank accounts.

We hope it is clear why we emphasized that the biggest problem with credit cards is how they are used. Being absentminded and innumerate is very costly in this domain. And while auto-pay can solve the memory problem, an even better strategy would be to turn over the management of credit card debt to someone who will both do the math and not be forgetful. As they say, there is an app for everything, and this is no exception. An app we particularly like is called Tally.[13] (Full disclosure: Tally was started by Jason Brown, who, when he was a student at the University of Chicago Booth School of Business, took Thaler's class. We have no financial stake in his company.)

Here is what would happen if Dan, the guy with the $3,000 owed to two credit cards, signed up for Tally: After doing a soft credit check, Tally would automatically pay off all $3,000 of Dan's credit card debt and take responsibility for managing his accounts. Tally would then monitor all activity on those cards and Dan's checking account, and make sure that all bills were paid on time. Most important, every month Tally would nudge Dan to pay off his debt faster by recommending a higher default payment based on his available cash and upcoming expenses. For using the service, Tally would charge Dan interest on the money it lends him, but at a lower rate than charged by the credit card.

Tally would also save Dan a lot of money by making sure that he never gets hit with a late fee or has an unpaid balance at the end of the month, because that is when using a credit card gets really expensive. If you have a zero balance and buy something for $1,000, you will not have to pay any interest to the credit card until the due date on your next bill, which can be as many as fifty-five days away. But if you paid just a penny less than the full amount some month, interest would start accruing on that $1,000 purchase starting the day you bought it. Ouch.

How can Tally pull this off? Jason is a nice enough guy, but Tally is supposed to be a business, not a charity. The answer is that credit cards charge really high interest rates even to people with pretty good ratings. This means that Tally can borrow at lower rates directly from banks on a person's behalf and then get paid a small fee by the bank.

Even if you have never missed a credit card payment and have plenty of money in the bank, if you slip up and miss a payment, you will be charged an interest rate close to 20 percent, even now when banks can borrow essentially interest-free. Remarkably, 20 percent of all late fee revenue comes from people with "super prime" credit,[14] because even people making good salaries can be absentminded. This is one reason that credit cards are such a profitable business. If you can afford to keep a reasonable balance in your checking account but tend to be absentminded like us, make sure you are on auto-pay.

Early in this chapter we introduced the distinction between choosing and using, and suggested that choosing is more important for mortgages, but using is more important for credit cards. For mortgages we are hoping that Smart Disclosure and EZ loans lead to better choices, and we urge people to use auto-pay to make sure they don't miss a mortgage payment. For credit cards, Smart Disclosure would allow choice engines to emerge as well, especially if user data were included. If you pay off your card each month, then you might care most about airline points, but if you run a balance, you should care most about interest rates and fees.

But Tally is not a choice engine. It is a *user engine*. Wouldn't it be nice if there were more of those in life? Although we like Jason and wish him well, we hope his business model spawns lots of imitators and competition. Anyone who can help people reduce the costs of their credit card habit gets a thumbs-up from us. And though Make It Easy remains our mantra, one of the best ways to make it easy is to make it automatic.

12

Insurance:
Don't Sweat the Small Stuff

There was a popular self-help book with the title *Don't Sweat the Small Stuff . . . and It's All Small Stuff*. The book's sensible message was that we should not get obsessed with minor annoyances that, in and of themselves, are not really a big deal. This is certainly good advice that applies in nearly every aspect of our lives. (Even coauthors who have worked together for decades sometimes forget this point.) Although that book is about emotional well-being rather than financial planning, the title serves as an excellent guide to insurance purchases.

Economists agree about the right way to think about insurance. The most important principle is to get protection against rare but significant mishaps that can lead to financial ruin. The sorts of risks that should be insured are homes being destroyed by floods or fires, major health problems, the death or disability of a family income earner, and the crash of the family car (if it is still worth anything). Any of these events can put a household in debt for years, or even lead to bankruptcy. Paying a company to share those risks makes good sense. We should not be insuring against the possibility that our team will lose the championship game, that our coffee machine dies, or even that we dent our car backing into a parking spot at night.

Of course, what constitutes a "large" loss will depend on one's financial situation. Billionaires don't need any kind of insurance, while poor families are in a more precarious situation. But the key principle remains the same. "Don't insure the small stuff" is really good advice, but people do not seem to follow it. In fact, people sometimes fail to insure the big stuff! Those living on a floodplain often fail to purchase insurance against a flood and can be wiped out by one of those so-called hundred-year floods that seem to happen about once a decade now. These losses are tragic. But in this chapter, we concentrate on the mistake at the other end of the loss spectrum, the error of insuring the small stuff. We will show that can cost families thousands of dollars a year.

The earliest forms of insurance did cover the sorts of risks that are sensible to insure. Merchants would buy insurance to cover the risk that a sailing ship would not return with its cargo for whatever reason.[1] Fire insurance became common after the Great Fire of London in 1666.[2] Mortgage lenders now require homeowners to have property insurance to make sure that the bank's collateral does not go up in smoke. Because insurance contracts can be complicated and crammed with fine print, you will not be surprised to learn that Humans often stumble when they have to choose which policy to buy. And you will be even less surprised to find out that we think some improvements in choice architecture can help here, too.

Even if you have paid off your mortgage, it is completely sensible for you to have an insurance policy that will protect you in case your home is destroyed by a fire or damaged by a storm. For many families, their home is the most valuable asset they own, and you should make sure that your policy would cover the replacement cost of your home (not the land) in case of a total loss. However, homeowners insurance policies, like many other kinds of insurance, are usually sold with a deductible, which is the portion of any loss that the policyholder has to pay. It is important to understand how deductibles work, because choosing the wrong deductible is the single most common mistake consumers make in purchasing any kind of insurance. If you are tired of reading about money mistakes, you can skip the rest of this chapter if you promise to follow this one rule of thumb: *when purchasing insurance, choose the largest deductible available.*

Of course, there are exceptions to any rule of thumb, including this one. If you are offered a deductible so large that paying it would cause a serious financial hardship, we give you permission to choose a lower one. But in general, people choose a deductible that is too low. In fact, we have a name for this mistake: *deductible aversion.*

Extended Warranties

The general principle that underlies our advice about deductibles is that you want to "self-insure" as many risks as possible. After all, it is costly for the insurance company to sell you a policy and to process a claim. That makes insuring small risks a bad deal for the consumer, which is why you should almost always decline the opportunity to buy them.

Consider an example. We just checked online and found a nice microwave oven for about $100. The seller offers an extended warranty for an extra $10. Is that a good deal? Just ask yourself: When is the last time that your microwave oven stopped working? For us, that would be never. But you might ask: What if one of my kids stupidly puts something metal inside the oven and its wiring gets fried? We would say two things. First, it probably isn't covered by the policy. Look at the fine print. And second, it is $100— not nothing, but not a whole lot. Buy a new one!

To make your life happier, especially if your spouse is likely to blame you on the rare occasions when you would have been better off having bought the policy, we recommend setting up a special mental account that we call an On My Own Account. It can be a real savings account at the bank or just a ledger or spreadsheet. Every time you do not buy the extended warranty, or trip insurance, or decline the collision damage waiver on a car rental (which is probably covered by your credit card anyway), or take a larger deductible on an insurance policy, deposit the money you saved into that account. On the rare occasions when such choices turn out to be unlucky, just deduct the cost from your On My Own balance. The money in that account will build up quickly if you follow our advice about deductibles.

Deductible Aversion

Insurance policies usually offer a choice of deductibles. In the United States, this includes policies for homes, cars, and health care. In a study titled "(Over)insuring Modest Risks," economist Justin Sydnor documents the case for choosing a higher deductible.[3] He analyzed the data from fifty thousand homeowners insurance policyholders in the early 2000s at an insurance company selling such policies. (The results would be similar for other kinds of insurance.) At that time, the insurance company offered four deductible choices: $100, $250, $500, and $1,000. Very few customers select the $100 deductible (which is very expensive), so we will just say don't take that option.

The question we want to answer is whether it would be smart for consumers to increase their deductible. Let's take one example to see how the analysis works. On average, policyholders would save about $100 per year in premiums by increasing their deductible from $500 to $1,000. Of course, if they have a claim, they will have to pay up to an additional $500. So, they would have to have a claim about once every five years to break even. Got it? But claims occur much less often than that. In Sydnor's sample, only about 5 percent of policyholders make claims each year, so increasing the deductible is a really good deal!

If all the policyholders took our advice to increase the deductible and deposit the savings into their On My Own accounts, they would each be adding $100 a year into the account and would have to dip into it just once every twenty years or so. Another way to look at it is that after twenty years, such policyholders would, on average, have $1,500 (plus interest) in their On My Own account. Not bad for one smart choice! Similar savings would be available on automobile insurance as well as health insurance, to which we now turn.*

Health Insurance: Choices Guaranteed to Be Bad

Remember Carolyn and the cafeteria? When discussing that example, we mentioned that some people think choice architects should try to create what might be considered a neutral choice environment so as not to nudge people in any particular direction.

---

* Another interesting finding from Sydnor's paper: he finds lots of evidence of inertia. Deductibles have gone up over time with inflation. We mentioned that only about 5 percent of policyholders take the very expensive $100 deductible. Who are they? Mostly longtime policyholders who took that option long ago. On average, newer policyholders have higher deductibles. As with the Swedish social security system, this illustrates what can happen if users make a choice once and then go on autopilot. Maybe now would be a good time to see what deductibles you have on any insurance policies you carry, and start that On My Own account at the same time.

We said this is generally impossible. Whenever people are choosing, there has to be *some* underlying structure. However, thanks to research by behavioral economists Saurabh Bhargava, George Loewenstein, and Sydnor, we do have good evidence about the influence of that structure, and the difficulty of achieving neutrality.[4] We also show that a seemingly sensible design can produce terrible choices and therefore costly outcomes.

The team studied what happened when a large U.S. company decided to change the design of the health care options it offered to its employees. It offered what we call the "salad bar" approach, meaning that participants would select exactly the ingredients they wanted in their health insurance. An important feature of this case study is that the only factors that differed among policies related to costs—all participants would have exactly the same set of options regarding where and from whom they could receive care, whether they needed permission for some procedure, and so forth. The salad-bar aspect was only about money.

Employees could choose their annual deductible from four options ($1,000, $750, $500, $350), their maximum out-of-pocket spending above the deductible from three options ($3,000, $2,500, $1,500), two coinsurance rates on coverage above the deductible and before the out-of-pocket threshold is reached (80 percent, 90 percent), and two office copayments ($15 for primary care/$40 for specialist, $25 for primary care/$35 for specialists). If you don't understand what all those terms mean, don't fret; it will not spoil the story. Since any of the possible combinations was permitted, there were 48 plans available (4 x 3 x 2 x 2), each with its own price.

This new health care plan was introduced with considerable internal fanfare, and employees were encouraged to build their own plan, much like the effort in Sweden to encourage people to build their own portfolio. However, one of the options, the one with the lowest monthly premium and highest levels of cost-sharing by the employee, was selected as a default plan for anyone who did not want to go through the choosing exercise. Okay, here is a quiz: What percentage of employees do you think made an active choice by designing their own plan?

There are plausible arguments for why one might think that many people would opt out of choosing. Just reading the paragraph listing the forty-eight different options is enough to give Sunstein a major headache. On the other hand, choosing the default seems to go against the grain. It is a bit like going to a costume party wearing your normal weekend outfit. Still, make your guess before going on.

Before we reveal the answer, we have to say that it is not quite possible to know exactly how many people just opted out because, as in the Sweden example, the default plan was also one of the options one could actively choose. Altogether, just 14 percent of the employees enrolled in the default plan, and the authors of the study believe that most of those actively chose that plan. They estimate that only 2 percent of the employees passively took the default. Regardless of whether this inference is precisely right, it does provide another example in which most people decline the default. And similar to the case in Sweden, the default plan was a pretty good option and, as we shall see, *demonstrably better* than many of the policies people chose instead.

Although choosing a plan may seem like a daunting task, the firm took some care in making the process user-friendly. As the authors put it: "Employees were asked to construct candidate plans by sequentially selecting levels within each of four cost-sharing attributes (for example, 'Which annual deductible meets your needs?') and were urged to consider the trade-offs between price and coverage (for example, 'Remember, a lower deductible means higher annual paycheck costs'). After building a first plan, employees were shown the monthly plan premium and could either enroll in that plan or build a subsequent plan through the same sequential process."

How, then, did the employees do as plan designers? Not so well. One might think this would be difficult to judge; after all, who is to say whether Sunstein's salad is better than Thaler's? Can't we apply the dictum "De gustibus non est disputandum" (one can't argue about tastes)? No! In this case, that dictum does not apply because many of the choices people made violated a fundamental principle of rationality, a word we rarely use in this book (not least because it creates a lot of trouble). The principle is *dominance*: if option A is better than option B on at least one dimension, and no worse on any of the others, then A must be preferred to B. If we give Sunstein a choice between two identical cans of Diet Coke, his drink of choice, and one is cheaper than the other, then the cheaper option dominates the more expensive one. No one who understands this principle would knowingly violate it. But remarkably, *a majority of employees selected a plan that was dominated by another one.*

Let this result sink in. The firm gave its employees total freedom of choice, and a well-functioning interface in which to compare options, but a majority of employees selected a plan that was unequivocally worse than at least one of the options they had rejected. Furthermore, these poor choices were costly. The employees who selected dominated plans ended up paying an average of 28 percent more for their health care than if they had switched to a better version of the plan they elected. The authors titled their paper "Choose to Lose."

The poor choices all had something in common: low deductibles! In many cases, low-deductible plans were dominated by an identical plan with a higher deductible. For example, one plan had an annual deductible of $1,000 and an annual premium of $930. It dominated a plan with all the identical features except for a deductible of $500 and a premium of $1,568. Do the math. By choosing the latter an employee is paying $638 to reduce the deductible by $500, while keeping everything else the same. That has to cost at least $138 more, and if there are no claims, the entire $638 would be saved. Any employee who had followed our handy rule to take the highest deductible would have avoided this trap.

The fact that many low-deductible plans at this firm were dominated by higher-deductible alternatives is not unique to this one large firm. A follow-up study by Chenyuan Liu and Sydnor used a survey of health insurance plans in a large sample of U.S. employers.[5] They searched for companies that offered comparable insurance policies with both high and low deductibles. They found 331 firms that met these criteria. If workers in those plans had followed the "take the higher deductible" rule of thumb, they would have been better off at 62 percent of firms, even in years when they had lots of medical bills. At roughly half of the firms, the high-deductible plan virtually guaranteed lower costs. The expected savings from selecting the high-deductible plan are typically more than $500 per year, often with no increase in financial risk. That is a potential $500-a-year contribution to the families' On My Own accounts.*

---

* A good question to ask is why firms offer these dominated plans. There is no definitive answer to this question. Most large firms in the United States are "self-insured," meaning that they bear the risk of total employee health care spending, and use insurance companies just to arrange care networks and administer the claims. So, employers' and employees' interests are well aligned. Liu and Sydnor offer this explanation for why high-deductible (HD) plans are so cheap: "The mechanism is that a combination of adverse selection and moral hazard may cause a wider disparity in the average costs (from the insurer perspective) for enrollees in the HD plans versus the low-deductible (LD) plans than would be expected simply from the reduction in coverage levels between those plans. Firms appear to roughly equalize their total contributions to health care across plans in their menu, which means they pass through these large average cost differences to employees enrolling in the HD plans. This can generate substantial savings for those who enroll in the HD option and when the difference in deductibles and out-of-pocket limits between plans are not large, can cause the HD option to become financially dominant."

Deductible aversion is not just an American affliction; the Dutch suffer from the same problem. In the Netherlands, everyone is required to buy health insurance and (as of 2020) all policies were required to have a deductible of at least €385 per year,[6] but families can elect a deductible of as much as €500 more. Roughly speaking, increasing the deductible by €100 reduces the premium by about €50. Apparently, our deductible rule of thumb is not (yet) well known in the Netherlands, because only about 10 percent of the public choose a deductible above the minimum.[7] Yet a team of economists from Berkeley and the London School of Economics find that most would gain from doing so.[8] This applies even to those for whom the choice should be most obvious, those who are very unlikely to spend more than the minimum deductible, and so bear little risk that they would have to pay more. Even among this group only 15 percent choose a higher deductible, although if they were Econs, everyone would do it.

In the United States, households that elect a high-deductible plan have the option of creating something better than a notional On My Own Account, which is only a mental account, after all. They can create something called a health savings account (HSA), contributions to which are tax-sheltered. Many employers try to encourage employees to choose the high-deductible (HD) plan by making contributions to the HSA for any employee who does so. Any money contributed to the HSA that is not spent at the end of the year simply rolls over to the next year and eventually just turns into a retirement savings account. The existence of these accounts deepens the mystery as to why high-deductible plans get so little take-up, even in cases when they are a certain money saver.

Part of the explanation for the low take-up rate of HD plans may be that consumers do not realize that an HSA account is about as sludge-free as one could wish. The account is opened automatically by the employer, often with a starting balance already deposited on January 1. Policyholders receive a debit card that is linked to the account, and any medical bill or purchase can be paid with the card. No paperwork or prior approvals are necessary. Workers might be confusing this with an older (but still existing) benefit called a flexible spending account (FSA) that we mentioned earlier in the book. These accounts are hassle nightmares with sludge lurking at every turn. Bills have to be submitted and are often rejected for no apparent reason. Worse, users have to guess how much medical spending they might need in the coming year and can lose money if they do not deplete the account by March 31 of the following year. This provision provides a boost to stores selling eyeglasses, which do a booming business to customers whose accounts are about to expire.

Deductibles now can be as high as $4,000 or more for a family plan, so one might think simple risk aversion could explain why more people don't elect them, but in the case of dominating plans there is no risk to bear. Households pay less no matter how much health care they consume! Consider this (simplified)* example: The employer offers two deductibles, $1,000 and $4,000, and contributes $1,000 to the HSA of any employee who elects the high deductible. Premiums are $300 a month lower for the HD plan, meaning $3,600 a year. Suppose a family puts all of the money saved on premiums into the HSA and considers it an On My Own Account. That means that by the end of the year $4,600 will have been deposited in the health savings account, enough to cover the deductible and, almost certainly, any other out-of-pocket spending.

We suggest that the family adopt the following mental accounting plan: Whenever a medical expense is incurred, until they reach

---

* We are leaving out other costs such as coinsurance just to make the calculations easier. In a case in which the HD plan dominates the LD plan this simplification does not affect the analysis.

their deductible, they pay for it using the debit card that comes with their HSA. After that, the insurance takes over. Notice that the family never has to pay for anything out of pocket, unless—and this is a big unless—a large medical expense happens early in the year, and before the family has extra money left over from previous years. For families that are living on a tight budget, this can be a crisis. But this is a problem that is easily fixed.

Remember that employers are contributing to the HSA because they want to encourage families to join the HD plan. If that is indeed their goal, we suggest they offer one additional benefit: interest-free loans to anyone who incurs a large medical expense early in the year. If properly communicated, this might increase take-up by low-income employees who may be most likely to worry about a liquidity crisis. Notice that because the HD plan is cheaper, these are families that could benefit most from the extra cash.

One important proviso. Although we are sticking to our rule of thumb for consumers in choosing deductibles, we remain agnostic about whether high deductibles actually make the health care system more efficient. It does seem that consumers spend less when they face a deductible, but whether that is a good thing is less clear. The usual argument for high deductibles is to mitigate what economists call "moral hazard," which is the idea that if patients face no costs of medical care, they will spend too much. They want consumers to have "skin in the game." Think of your experiences at open bars or all-you-can-eat restaurants to get the idea. And certainly, patients will think twice about going to the doctor or filling a prescription if they have to pay. The question is whether they cut back on the right things. Unfortunately, the evidence suggests that they do not.

Economists Katherine Baicker, Sendhil Mullainathan, and Joshua Schwartzstein argue that health care designers need to worry about what they call "behavioral hazard" at least as much as moral hazard.[9] Recall that for many medical conditions, a major problem to overcome is what doctors call "adherence" or "compliance." For diseases such as diabetes, hypertension, and high cholesterol, taking prescribed medication is essential to good health, and failing to do so can create costly medical emergencies. In a well-structured system, the price of these medications would be negative, meaning we would reward patients for adhering to their prescribed medications. The evidence suggests that when patients have to pay for some or all of the cost of their medications, they are as likely to cut back on high-value drugs such as insulin or beta-blockers as they are to cut back on nearly useless drugs such as those for the common cold.

One experiment conducted by a team of medical researchers led by Niteesh Choudhry is particularly telling.[10] They randomly assigned patients discharged after having suffered a heart attack to either a control group with usual coverage under which prescription refills would usually cost between $12 and $20, or a treatment group for whom statins, beta-blockers, and ACE inhibitors (drugs of known efficacy for such patients) were provided for free. They then tracked adherence rates and clinical outcomes over the next year. Faced with lower prices, consumers used more drugs, just as economic theory would predict. But how does this behavior affect health outcomes. One recent experiment tracked new enrollees in Medicare's prescription benefit program.[11] Due to a quirk in the way eligibility works, those born earlier in the year (e.g., February) are more likely to face cost-sharing by the end of the year than those born later (e.g., September)—meaning they paid more for each drug out of pocket. While the change was small, about $10 per drug, patients cut back on their drugs, as in the previous study. But as medical science would predict, patients who cut back had a much higher risk of dying—about 33 percent higher! What's worse, the people at the highest risk of problems like heart attack and stroke—exactly the ones that economic theory would predict should cut back the least—were the *most* likely to drop life-saving drugs like statins, beta-blockers, and ACE inhibitors when the price went up. Here, charging people for proven medications costs both money (in terms of higher health costs) and lives. So, requiring patients to share the cost of medical expenses may drive down spending in the short run, but it remains an open question whether that lowers costs in the long run, and whether it is a good idea, even if so.

In light of this, we think that our On My Own-HSA mental accounting may help on two fronts. First, it may help households choose financially superior plans. There is no point in paying $800 to reduce the deductible by $500. When we encourage using the On My Own to "pay" for the health care costs that come in before reaching the deductible, we are hoping to thread the following needle: we hope that families will not skimp on necessary medical services because of an out-of-pocket cost, but at the same time we want to discourage wasteful spending by reminding people that they get to keep and invest the money in their HSA for future medical expenses or retirement spending. If this worked, it would be helpful nudging via mental accounting.

While we have focused specifically on the American healthcare system here, similar dynamics exist in many other countries. And our maxim of choosing the largest deductible can be usefully applied around the world.

 PART IV

SOCIETY

In the previous section, in which we tried to show you the money, the level of analysis was primarily the individual or household. Although third parties were lurking in the background in some places—such as patients who fail to take their medicine and thus increase the price of health care (or waiting times to get access to a doctor) for others—they were not our main focus. In the following two chapters we switch to a wider-angle lens and address two topics in which the primary goal is to encourage people to take actions that mostly help others. Using the analogy of COVID-19, we are switching from nudges to encourage people to stay away from crowds where they might get sick, to nudging them to stay home if they have been exposed to someone who tested positive.

The first topic is organ donations, in which the goal is to increase the supply of organs to people who need transplants, while respecting the rights of people to decide what happens to their bodies, even after they die. The second is climate change, in which we all have to make sacrifices that produce benefits shared by everyone, including people not yet born. Fortunately, the tools of choice architecture can help with both problems. We hope that the analysis will have broader lessons for use of those tools to address many problems in which the actions of individuals can strongly affect third parties, for good or bad.

13

Organ Donations:
The Default Solution Illusion

Policymakers have become increasingly sophisticated in their use of choice architecture to achieve policy goals. It is therefore surprising that a domain in which the details of choice architecture have been prominently discussed is one in which we think poor choices have been made. The topic in question is organ donations, to which we devoted a chapter in the original version of this book. Like this chapter, that one came pretty late in the book, so maybe no one read it. Or maybe we did a bad job of writing it. Or possibly no one thought that they had to read the chapter because they could pretty much guess what our position would be. So, we are giving ourselves what golfers call a mulligan, which is a euphemism for pretending that a poor shot never happened and trying it again. Here we go.

When we began working on that original version, we made a list of potential topics that we might include. Organ donation was one of the first topics on this list. We thought this would be a good topic because we knew about a result from a study written by our friends Eric Johnson and Dan Goldstein.[1] The question they addressed was the effect of default rules on the expressed willingness of people to donate their organs if they should happen to die suddenly. Johnson and Goldstein obtained a dramatic

finding. In countries that classified people as willing donors by
default (so-called presumed consent countries), very few people
chose to opt out. But in countries in which people have to take
some action to become a donor (this policy is called informed
consent, explicit consent, or in the United States, explicit authorization), most people failed to opt in. Their paper included what
has been called the most famous graph in social science.

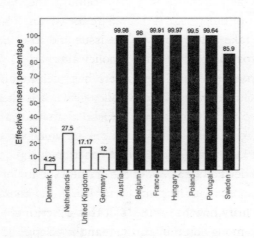

Figure 13.1. Effective Consent Rates by Country (Source: Johnson and Goldstein, 2013)

Although the results should not be a surprise to anyone who has
gotten this far, they are still quite striking. Only 12 percent of Ger-
mans agreed to be organ donors, while more than 99 percent of
Austrians had failed to opt out. Amazing!

Naturally, we figured that in our chapter on organ donations,
we would advocate the adoption of a presumed consent rule. And
most people who know about our book, including many who have
even read it, came to the same conclusion. But, surprise, that is
not the conclusion we reached. After doing research on the topic,
we advocated a different policy, one we call *prompted choice*.

To our dismay, in the years since, several countries, including Wales, England, and Germany, have considered or made the switch to presumed consent. After such laws are passed, we often get notes of congratulations via Twitter! It is frustrating that on the single topic on which the selection of default rules has gotten the most attention, countries are adopting what we think is the wrong system. Cue the sound of our teeth grinding. Why has this happened? One possibility is that we came to the wrong conclusion, so part of our research to prepare for writing this new edition was to take a deep dive on the issue and to think carefully about the pros and cons of various policy alternatives. To preview what is to come, we think that there has been some confusion about the desired goals of this policy. The goal is not just to choose a system that gets the bars on that chart to be as high as possible. A central goal is to save lives, by making more organs available for use. But that is not the only goal; it is also important to consider potentially competing interests, preferences, and rights.

To help clarify how to think about this policy, it is essential to distinguish among three important (and overlapping) groups of people. The first are people who need or will need an organ to save their life. Let's call this group Patients. In the second category are the people who at some point in their life may be close to death and whose organs could help save lives. These are the people to whom the default rules directly apply, and we call them Potential Donors. This category includes all healthy adults in a country, and policy discussions tend naturally to focus on them. One useful fact: you are about three times more likely to be a patient in need of an organ than to be an organ donor.

The third group we consider are the family members of the tiny subset of Potential Donors who actually die and have healthy organs that could be used. We call this group Families. Families are relevant because transplant teams normally have conversations with the next of kin before organs are removed, typically in extremely trying circumstances because organ donation candidates are often the result of a sudden death and that death might be of a child or life partner. The nature of those conversations varies considerably across countries. We think that the role of these grieving Family members is often neglected in policy discussions.

Although a primary goal in this domain is to maximize the number of Patient lives saved, the policy should also respect the rights and preferences of Potential Donors and Families. This is a case in which the philosopher John Rawls's notion of the veil of ignorance can be usefully applied. Everyone is a Potential Donor but could also, at some point in their life, be a Patient or member of a Family. We should design a policy that is best before anyone learns what role(s) they might play.

We discuss this issue in detail not only because it is important in itself, but because it offers some general lessons on the way default options work. As we saw in the case of pensions, people who have been automatically enrolled in something are not necessarily treated identically to those who elect to join on their own. The same issue is at play here. A Potential Donor who has failed to opt out in a presumed consent country is treated differently than someone who has decided to register as an organ donor in a country where explicit authorization is the law of the land. That important distinction makes the analysis more complicated than it is sometimes portrayed. We favor the policy of prompted choice because there is no evidence that a viable alternative system would save more lives (and hence is superior in terms of the interests of Patients), and because we think it does the best job of respecting the rights and interests of Potential Donors and Families. At the same time, we favor more nudges, and better choice architecture, to increase the prompting.

Some Background

The first successful organ transplant took place in 1954 when a man offered his twin brother a kidney. The first transplant of a kidney from a deceased donor occurred eight years later. As they say, the rest is history.

Since 1988, more than 819,000 organs have been transplanted in the United States, with nearly 80 percent of them coming from deceased donors.[2] Unfortunately, the demand for organs greatly exceeds the supply, which means that a lot of lives could be saved if we could find a way to make more organs available. As of November 2020, there were more than 108,000 Patients waiting for an organ transplant, mostly for kidneys, in the United States alone, and hundreds of thousands more worldwide.[3] Many (possibly as many as 60 percent) will die while on the list, and although the number of people on the waiting list has declined in recent years, the number of transplants continues to be much lower than the demand. Almost thirty-five thousand people on the current waiting list have waited more than three years for an organ transplant. The U.S. government estimates that every day, seventeen people die waiting for a transplant.[4]

The primary sources of organs are patients who have been declared brain-dead, meaning that they have suffered an irreversible loss of all brain function but are being maintained temporarily on ventilators. In the United States, roughly twelve thousand to fifteen thousand Potential Donors are in this category each year, but fewer than two-thirds become donors, either because of medical conditions like cancer or infection that rule out a transplant, or because the transplant has not been authorized.[5]

Living donors are another source of kidneys, which is possible since we each have two. It is unlawful to offer payments to living donors (though some countries do tacitly permit a black market of this type). Nevertheless, people do donate their kidneys and might be promised priority on the waiting list if they are ever in need. Often these live donors are friends or relatives of the patient getting the kidney. But if the donor isn't a match for the donee, a hospital may be able to set up a matching system—the closest thing to a market that exists. In the simplest of these deals, if there is a patient with blood type A who has a willing donor who is type B, the matching organization looks for a patient who is type B and has a donor who is type A. The organization then arranges simultaneous operations. However, these kinds of bilateral trades can be hard to organize, especially for rarer blood types. Economists, most notably Alvin Roth, have helped solve this problem by creating mechanisms to facilitate more elaborate chains of multiple donors and Patients.[6] There are also a few Good Samaritans who donate kidneys just because they think it is the right thing to do. Unfortunately, there are not enough of them to meet demand.

When demand exceeds supply, as in this case, economists usually recommend using prices to eliminate the shortage. Gary Becker and Julio Jorge Elías, for instance, have advocated creating markets in kidneys.[7] Such markets would work by allocating available kidneys to those Patients who are willing to pay the most, the same way we allocate Maseratis and Saint-Tropez villas. The more Patients are willing to pay, the more people would supply their kidneys. It is not only economists who have this view. Some philosophers have vigorously defended the view that people should be able to buy and sell kidneys.[8]

Nevertheless, this policy has not gone very far. The only country that allows a legal market in kidneys is Iran.[9] As Roth correctly notes, most people find the very idea of such markets to be "repugnant."[10] People do not think that kidneys should be allocated strictly (or even partially) on the basis of willingness (and ability) to pay. It may be fine for luxury goods to be limited to the rich, but most people believe that life-saving operations should not be. Countries have decided instead that priority on the waiting lists for kidneys (and other organs) should be determined by medical factors, such as how urgent it is for the Patient to get a kidney, how long the Patient can be expected to live, as well as how long he has been waiting.

All of this means that to meet the demand for kidneys—and other organs, like hearts and livers, for which live donations are impossible—we need to rely on the organs of deceased donors. Because each donor can provide as many as eight organs for transplant, every extra donor is quite valuable.[11] Actions by both Potential Donors and their Families, who are often consulted, are important in determining how many organs are obtained. This is where default rules come in. When a potential organ donor is declared dead, what should the policy be? There are numerous options to consider.

Routine Removal

The most aggressive approach is called *routine removal*. In this regime, the state owns the rights to the body parts of people who are dead, and their organs can be removed without asking anyone's permission. Though it may sound grotesque, routine removal would surely save the largest number of Patient lives, so if that is the only goal, it might be best of all. And it would have that beneficial effect without intruding on anyone who has any prospect for life.

This approach is not used by any U.S. state. But in some states, medical examiners performing autopsies have previously been permitted to remove corneas without receiving anyone's permission. Where this rule was used, the supply of corneal transplants increased dramatically. In the state of Georgia, for example, routine removal increased the number of corneal transplants from twenty-five in 1978 to more than a thousand in 1984.[12] A widespread practice of routine removal of kidneys would undoubtedly prevent thousands of premature deaths, but it would do so by trampling on what many people believe to be the rights of Potential Donors. Many people who would gladly agree to be organ donors (including the two of us, who have in fact so agreed) would nevertheless object to a law that allows the government to take parts of people's bodies without their explicit consent, even if they are about to die. Such an approach violates a generally accepted principle, which is that within broad limits, individuals should be able to decide what is to be done with and to their bodies. Although we recognize its potential benefits, we will take these objections to routine removal as decisive going forward.

Presumed Consent

Some countries have adopted the opt-out policy that is usually called *presumed consent* (or deemed consent). In a strict application of this policy, all citizens are presumed to be consenting donors unless they explicitly register as unwilling donors. Since we know from that famous graph that few people will in fact opt out, this policy has considerable appeal. From the standpoint of saving lives, it might seem likely to have significant benefits. And from the standpoint of the rights of Potential Donors, it might seem pretty good. After all, they can opt out. For that reason, presumed consent might appear unobjectionable in terms of the interests of Families as well.

But not so fast! In any context, the very fact that nearly everyone goes along with the default might give us pause, or at least encourage us to ask what, exactly, is happening here. If people are not opting out, it might be because of inattention or inertia, not because the default captures what they would do if they were actually to make a decision. If most people are not carefully considering this choice or don't even know about the policy's existence, then perhaps we should not be comfortable taking their inferred preferences seriously. In fact, we believe that in countries where only a tiny number of people have opted out, it does not make sense to give a lot of weight to people's failure to opt out—in the sense that their failure to do so should not necessarily be taken to reflect their true convictions.

To examine this issue further, let's think a bit more about the ethics of choosing default rules. We have argued that choice architects should strive to pick defaults that are consistent with the choices people would make if they had all the relevant information, were not subject to behavioral biases, and had the time to make a thoughtful choice. Because surveys indicate that in many countries a large majority of citizens do want to be organ donors, presumed consent seems broadly consistent with this rule (and again seems a way to save the lives of others; we will get back to the word *seems*). But there is another factor to consider. *How strongly do we want to infer someone's preferences from their failure to take some action?* Especially when opt-out rates are quite low, two equally plausible explanations for inaction are lack of salience (they didn't know they had a choice) and sludge (opting out is costly).

So, given that the failure to opt out is not always a clear signal of preference, we have to be careful how we choose the default. To illustrate, let's compare two opt-out policies: presumed consent and automatic enrollment in a retirement savings program. If someone is enrolled in a retirement plan by default, it is important that she be clearly notified that that is what has happened; clear notification is necessary to ensure that the right to opt out is real. If she nonetheless notices that fact only sometime later, or just said "yeah, whatever" without much thought, and really prefers not to be saving, she can always opt out, either by stopping the contributions or by withdrawing all her money. There might be a tax penalty for early withdrawal, but in any case the harm that can be done to the person who is automatically enrolled is pretty limited.

By contrast, there are people who are strongly opposed to anyone doing anything to their bodies after they die—but who may not even be aware of the policy, much less know what they need to do to opt out. Reminders can help, but they might not be sufficiently salient, and people might procrastinate. If they do not want to be organ donors, should their wishes be ignored? As we have said, many people insist that the answer is clearly no. Wills are legal documents that determine how money and other possessions are distributed among heirs. If we think that the dead should have the right to determine how their money is spent, shouldn't they also have the right to decide what is done with their body? Similarly, we honor the previously stated wishes of patients regarding how they wish to be treated in end-of-life care.

Now consider the interests of the third group we identified earlier, the family members of the deceased. Very few if any countries actually implement a strict (or "hard") presumed consent policy, in which organs are taken from deceased patients without consulting family members. (As we shall see, this point turns out to be crucial for our analysis.) Instead, the family members of the deceased are informed of the desire to use the organs, and if they object, no organs are removed. Indeed, many countries that have recently adopted presumed consent have explicitly called their policy "soft" presumed consent because the law requires that Families always be consulted and their wishes honored. In our view, this policy imposes cruel and unusual punishment on Families, many of whom are already coping with the death of a loved one, often with little notice. (Accidental deaths such as those on the highway are a frequent source of young, healthy organs.)

Under presumed consent, the problem, as we see it, is that it is actually a Families consent policy, and *Families have very little information about donors' wishes.* The fact that someone failed to opt out of some policy may not be very informative, especially if almost no one is doing so. In many countries with a presumed consent system, there is not a registry of people who have made an active decision to become an organ donor. Wales and England, which recently switched to soft presumed consent, are exceptions in that they are retaining their existing list of registered organ donors and are encouraging new sign-ups. Still, we worry that over time, people will not be inclined to register as donors if they think the existence of a presumed consent policy means that they have already been registered by default. Why should I bother to register if my consent has already been presumed?

One other point is worth noting. If a country were to adopt a hard presumed consent rule and nearly everyone went along with the default, then routine removal and presumed consent would be nearly identical policies. It is puzzling that between two policies so similar, one can be viewed as grotesque and the other as thoughtful and modern. Admittedly, presumed consent would, in such circumstances, save a lot of Patients' lives if opt-out rates did not increase (an assumption that may not hold). It is true that under presumed consent, unlike routine removal, Potential Donors have the opportunity to opt out, at least in theory. If they are clearly given that opportunity, and if it is easy to do so, the ethical objection would be much weakened.

It is worth noting that there are many differences between automatic enrollment in savings programs and automatic enrollment as an organ donor. The goal of the first is to help employees save; the goal of the second is to save the lives of third parties. Some people believe that in cases in which the health of third parties is at stake, a stronger nudge, or even a mandate, may be justified. We believe that too! But in the context at hand, we are assuming that Potential Donors should be entitled to do as they wish with their bodies and that the choice architecture should not violate their wishes. Fortunately, there are other options to be considered.

Explicit Consent

Presumed consent is an opt-out rule. The obvious alternative is to adopt some kind of opt-in rule, the most common being what is called an *explicit* (or informed) consent rule, meaning that people have to take some concrete steps to state that they want to be donors. Typically this now means joining an online registry of willing donors. It is clear that many people who say they are willing to donate organs nevertheless fail to take the necessary steps. That was the main point of the Johnson-Goldstein graph.

For example, according to a recent poll conducted by Gallup, more than 90 percent of Americans said they supported or strongly supported the donation of organs for transplant, but only 55 percent said they had registered as donors.[13] True, it is possible that people do not quite tell the truth in surveys, but it is also possible that people have limited attention, suffer from inertia, and procrastinate, and that the concrete steps necessary to register as an organ donor are deterring would-be donors from doing so. If so, an opt-in approach may not reflect how Potential Donors would answer if they focused on the question, were properly informed, had appropriate trust that being a willing donor would not ad-

versely affect their treatment in a hospital, and did not procrastinate. If an opt-in approach is "unadorned"—if it is not supplemented
in some way—then it really is not very good from the standpoint
of capturing the true preferences of Potential Donors. Perhaps
they need a nudge.

Prompted Choice

How can we induce more of the people who wish to be organ donors to register those preferences? Defaulting them into that status is one way, for sure, but doing so has drawbacks, as we have
seen. Fortunately, default rules are not the only tools available to
choice architects. We call our preferred design *prompted choice* because it enhances explicit consent with a concerted effort to nudge
willing donors into becoming registered donors. A primary function of prompted choice is overcoming procrastination, inertia,
and limited attention.

The first step along those lines is our usual prescription: Make
It Easy. If you live in the United States, you can register online in
a couple of minutes. Go to the Donate Life website (donatelife
.net). Maybe do it now? It had once been common practice to require people to sign the back of their driver's license or a special
donor card and in some cases to get two witnesses to sign as well.
These were barriers to joining the registry that modernity and
sensible laws have usefully erased. Sludge reduction at work!

The next step is to get people's attention, which is where the
"prompted" part comes in. We cannot count on everyone to go
through the bother of signing up even if it is easy, so why not ask
them to sign up when we have their attention? Every state now
does so when people renew their driver's license, though in some

places that does not happen very often. After getting a picture taken and paying the fee, people are asked whether they are willing to be an organ donor. If they are, their name is added to the registry and their driver's license is marked "Donor."* This is increasingly done through online renewals. There are now about 170 million registered donors in the United States, and nearly all of them have been registered through the driver's license process.[14]

The last step is to make sure that the donor's wishes are honored. In the United States, every state has passed a "first-person consent law" that requires precisely this. If an individual registers as a donor, that constitutes legal permission for donation after death. The law even provides good faith immunity to the teams who act on that legal authority. While Families who object may make a stink, the legal clarity helps the donation team that is talking to the family members to be able to say that they are required by law to honor the wishes of their loved one. This is a big plus for the Families—they no longer have to make a decision under high uncertainty and emotional stress. It is also good for Patients. In the United States the "conversion" rate of registered donors who have died and are medically suitable for organ donation is close to 100 percent.

Still, we think it is possible to improve on the choice architecture here. We understand the approach of asking people whether they want to be donors every time they have to renew their license; we applaud that approach with respect to people who once said no but might have changed their minds. Still, we wonder whether the authorities should be asking people who have said

---

* A subtle point to consider: In a state that uses this system, should the people who agreed to become donors the last time they renewed their license be asked again, or should their previous answer be presumed? The last time Thaler renewed his license the clerk offered what seemed to be a gentle nudge: "You still want to be an organ donor, right?"

yes to donation the last time they renewed their license. Maybe it makes sense to presume that yes once still means yes? And it is possible that if people who once said yes are asked again, they are getting an unintended signal, such as that their organs might no longer be usable or that officials think they are making a mistake. We agree that people who once said yes should be able to change their minds, but we are not sure how regularly they ought to be prompted again.

In addition, the Department of Motor Vehicles may not be the best place to make an organ donation decision. Since it is possible to add one's name to the donor list online, recruitment could be done anywhere. One approach along these lines comes from Israel, where voters were prompted to become donors when they cast their ballots. This clever idea has been a successful innovation. In some U.S. states (for example, New York), you can also sign up when you register to vote, another good idea.[15] Making this an option when you file your tax return could be another option.

People can also be nudged to register in other ways, such as smart media campaigns. An excellent example of such a campaign was conducted by the Brazilian football team Sport Club do Recife. At home matches, the team showed a video encouraging fans to sign up for a donor card with the team's logo. You can find the video online by searching for "Immortal fans."* It is well worth watching. A woman who has received a new heart promises that her new heart will be beating only for Recife! Those behind the promotion report that it yielded more than fifty thousand sign-ups. We hope that other sports teams or, even better, leagues follow this example.

---

* You can also go straight to the video: https://youtu.be/E99ijQScSB8. Another ad we like—because or in spite of the fact that it is a bit edgy—comes from Donate Life: https://youtu.be/BH04JOjzYu4.

Belgium, and Flanders in particular, has been a pioneer in this sort of recruitment. In 2018, the TV show *Make Belgium Great Again* dedicated an episode to organ donation, combining emotional appeal with a clear call to action. The show also coordinated with 240 municipalities across Flanders to open their offices on the following Sunday and allow people to come in and complete an organ donor form. The initiative resulted in more than 26,000 new registrations, an amazing accomplishment considering that the average number of organ donor registrations in Flanders was previously between 7,000 and 8,000 per *year*.[16]

The show also aired a special episode in 2020 to raise awareness of a new online registration function, and accompanied the episode with a special campaign in the Flemish city of Kortrijk. Overnight, bicycle paths were sprayed with the message "Call 0491 75 71 63 for the deal of a lifetime." Once people called the number, they received a message from the town's mayor and the show's presenter encouraging people to register via the online function. Belgium also allowed citizens to register as organ donors during municipal elections, and the government introduced the Federal Truck, which toured the country between 2015 and 2019 to educate schoolchildren about transplantation and initiate discussions within Families about organ donation. With these sorts of efforts, it is no surprise that the country was able to more than triple the number of people registered as organ donors in the years since 2009, while opt-outs have been stagnant.[17]

Finally, one last initiative we applaud is a true nudge for good, and we are pleased to say that it came from Apple, whose founder Steve Jobs received a liver transplant. When Americans buy a new iPhone or set up the health app for the first time, they are prompted to register as an organ donor via the Donate Life registry. From its start in 2016, this initiative has produced more than six million registrations so far.

Mandated Choice

There is another option, which is to *require* everyone to declare whether they want to be an organ donor. Whether it is actually feasible to require this of everyone will vary from one country to another. In the United States, there is no obvious way to reach everyone, because not everyone has a driver's license or a passport. Nevertheless, one could use a mandate instead of a request when asking those applying for a driver's license. The plan could be implemented more universally in countries where everyone is required to have a national ID card that is renewed reasonably often. (This is not the sort of question to which an answer given at age eighteen should be considered final.) If the goal is to save lives, mandated choice might seem to be a bit better than prompted choice because more people will register a choice, and from the standpoint of protecting the rights of Potential Donors and Families, it might seem at least as good. Is it?

To answer that question, we need to ask another one: What is the difference between prompted choice and mandated choice? The difference is a subtle one, and in fact, what we call prompted choice has long been called mandated choice in the organ donation literature, causing considerable confusion. So let's try to be clear. Suppose the driver's license application is administered online. If a response to the organ donation question is required, then the application will not be considered finished unless this question is answered. If it is merely prompted, then people can simply choose not to answer.*

---

* New York state currently uses a peculiar hybrid approach. The organ donation question has to be answered for the application to be considered complete, but one of the options offered in the organ donation section is "skip this question." We are not sure how to categorize this method. Is it a mandate if one of the options is to skip the question? We think it is best considered a strong prompt or reminder.

That is a plus because the failure to register is not a no to donation. It is no decision. This allows us to ask the family at death. There are people who want their family to decide, especially in certain cultures. If we force a yes or no to donation then we eliminate one of the best aspects of an opt-in choice architecture, which allows two pathways to a yes.

Which is better, a mandate or a prompt? The answer is not obvious. A mandate might be warranted if people are not paying enough attention to this question, but that could also be accomplished with just a reminder, such as "You did not answer the organ donation question. Would you like to do so before completing?"

As libertarian paternalists, we try to resist imposing mandates when we can, and in this case, we see some solid reasons to oppose it. For one thing, there is some evidence that mandated choice can backfire, which is to say that from the standpoint of saving lives, it might be inferior to prompted choice. When Texas implemented a mandated choice system, only 20 percent of citizens agreed to be donors.[18] Virginia had a similar, if less drastic, outcome, obtaining just a 31 percent sign-up.[19] And there is also experimental evidence from economists Judd Kessler and Alvin Roth that fewer people agree to join if the choice is forced. Their conclusion is well summarized by the title of their paper: "Don't Take 'No' for an Answer."[20]

Citizen backlash is another reason we prefer the kind of prompted choice that has been adopted in most states. People who chose not to answer the question are not recorded as organ donors but are still issued their driver's license. Also, these states keep track only of people who have opted in, not those who have opted out. It is a registry of donors, not donation decisions—an important distinction. That raises an interesting question about mandated choice. Would answers of no be officially recorded? It seems like that would be a logical implication of the mandate, and if so, that information would be considered a legal refusal under the law and therefore be shared with Families. Keeping a registry of those who do not wish to be donors would almost certainly decrease donations.

If mandating choices saved lives, that would surely be a strong point in its favor, but we think the evidence suggests that prompting should be preferred to mandating in this context.

Incentives

Although societies (aside from Iran) have ruled out paying living donors, it is possible to augment any system with additional incentives. For example, live kidney donors are now eligible for compensation for all health expenses and (up to some limit) lost wages.[21] Israel has implemented an interesting incentive-based policy along these lines that provides some useful lessons.

Although Israel has an opt-in donor list, the next of kin makes the ultimate decisions about organ donations, so getting permission is key. (There is no "first-person consent" law.) Realizing this fact, the Israeli parliament first passed a law in 2008 that granted priority to wait-list candidates who had registered as organ donors at least three years prior to being placed on the wait list. Second, it gave even higher priority to wait-list candidates with first-degree relatives whose organs were donated at their death.* This second factor means that the relatives who are making the ultimate decision can benefit directly from approving the organ donation. Singapore also offers incentives, but they switch the frame to one of

---

* Highest priority is given to those who had been living donors, as is done elsewhere.

loss. They have a pretty hard version of presumed consent, with a registry for those who want to opt out. But anyone who does opt out is told they will be placed at the bottom of the waiting list if they should ever need a donor.*

The Israeli policy appears to be helping. In the five-year period following the changed policy, the authorization rate by family members increased from 45 percent to 55 percent.[22] The campaign also increased registered donors. It seems worthy of serious consideration, especially in countries with low registration rates. (Recall that in the United States about 55 percent of the adult population are registered.)

Lives Saved?

Several countries have recently switched from opt-in systems to presumed consent, and some U.S. states have considered the policy as well. The changes are usually justified on the grounds that the presumed consent policy saves lives. The issue is not simple, but we do not think the evidence for that conclusion is compelling. Moreover, we think there is confusion about several issues we have raised in this chapter.

To begin with, we think that people have drawn the wrong conclusion from that famous Johnson-Goldstein graph. The demonstrably correct conclusion to draw is that defaults have a huge impact on the elicitation of preferences. We have seen evidence to support that conclusion throughout the book, and this example

---

* China has offered a more direct incentive for relatives to authorize the donation: cash. We are not aware of an evaluation of this policy and note that it would be illegal in the United States.

remains one of the best empirical tests of that finding. But it is wrong to conclude that adopting a presumed consent policy and obtaining a low opt-out rate will *necessarily* save lives.

That would be a reasonable conclusion if countries were implementing a hard presumed consent rule, meaning that Families would not need to be consulted. Donor consent would literally be presumed. Such a policy would completely eliminate the time and effort needed to get the permission of Families in a process that is highly time sensitive, as well as remove the risk that Families will block the donation. However, we have found that few if any countries actually implement that policy. To give just one example, in Italy, which is nominally a presumed consent country, the official website says this about the role of Families (our translation): "In the case in which the deceased person did not leave a statement regarding organ donation, the donation of an organ is allowed only if the relatives (in order: spouse, partner, adult children, and parents) are not opposed to the donation. For minors, it is always the parents who decide; if even one of the two is against, the donation will not take place."[23]

Even in countries that have legally adopted hard presumed consent, such as Austria and Singapore, in practice doctors consult with Families before organs are removed. In Sweden, another supposedly hard presumed consent country, Families can overrule unless the donor has actively opted in during his lifetime. These policies are understandable. In a highly emotional situation, with uncertainty about the wishes of the deceased, doctors are reluctant to press grieving family members about organ donation, even if they are legally within their rights to coordinate the donation. Doing so might also run the risk of creating blowback against organ donation in general.

For the recent adopters England and Wales, as well as many other countries, the law explicitly stipulates that the policy is one of soft presumed consent. Families or close friends are always consulted before organs are used, and if no one can be reached, no surgery is performed. Given these rules and customs, it is less than obvious how a presumed consent policy actually saves lives.

To clarify the policy as we see it, let's classify people according to the system present in their country (opt-in or opt-out) and their preferences as indicated by either their action (an expressed preference) or their inaction (no expressed preference). There are four possibilities shown in Table 13.1.

Table 13.1. Implied preferences from action and inaction in organ donation schemes*

	NO EXPRESSED PREFERENCE	EXPRESSED PREFERENCE
Country Is Opt-Out (Presumed Consent)	A *Ambiguous. Ask my family.*	B *No, do not donate my organs.*
Country Is Opt-In (Explicit Consent)	C *Ambiguous. Ask my family.*	D *Yes, donate my organs*

The default system would matter a lot if the A and D groups (which are either implicitly or explicitly agreeing to be organ donors) were treated the same way, or even similarly, but they are in

* Astute readers may object to this simplified four-cell table. There are two notably absent groups, call them A* and C*—those who would actively register as donors or objectors if they could. In fact, this would be possible if their country maintained a national registry of donors and objectors. Increasing numbers of countries now keep national registries, but explicit consent countries are less likely to keep a registry of objectors, while presumed consent countries seldom register who is actively willing to donate (with some notable exceptions such as Belgium, Wales, the UK, and the Netherlands). That is because countries keep registers of willing donors, not donation decisions.

fact handled very differently. Those in Group D (registered donors) in the United States, with its first-person consent laws, are treated in the most organ-donation-friendly manner: the law backs the donor's active wishes. But those in Group A, who have merely failed to opt out, are treated similarly to those in Group C, those who have not registered. There is some logic to this: *treat those who have not actively indicated a preference the same way, regardless of the system.* And we know from that famous graph that this applies to most people!

In contrast, the wishes of Groups B and D are generally accepted since they made active choices. A benefit of the opt-in architecture is an additional opportunity for a yes—if an individual doesn't register, the family will be asked for permission. Alexandra Glazier, an organ donation expert, refers to this as "two bites of the apple."[24] By contrast, under presumed consent, especially in the absence of a registered donors list, there is only one chance to say yes, and it comes from Families.

All of this means that in practice, the phrase "presumed consent" is misleading. No one's consent is ever presumed. We think part of the allure of presumed consent laws rests on confusion about the implications of changing the default. Presumed consent would certainly save lives if it were implemented, allowing the routine removal of organs for any donor who had not opted out. But as we have stressed, we have not found *any* country that does this in practice, even if, as in Austria and Singapore, the law technically requires it.

Still, it is an empirical question. Does switching to presumed consent save lives? Many studies have tried to answer this question by comparing actual organs transplanted across countries, but the conclusions vary. One reason for the lack of clarity is that the number of countries studied is less than fifty, which is a pretty small sample, and the countries studied differ in important ways that can affect organ donations. To cite just one example, Catholics tend to be favorably disposed toward organ donation, and predominantly Catholic countries are more likely to adopt presumed consent. So, if presumed consent countries have higher rates of organ donation, is that because of religion or public policy? Yes, multivariate analyses can try to untangle this mess, but this is why the small sample problem looms large.*

An even more basic problem for empirical analyses is deciding which countries should be categorized as using presumed consent. Consider the case of Spain, which has long led the world in organ donations. Spain is usually included in the presumed consent category, in part because it was one of the first countries to enact a presumed consent law, back in 1979. But that law was clarified just one year later to make clear that Families should always be consulted. Consent by the donor is never presumed, and there is not even a registry of those who wish to opt out. Thus, de facto, Spain is an opt-in (by Families) country. There is certainly no sense in which that old law has any bearing on its outstanding organ transplant record.

Rafael Matesanz, the creator of Spain's National Transplant Organization, and Beatriz Domínguez-Gil, the organization's current director general, clearly state that their success cannot be attributed to that law: "To the contrary, infrastructure, organization around the process of deceased donation, and continuous innovation are deemed the keys for success."[25] A core aspect of the "Spanish model" is the country's three-layered transplant coordinator network. At the local level, each procurement hospital appoints a

---

* Footnote for statistics geeks: Many studies use multiple observations from each country, but this only creates the illusion of a bigger sample size. The multiple observations for a single country are not independent. Once you take this into consideration, there is not enough power to draw any conclusions.

dedicated transplant coordinator, a physician who is responsible for ensuring the early detection and referral of organ donor candidates at her hospital. Medical staff involved in organ transplants are also specifically trained in the entire donation process, and deaths in critical care units are routinely audited by external and internal experts to determine whether potential donors have been missed—and how to further improve the system. There has also been an emphasis on ensuring that hospitals are adequately reimbursed for organ donation costs so that there is no financial incentive to decrease donations.[26]

Certainly, miscategorizing Spain as an opt-out country can skew empirical tests because it has the highest number of deceased donors per capita in the world. But more basically, because few, if any, countries actually practice hard presumed consent, we are not even sure what it means for any country to be included in this category. We believe the fact that a country enacted a law a long time ago that is not currently being implemented as written (because of regulations or customs) is more accurately viewed as a signal that the country has (or had) a favorable attitude toward organ donation, rather than as a legal framework that overcomes the problem of obtaining permission from the family members of brain-dead patients.

There are also studies that conduct a before-and-after analysis when a country changes the policy, but they are not definitive either. When Brazil introduced presumed consent in 1997, the government failed to invest in the other aspects of the infrastructure and then reversed course a year later. Following Wales's change of policy, there was an increase in organ donations from deceased donors, but there are many confounding factors. When Wales introduced the opt-out system, accompanying the change were lots of other activities, including a £2 million media campaign, increased staff training, and ongoing efforts to encourage people to actively join the register of willing donors.* From 2016 to 2020, more than 150,000 people actively registered as organ donors in Wales, compared with fewer than 17,000 opt-out registrations.[27] These other factors make it difficult to attribute the increase in organs donated to any specific cause. In fact, it is possible that if Wales had devoted all its efforts to these other activities, rather than focusing on a nominal policy change, it would have achieved as much or even greater success.

One simple way to evaluate the organ donation process in a state or country is to use the number of organs donated per ten thousand deaths. This controls for the fact that some jurisdictions have higher death rates than others. Using this measure, the United States, with its prompted choice opt-in system, has one of the highest donation rates in the world, with some individual states outperforming Spain.[28] In fact, treating U.S. states as countries, Alexandra Glazier and Tom Mone estimate that donations are 27 percent higher in opt-in jurisdictions than in those using opt out. In looking at the potential benefits of switching to a different system, it is important to evaluate the possible risks. Countries that have seen some apparent benefit to switching to presumed consent started with donation rates far below where the United States is currently performing. Also, the Gallup poll from 2019 that we mentioned earlier found that as many as 37 percent of those surveyed in the United States say they would opt out if the United States moved to a presumed consent system—a number that might include cases of reactance, meaning that some people can react badly if their preferences are presumed about anything.[29] If this figure proved to be accurate, the United States

---

* That England and Wales are still prompting people to be on the registration list, which we applaud, highlights the fact that these countries realize a presumed consent law does not solve the problem by itself.

could actually experience significant *decreases* from its current rate by changing to presumed consent.

The Bottom Line

We have emphasized that although defaults can be a powerful tool, changing the default is not the answer to every problem. The topic of organ donation is a good illustration of that point. The crucial factor is that Potential Donors are not the only relevant actors. The challenge is that Families are part of the process, which makes presumed consent a much weaker tool than it may seem. As we have seen, the other aspects of the organizational processes are the secret ingredients to success. These procedures are what Spain is managing so well. They are a combination of organizational choice architecture and well-designed communication strategies used when approaching Families—factors that have proved to be more important than the choice of a default.

In the United States, such duties are carried out regionally by fifty-eight organ procurement organizations (OPOs) that are responsible for handling deceased organ donations in their territory.[30] For example, the Gift of Life Donor Program, an OPO based in Philadelphia and responsible for eastern Pennsylvania and Delaware, is well recognized as a top performer, and unsurprisingly Pennsylvania and Delaware consistently have high organ donation rates. Unfortunately, the underlying pool of potential donors varies by region, and the procedures used by OPOs are rather opaque (at least to us), which makes it difficult to identify which specific OPO practices lead to higher donation rates.

In this context, the goals should be to save the lives of Patients, to respect the rights of Potential Donors, and to do whatever can be done to protect the interests of Families. With those goals in mind, we think that states and countries should concentrate on two priorities in dealing with this problem. First, learn the best practices from Spain and elsewhere, and second, experiment with alternative ways of prompting more sign-ups to the willing donor list, in terms of locations for prompting, incentives for joining the list, and media campaigns. Changing the default rule can be a distraction from these more promising paths.

14

Saving the Planet

Come gather 'round, people
Wherever you roam
And admit that the waters
Around you have grown
And accept it that soon
You'll be drenched to the bone
If your time to you is worth savin'
And you better start swimmin'
Or you'll sink like a stone
For the times they are a-changin'

—BOB DYLAN

As anyone who has been paying even a little bit of attention knows, the world faces a crisis known as climate change. Gradually the planet is getting hotter and the climate is getting more volatile, with a host of harmful effects on public health and welfare. People in poor countries are especially vulnerable, but those in wealthy countries are also at serious risk. Violent storms and gigantic fires do not spare anyone.

Because this is such an enormous problem, we might expect that everyone would be united in working to respond to it. And indeed some countries have adopted bold initiatives, incurring significant costs in order to reduce greenhouse gas emissions. But to date, progress has been limited. A key reason is those significant costs; large reductions in emissions are not going to come cheap.

For the sake of simplicity, our focus here is on reducing emissions, but unfortunately it is inevitable that the world will have to find a way to deal with the effects of climate change over time. Temperatures, sea levels, storm intensity, and wildfires will be rising over the coming decades even if the rate of growth of emissions is greatly slowed. That means that policies to adapt to these adverse effects will be needed, and those policies should incorporate choice architecture best practices and a host of nudges. Adaptation is essentially a means of reducing the harm of climate change. For example, many interventions can make wildfires less frequent and/or easier to control. Building sea walls can reduce the risk of flooding from higher sea levels, and if we can shift home building toward places where flooding is less likely, we can do even better. It is possible to develop hybrid crops that are more resilient to heat drought, but farmers might need to be nudged to switch to those crops, having grown something else for generations. You get the idea. An understanding of choice architecture could spur many reforms to reduce the harms of a warmer world.

A Perfect Storm

Some basic lessons of behavioral economics help explain why nations have not done more. Sadly, we have what amounts to a perfect storm, a confluence of factors that make collective action difficult. Here are the main obstacles:

1. *Present bias.* As we have seen, people tend to be much more concerned with now as opposed to later. Although scientists have been warning about the perils posed by climate change for decades, the most serious risks have often been seen to be off in the future,

perhaps decades away. People have bills to pay now! It's true that all over the planet, people are *now* facing risks and problems related to climate change. But at important moments, many leaders, and many voters, have seen climate change as a challenge for future generations, and they don't vote. There is a big contrast here with COVID-19, in which the toll, in terms of illnesses and deaths, was felt in the here and now as friends, families, and political leaders got sick.

2. *Salience*. People can see smog, and they really don't like it. Dirty air and water are both visible and scary. In many nations, including the United States, the public has demanded (and often received) cleaner air and water. By contrast, greenhouse gases are invisible in the air. If you can't even see them, you might not worry about them.

3. *No specific villain*. For some threats, there is an identifiable perpetrator—a wrongdoer whose terrible deeds capture public attention. It's not so hard to mobilize public attention and to spend resources to combat terrorists, especially if they are led by prominent people and determined to carry out terrorist attacks. Climate change is faceless. It is a product of the actions of countless people—effectively all of us, over a very long time. After the attacks of 9/11, the existence of a specific villain (Osama Bin Laden in particular) helped fuel an aggressive response, even though one could have argued then, and could even more easily argue now, that climate change poses a greater threat than terrorism, in terms of expected lives lost.

4. *Probabilistic harms*. It's easy to see that some actions cause harms—as, for example, when one person hits another, or when a company dumps toxic materials into a local lake. The harms caused by climate change are often probabilistic, which makes it harder to reach consensus. If we see an increase in hurricanes or

fires or blizzards in some part of the world, is climate change responsible? To be sure, the science of climate attribution is rapidly
advancing,[1] and many scientists correctly emphasize that climate
change increases the expected frequency and severity of hurricanes and fires. Still, it may not be possible to insist that any particular event is attributable to climate change. For those who seek
to mobilize people, that is a problem. And even appropriately careful language is sometimes exploited by climate change skeptics.

5. *Loss aversion.* We have referred to loss aversion, which means
that people are more negative about anticipated losses than they
are positive about corresponding gains. Efforts to reduce greenhouse gas emissions require the imposition of immediate losses.
If everyone has to pay some new "climate tax," loss aversion kicks
in. It's true that climate change imposes losses too—but the very
worst of those losses are in the future and their magnitude is in
many ways uncertain.

We are not saying that these problems are insuperable! All over
the world, there is a lot of climate activism, especially but not only
from young people, and it has helped spur significant regulatory
activity. (Humans can overcome present bias; they often do care
about future generations; the losses from climate change are increasingly salient, and many of those losses are being experienced
right now; people buy insurance and know that it's good to avoid
probabilistic harms; and we can identify the big emitters.) But
two additional problems apply to climate change, and indeed to
environmental protection in general, and they help explain why it
can be so challenging to get an appropriate response.

First, people do not get clear feedback on the environmental
consequences of their actions. If your use of energy produces air
or water pollution or results in carbon emissions, you might not

be aware of that fact, at least not on a continuing basis. Even if you are told about the connection, it may not affect your behavior. Those who set their thermostat to a comfortable temperature and let the heating and cooling system perform its magic are unlikely to think, moment by moment or even day by day, about the costs those decisions are imposing on others. And even if you know that you will contribute to climate change if you drive a lot, will you drive less or get an electric car? Maybe so, but maybe not. The same point applies even more strongly to decisions that most people do not clearly link to climate change, such as what foods they eat or what materials are used in the products they buy.

Second, and most fundamentally, there is the problem of free riding. Progress on climate change depends on the actions of many nations and their citizens. If one family, one large company, or even one country reduces emissions, that is definitely progress. But if other families, companies, and countries are increasing their emissions, the world can end up losing ground. At times, for example, prominent leaders in the United States have thought: Why should we scale back emissions if China and India are not doing anything like that? Why should we spend a lot of money and help the rest of the world if other nations are continuing with business as usual, and thereby harming us? For their part, leaders in China and India have sometimes thought: Why should we act aggressively to reduce emissions when other, richer countries created the problem in the first place? (We'll return to that point shortly.)

This is what is often called a "tragedy of the commons." Each dairy farmer has an incentive to add more cows to his herd, because he obtains the benefits of the additional cows while suffering only a fraction of the costs; but collectively too many cows will eventually ruin the pasture. Dairy farmers need to find some way to avert this tragedy. Similar problems plague the fishing industry, and they help to explain air pollution and climate change, with the latter sometimes described as a "wicked" commons problem because of the gravity of the threat and the sheer number of people and nations involved.[2] When a tragedy of the commons is involved, the standard remedy is coercion, agreed to by all. For example, dairy farmers might all agree to limit the number of cows they will add to their herds—and they might agree to punish those who violate the deal. Norms can also help,[3] and choice architects can help create those norms, though that takes time.

Now, if you are reading this chapter hoping to hear that you shouldn't worry because low-cost nudges will make this problem go away, we are going to disappoint you. As we have often stressed, not all problems can be solved with light-touch interventions. If an earthquake creates a tsunami that sends a gigantic wave speeding toward your town, we don't think you should try telling the wave that 99 percent of all waves turn around before reaching the end of the beach. Racing uphill is a better idea.

Unfortunately, we do not have the option of running away from climate change, but unlike in the case of a tsunami, we do have a bit more time to act. And although it is true that nudges will not solve the problem, they can help, and we need all the help we can get. It also helps to think about climate change as a global choice architecture problem. The findings of psychology and behavioral economics can help us understand how to make progress.

Creating Cooperation

Although the phrase "tragedy of the commons" was popularized by Garrett Hardin in a famous article published in 1968, the concept has been well known by social scientists for much longer.[4] In economics, Paul Samuelson, a giant in the field, wrote about what he called "public goods" problems in a three-page (!) paper published in 1954.[5] He defined a public good as one that everyone can consume without diminishing others' enjoyment. Fresh mountain air is a good example. No matter how many deep breaths you take up on the top of the hill, there will be plenty of air left for everyone else.

Samuelson's analysis was based on the generally accepted assumption of economists at that time, which was that people act like Econs: they are both rational and selfish.* In this context, that means people understand the situation they are in (even though Samuelson had just figured it out himself) and act to maximize their own welfare, ignoring the preferences of everyone else. Under those assumptions, public goods present a real problem, because no one will be willing to contribute anything to their creation. It is easy to see how this applies to individuals: if you make environmentally friendly choices in your life, everyone shares in the benefits you create, so you might not make those choices. Thankfully, Humans are less selfish than Econs, and some people and governments do take it upon themselves to act, though not as much as we might hope.

This analysis is even more important when applied to big companies such as utilities and automobile manufacturers that are responsible for a large portion of global carbon emissions. Usually their primary goal is to make money. When they scale back pollution, they might not reap many benefits (unless consumers reward them). To be sure, both employers and employees are affected by

---

* In this chapter, we are breaking our self-imposed ban on using the word *rational* and we will use the term simply to mean that people do the math correctly. We also add the word *selfish* because it is a completely different concept. It can be perfectly rational for people to care about the welfare of others. Standard economic models generally assume that we care just about ourselves and perhaps our immediate family members, or at least most of them.

climate change, but even taking those considerations into account, a narrow profit maximization analysis might not call for large reductions in greenhouse gas emissions. We are aware that even so, many corporations are taking substantial (and costly) steps to reduce those emissions. Those who run companies have consciences— and they can be nudged by their employees, investors, customers and maybe especially their children. Still, investors do care about profits, and in this context that creates a real challenge.

The free-rider problem is more important still at the governmental level, because the only way we can make the required progress on climate change is through coordinated actions by governments around the world. You can think of nations as akin to those farmers deciding how many cattle to add to the pasture. Unless they face a lot of public pressure or pressure from other nations, or have leadership that is strongly committed to addressing the problem, China, India, and the United States might be reluctant to scale back a lot on their own; they might need some type of enforceable agreement. (We emphasize that in some periods, all three nations have done a great deal to reduce their emissions, acting largely on their own; the only point is that because of the free-rider problem, it is challenging to get them, or the world as a whole, to do what should be done.)

Social scientists have studied an interesting experimental game that illustrates some of the nuances of this situation, and this game can provide useful insights into many international agreements, including the Paris Agreement of 2015. It is called the public goods game. To see how it works, pretend that you are a participant along with nine strangers whom you will never meet. Each of you has been given five one-dollar bills and told that you can keep all of them and take them home. However, you can also decide whether you would like to contribute anonymously any of the dollars to a "public good pot." Each dollar you or anyone else contributes will be doubled by the experimenters, and then the pot will be divided equally among the ten players. If no one contributes anything, each player takes home five dollars. If everyone contributes all five dollars, then everyone takes home ten dollars.

How much do you contribute? If it helps you to think about it harder, multiply the stakes by a hundred or a thousand.

While you are deciding, we will do the arithmetic for you. If you contribute one dollar, the public good pot grows by two dollars, of which you will get your share (10 percent, or twenty cents). That means that the more you contribute to the public good pot, the less money you take home. But before you decide not to contribute anything, keep in mind that the more everyone contributes, the more everyone gets. With full cooperation, everyone doubles their money in just a few minutes!

What have you decided? Are you going to be a selfish Econ or a generous Human, or something in between?

Versions of this game have been played hundreds if not thousands of times, and it turns out that people are not as selfish as economists thought them to be, so the prediction that no one will donate anything is wrong. On average, groups contribute about half their money to the public good. That is the (somewhat) good news. The bad news comes if we repeat the game several times. When that happens, contribution rates gradually drop off to about 15 percent. Roughly speaking, people are *conditional cooperators*. They are willing to contribute to the public good as long as others are doing so as well, but if others are free riding, contributions gradually dry up. Interestingly, if you let the members of the group talk to one another before they make their decisions, contribution rates go up.[6] Subjects make speeches urging cooperation and pledging to donate themselves, and even though these pledges are not binding (economists call such statements "cheap talk"), they still help raise contribution rates and maintain them over time.

This simple game illustrates what has happened in some of the less successful attempts to achieve international cooperation in the fight against climate change. As in the experiments that allow communication, international conversations at the highest levels start with lofty, idealistic language about the need for cooperation and how we are all in this together, producing a universal plea: if we all pitch in, we can give future generations a chance of continuing to inhabit our planet with a hospitable climate. That can help. But eventually, countries argue about how much each should be doing to reduce the problem (by reducing their emissions), and then start to discuss potential long-term plans and how firmly to commit to stick to them. As the difficult debate that ultimately led to the Paris Agreement shows, this is where things get tricky. Each country has its own point of view. *Who's going to contribute how much to the public good pot?*

To flesh things out just a bit, let's give a highly simplified version of the science of climate change. For as long as humans have inhabited the earth, or at least since we learned how to keep a fire going, we have been emitting greenhouse gases. Such gases stay in the atmosphere for a long time. Rich countries, such as those in North America and Europe, have contributed a large percentage of the cumulative total, because modern inventions such as electricity, transportation, factories, heating, cooling, and so forth produce a lot of emissions. The United States continues to be the champion cumulative emitter, having contributed about one-quarter of the global total since 1751.[7] (To be sure, its share goes down every year.)

Meanwhile, historically poorer countries, such as China, India, and Brazil, long lagged behind. In international negotiations, they often argued that wealthy countries had gotten rich using a lot of energy—and that it was deeply unfair, and not at all in their interest, for poor countries to suddenly face strict emissions limits. It is true that as early as 2006, China had surpassed the United

States as the world's largest annual emitter, and it is now the largest annual emitter by far.[8] Nevertheless, China argued that it would not be just for it to face the same restrictions faced by the wealthier nations that had been emitting more for centuries—and getting rich as a result.

We can spend the rest of our days on earth arguing about what would be fair in this situation, but it is safe to say that achieving an agreement on that question is difficult. The philosophical issues are extremely complicated. In any case, humans have been shown to have self-serving biases when it comes making judgments about what is fair.[9] Just observe a couple dividing up the possessions during a divorce if you want to see this behavior up close. In the area of climate change, self-serving judgments about what is fair can be found on all sides in international negotiations, and they have been a serious obstacle to progress.

The behavioral economics literature does offer an idea about one possible way forward. Recall that people playing the public goods game are conditional cooperators; they cooperate if others do. In a series of experiments, the behavioral economists Ernst Fehr and Simon Gächter have shown that cooperation in repeated public goods games can be increased if players are allowed to punish noncooperators *at their own expense*.[10] The way this works in the game described earlier is that if Player A observes that Player D (whose identity is masked) is not contributing, A can punish D. For each dollar A is willing to pay, D's payoff is reduced by three dollars. Note that A gains nothing directly from punishing—and indeed has to pay for the privledge of punishing a noncooperator. As a result, Econs would never punish anyone in this game. But well-meaning (or possibly spiteful) Humans do punish! It turns out that the introduction of an option that no Econ would use greatly increases cooperation. In fact, with these rules in place, cooperation *increases* as the game is repeated—just the opposite of what is observed under the normal rules.

We believe that these findings provide a useful behavioral underpinning to an idea that has been proposed by economics Nobel Laureate William Nordhaus, a climate expert. Nordhaus has suggested that countries form what he calls Climate Clubs.[11] As with other kinds of clubs, such as a tennis club, members would enjoy certain benefits (use of the courts), but would also have to agree to the club rules (no racket throwing, paying dues on time). Failure to follow the rules can get you kicked out of the club. The key to the Climate Club idea, however, is that countries that do not agree to join and follow the rules would be subject to punishment by club members (perhaps via some kind of tariff).

We are enthusiastic about the concept of Climate Clubs although we have some misgivings about the term itself; described in that way, it can seem a bit cute, and not serious enough for actual nations to adopt. Nations like treaties and agreements, not clubs, and labels matter. Nonetheless, the concept is highly suggestive—worthy of general attention and grounded in good social science research. In fact, the idea is closely related to what happened in Paris in 2015 to produce the Paris Agreement, which became effective in 2016. Under the Paris Agreement, most of the world's nations are in something akin to a Climate Club. The signatories have agreed to "nationally determined contributions," which, it is hoped, will become increasingly ambitious over time. After the election of Joe Biden in 2020, the United States immediately resumed its important role, and we are hopeful that genuine progress can be made. Fingers crossed.

But how should nations go about fulfilling their commitments? How would they bring about the reduction of emissions that is required? There are many possible answers. Ideally, the first step would involve monetary incentives.

Better Incentives

When incentives are badly aligned, it is appropriate for government to try to fix the problem by realigning them. In fact, although economists are often a contentious group, this is one topic on which there is nearly unanimous agreement: if we think we are emitting excessive amounts of greenhouse gases (or any other pollutant), then we should make sure decision makers face costs that give them the correct incentives to cut back.[12] In the environmental arena, two broad approaches have been proposed.

The first is to impose taxes or penalties on those who pollute. A tax on greenhouse gas emissions is one example. The second approach is called a cap-and-trade system. With cap-and-trade, those who pollute are given (or sold) a limited number of "rights to pollute" (the cap), and these rights are then traded in a market. If polluters exceed their allowances, they are in violation of the law. Although each approach has its adherents, we will not take a stand on which approach is better. That's a tough question, and reasonable people disagree. The two methods come at the problem from different directions.

Green Taxes

If the tool of choice for governments is a tax, then they are trying to set a price that they think will give people the right incentives to reduce the amount of emissions they produce. Some of the desired changes will take time. If the price of gasoline quadruples tomorrow, many people cannot immediately change where they live and work, and many will not immediately change how they commute. But high carbon prices inevitably alter behavior and lead firms to alter how and what they produce. People in Europe drive smaller and more fuel-efficient cars than Americans do in part because they have had higher fuel taxes for decades. Using a tax as the way of setting incentives also has the advantage of bringing in revenues to governments that have been running large deficits fighting the Great Recession and COVID-19. A particular advantage of a carbon tax is that it would create incentives to innovate—for example, by producing cheaper sources of energy that produce little or no carbon emissions. In many nations, incentives, including taxes, have helped spur innovation with respect to solar, wind, and other forms of green energy, and have also helped spur the rise and spread of electric vehicles.

We leave it to others to decide how to structure any carbon tax and what to do with the tax inflows. We would favor structuring the tax in a way that makes sure that the tax burdens do not have adverse effects on poor people. To assure progressivity, and to overcome loss aversion, we believe that a carbon tax should be "bundled" with economic help, so as to ensure that lower-income people are not net losers from the tax (at least on average). For example, it might be possible to bundle the carbon tax with a combination of payments to lower-income people who are hurt by that tax and expenditures on government programs that benefit them or that are otherwise popular. Free high-speed internet, anyone? Because wealthier people engage in actions that result in more carbon emissions, they would generally pay more than their per capita share of the total bill, but we would also favor making some portions of a carbon tax explicitly progressive (for example, by taxing emissions from larger houses and more expensive cars at a higher per-unit rate). In some cases taxes can be negative, such as with subsidies. The United States now subsidizes the purchase of electric cars and home solar energy systems, for example. The fact that the tax would raise revenues creates opportunities for creative use of that money. The tax approach sets the price and then

lets the market react, leaving the aggregate level of emissions uncertain. Over time, if emissions do not fall enough to reach appropriate targets, or if the climate crisis grows even more urgent
(alas, this is entitely possible), then the tax rates can be adjusted.

Some environmentalists are deeply suspicious of carbon taxes.
They want strong and immediate reductions in emissions, and
they doubt that taxes can get us there. In our view, their skepticism is unwarranted. If you want strong and immediate reductions, taxes can definitely get us there; everything depends on
their size. The higher the tax, the greater the reduction in emissions. In view of the magnitude of the problem, a low or nominal
tax would be tough to defend. While many people, and some nations, embrace the goal of "net zero" emissions by a specified
date, the world cannot, and should not, try to reduce global emissions to zero in the next year; humanity is not ready to immediately do without transportation and electricity, for example
(sacrifices we might have to make to get to zero very quickly). But
we can reduce emissions significantly with a stiff tax that becomes
increasingly stiffer over time. That could drive carbon emissions
way down over the next decade or two.

In theory, the tax should be equal to the "social cost of carbon," a number that is designed to capture the damage done by a
ton of carbon emissions. Of course, reasonable people disagree
about how this number should be calculated, and numerous assumptions, not always based on clear evidence, have to be made
before an estimate is produced. In 2016, the United States chose a
social cost of carbon of about $50, and that figure influenced the
assessments of a number of other nations. Many experts now
think that $50 is too low and that in light of new scientific find-
ings, continuing uncertainty, and the risk of catastrophe, nations
should choose a much higher figure. This is not the appropriate
place to go into the nuances of this calculation. Let's leave it that

if we pick some date by which we want to be carbon neutral, it is possible to design an array of taxes that could get us there.

Sweden currently has the highest carbon price in the world, about $130 per metric ton.[13] Since the tax was introduced in 1991 at about $28, and gradually increased to its current level, the country has seen an 83 percent increase in real GDP—comparable to that of other OECD member countries—and a 27 percent decrease in emissions.[14] Though the tax increased gasoline prices, the response to the tax promoted significantly larger behavioral changes than would be expected under a gasoline-price increase alone.[15] There is a general lesson here. If a tax is understood to be responding to a serious problem, people might respond even more than they would to the purely economic incentive. In this context, they might hear a signal that it's good to reduce greenhouse gas emissions—and they might be willing to do that even if it's not in their economic interest. Humans are like that.

We would also underline a point in Sweden's practice that you might have just skipped over. Since 1991, Sweden's carbon tax has nearly *quintupled*. The basic idea of starting with a low carbon tax and increasing it over time makes a lot of behavioral sense, and it has been adopted or given serious consideration in several countries, including Germany. Maybe it should be called Green More Tomorrow. Alert to present bias and loss aversion, policymakers (and private companies) might impose relatively low costs today, or soon, while committing to increase those costs over time. In an illuminating, broad-ranging essay on the use of behavioral economics to combat climate change, Helga Fehr-Duda and Ernst Fehr note, "The basic principle of committing to a policy today but delaying the consequences is routinely used by politicians, for instance to increase retirement age without losing voters."[16] They add that the principle can be used in multiple areas, including climate change policy. In nations in which the idea of a climate tax runs into serious political opposition, and in which less efficient alternatives are more popular, Green More Tomorrow might be the best path forward.

Cap-and-Trade

In contrast, a cap-and-trade system starts by specifying the desired level of emissions (the cap), then allows markets to determine the price of emissions permits. If technology makes it cheaper to produce clean energy, then the price of those permits will fall. In fact, a main goal of cap-and-trade is to create an incentive to produce cleaner energy.

For a cap-and-trade system, an important distributional concern is how the initial levels of permits are allocated. Should a factory that has been belching black smoke for years be allocated a large number of permits that it can sell by cleaning up its act? One worry is that because such laws do not get passed instantaneously, polluters would delay cleanup, hoping for a bigger initial allocation. Again, we are going to duck these questions, not because they are unimportant, but because they are complicated and we don't want to get distracted from the primary focus of this book. (Attention is a scarce resource, just like clean air.)

Readers might ask why we are putting so much emphasis on economic incentives in this domain, when we raised questions of the possible downsides of making patients pay for a portion of their health care expenses through deductibles and co-pays. That is a fair question. Our ambivalence about the importance of giving health care consumers incentives to economize on their use of doctor visits and prescription drugs stems from the evidence suggesting they are not very good at making these trade-offs. An economist would say that patients do not know their own health "production function." We do not want people who have had a heart attack to cut back on their drug regimen because their car broke down this month and they can't tell whether the hypertension drug is doing anything for them.

At the consumer level, the relation between energy consumption and behavior is at least somewhat more transparent. Raising the thermostat in the summer and lowering it in the winter has clear effects, which, by the way, could be made even more salient and transparent. We will get to that. In other domains, prices could help signal the implicit emissions, associated with consumption, that are less obviously related to climate change. For example, raising beef for consumption is one of the most greenhouse-gas-intensive ways of producing food. (Cows' "emissions" are not friendly to the environment, and the land required as pasture could have been used in some other manner that is friendlier to the environment.) If the price of beef goes up, even American Humans will eat fewer burgers.

The more important reason we favor economic incentives to deal with this problem is that much of the behavior that needs to change is conducted by firms. If firms see high prices for carbon emissions, they will have every incentive to innovate on every possible front, from producing Teslas to the plant-based Impossible Burger. (Which, by the way, is surprisingly tasty. Try it!)

In exploring economic incentives, we have focused on taxes and cap-and-trade, but there are alternative ways to align incentives. Political leaders (and some climate researchers) in many nations have called for subsidies, which in some circumstances might have the same effects as taxes, but which might be far more palatable to the public, because they offer gains and do not impose losses. For example, in the United States electric cars have received subsidies while gasoline taxes have remained low compared to most countries. This reflects a political judgment. The circumstances in which subsidies are an appropriate policy instrument raises complex questions that we do not engage here. Although we believe that subsidies can play an important role, they are inherently a patchwork approach, and let there be no doubt: someone has to pay for them.

The Energy Paradox

Despite all these points in favor of economic incentives, a growing body of economic and psychological research, rooted in behavioral findings, suggests that regulatory mandates might also be a good approach to environmental problems, much better than economists have long thought. And as a matter of practicality in the United States, and many other nations, national legislatures have not been willing to pass a comprehensive carbon tax or cap-and-trade system. This has led regulators who care about climate change to use other methods. Most economists think those methods are distinctly second-best. Maybe so, but maybe not.

How could blunt regulations possibly work better than incentives? A starting point is that when consumers buy motor vehicles and appliances, they might not take adequate account of the potential savings, to them, of fuel-efficient vehicles or energy-efficient appliances. This is known as the *Energy Paradox*[17]: Consumers, who are Humans, decline to spend an extra $100 on a more energy-efficient washing machine that could save them much more than that in just a few years. And if consumers neglect the economic benefits—to them—of fuel economy or energy efficiency, then a regulatory mandate could, in principle, generate large economic benefits, far in excess of those produced by the reduction of externalities alone.

Indeed, a great deal of research suggests that consumers pay too little attention to those benefits, and some analyses by government agencies suggest that the savings from fuel efficiency and energy efficiency mandates are both very real and very large. If so, we should add consumer monetary savings to the benefits stemming from reductions in greenhouse gas emissions and emissions of other air pollutants. As a result, the total savings from aggressive fuel-economy and energy-efficiency mandates can dwarf the costs. In principle, it is possible that their net benefits will actually be much higher than those of economic incentives, which will combat externalities but will not deliver consumer savings.

You might expect us to say that if consumers do not take adequate account of potential savings, they should be nudged, not coerced. And indeed, many nations have taken steps in that direction through mandatory labels pointing out the economic savings. Some of these are behaviorally informed and specifically designed to speak to Humans. We applaud those steps (and will have more to say about them). Still, we share the suspicion of many analysts who believe that while these nudges help, they do not adequately correct consumers' failure to give adequate consideration to economic savings. However, we do not intend to argue that position strongly, much less to settle the matter.[18] At the very least, we think it is worth recognizing the possibility that rules and mandates can get consumers big savings—while at the same time protecting the planet. One illustrative example is building codes. If home builders believe (perhaps rightly) that consumers will not pay more for a more energy-efficient home, then they will underinvest in such things as insulation, which is much cheaper to include when a home is being built than later on.

Regulators, please take notice. (And consumers, please consider those savings.)

Feedback and Information

As we have emphasized, the most important step in dealing with environmental problems is getting the prices (that is, incentives) right, and although we are hopeful that the nations of the world will eventually come to share that view, we realize that in many nations it is, and will likely continue to be, a hard political pill to swallow. In the United States, at least, presidential candidates have not been willing to campaign on a promise to raise gasoline prices and utility bills. It is a good sign that in his 2020 presidential campaign, Joe Biden said that he favored a carbon tax (he was the only Democratic presidential candidate to do so). But in many nations, including the United States, a serious obstacle to improved incentives is that the costs of pollution are hidden, while the price at the pump or on the utility bill is quite salient.

That is why we suggest a kind of "all tools on deck" approach to climate change. Sensible regulations, going well beyond nudges, might be imposed in many domains. But there are also a wide variety of useful interventions that fully qualify as nudges that should be part of the environmental tool kit. By themselves, those steps will not eliminate the risks of climate change. But they will help, and as former President Obama likes to say about initiatives that merely dent large-scale problems: "Better is good."

One class of sensible initiatives improves the feedback consumers receive on the implications of their actions through better information and disclosure. Such strategies can improve the operation of markets and government alike; they also tend to be inexpensive. To be sure, many people fear that disclosure by itself is ineffective and will accomplish too little. This view is often right. But sometimes, information can be a surprisingly strong motivator.

A particularly significant success story for disclosure requirements is the Emergency Planning and Community Right-to-Know Act, a law enacted by Congress in 1986 in the aftermath of an industrial chemical accident from a U.S. plant in Bhopal, India.[19] Understood as a modest and uncontroversial step, it was essentially a bookkeeping measure, intended to give the EPA and local communities a sense of what hazardous materials might be lurking undetected. The statute ended up doing a lot more. In fact, the requirement of disclosure, captured in the Toxics Release Inventory, counts among the most unambiguous success stories in all of environmental law.

To create the Toxics Release Inventory, firms and individuals must report to the national government the quantities of potentially hazardous chemicals that have been stored or released into the environment. The information is readily available on the EPA website to anyone who wants it. Tens of thousands of facilities now disclose detailed information on hundreds of chemicals, covering billions of pounds of on-site and off-site disposal or other releases. Users of hazardous chemicals must also report to their local fire departments the locations, types, and quantities of stored chemicals. And they must disclose information about potential adverse health consequences.

The surprising fact is that without mandating any specific changes by firms, the law had beneficial effects, spurring large reductions in toxic releases throughout the United States.[20] This unanticipated consequence suggests that all by themselves, disclosure requirements can sometimes produce significant emissions reductions. Disclosure requirements are used in countless other environmental areas and countries, from an Italian sea resort cleanliness and recycling initiative to a climate index for Swedish municipalities.

Why, exactly, has the Toxics Release Inventory had such beneficial effects? A major reason is that environmentally concerned groups, and the media in general, draw attention to serious offenders, producing a kind of "environmental blacklist."[21] This is a nice example of a social nudge. Few companies want to appear prominently on the Toxics Release Inventory list. The bad publicity can result in all sorts of harm, including lower stock prices.[22] Companies that end up on the list have strong incentives to reduce their emissions. Even better, companies are motivated to ensure that they do not end up on the list. The result is a kind of competition, in which companies enact more and better measures to avoid appearing to be significant contributors to toxic pollution. If companies are able to reduce emissions at low cost, they will do so, simply in order to avoid the bad publicity and the resulting harms.

Disclosing Greenhouse Gas Emissions

With this example in mind, we think there is an obvious nudge that all countries should adopt to help deal with climate change. Governments should be creating a greenhouse gas inventory (GGI), requiring disclosure by all significant emitters. The GGI would permit people to see the various sources of greenhouse gases in their communities and elsewhere and track changes over time. Seeing that list, governments could respond by considering legislative measures. It is inevitable that interested groups, including members of the media, would draw attention to the largest emitters. To be sure, an inventory of this kind might not produce massive changes on its own. But such a nudge would not be especially costly, and it would almost certainly help. (Compiling information about emitters is also a necessary prerequisite to enacting economic incentives.)

Early progress on this initiative has already been made. Some kind of GGI is required in a number of nations, including the United States. Indeed, the Paris Agreement requires parties to provide a national GGI. But well before the Paris Agreement mandated it, the EPA formally did so starting in 2011, explicitly with the hope that it would nudge high emitters to make real reductions. This same idea has picked up traction in the form of voluntary programs in the private sector; for example, the Carbon Disclosure Project (CDP) provides a standardized global disclosure platform that investors, companies, cities, states, and regions have used to document and manage their environmental impacts. CDP alone has disclosures from more than eighty-four hundred companies and eight hundred cities.[23]

We are not aware of a careful study of the actual impact of GGIs. At least in the United States, the disclosure does not seem to have had the large impact of the Toxics Release Inventory, perhaps because it has not been sufficiently salient to the public or because greenhouse gas emissions are not as scary sounding as "toxic" emissions. But that could be changing. As we were writing this book, much of the American West Coast was experiencing horrific wildfires and smoky air. Australia had experienced similar events and they were impossible to ignore. At the same time, there were a record number of tropical storms in the Atlantic, so many that the agency that gives storms names in alphabetical order ran out of letters and had to switch over to Greek letters, eventually reaching iota, the ninth letter (if you have forgotten your Greek alphabet).[24] Extreme climate events are becoming increasingly common, and a great deal could be done to draw attention to emissions trends, including which parties are part of the problem and which are creating solutions.

Automatically Green

If the goal is to make the environment cleaner, a simple idea is to *make the green option the easy option*. And if the goal is to make it really easy, make it automatic.

In many countries, our lives are increasingly accompanied by the equivalent of "green defaults" replacing dirtier ones. Consider motion detectors that turn out the lights when people do not appear to be in the room. In this way, motion detectors create the equivalent of an "off" default. If the default setting on office thermostats is turned down in winter and up in summer, we should expect significant economic and environmental savings—at least if the default setting is not so uncomfortable that people will take steps to change it.

Both policy and technology are making green defaults of this kind readily available. We have seen that inertia is a powerful force. In addition, a green default is a kind of signal. It tells people what it is right to do. When people reject it, they might feel conscience-stricken—and evidence suggests that they often do. There is a general lesson here. Architectural solutions, making things easy or automatic, can have a much bigger impact than asking people to do the right thing.

Now consider a much bigger question: the choice among utility suppliers in places where such choices are available. Typically, the default may not be environmentally friendly; it might even be generated with coal. To use green energy (such as solar or wind), people must seek out relevant information and choose it affirmatively (if it is an option at all). Most do not bother, but what would be the effect of switching to a green default, so that people are automatically green? The evidence is in, and it's very clear: many more people end up with green energy. They stick with it, even if it's a bit more expensive.

Vivid findings come from a randomized controlled trial conducted in Germany, specifically testing the effect of a default rule on the use of green energy.[25] The study involved almost forty-two thousand households, participating in a 4.5-week-long trial and randomly assigned to one of two treatments. In the first, people were asked whether they wanted to opt in to green energy; in the second, they were automatically enrolled into a green energy provider but were asked whether they wanted to opt out. In both treatments, green energy was slightly more expensive.

The default rule had a massive effect. Conditional on the purchase of an energy contract, only 7.2 percent of purchased contracts in the opt-in treatment were green. But in the opt-out treatment, a remarkable majority of 69.1 percent of purchased contracts were green. Notably, this effect was robust after controlling for service quality of the chosen contract, base prices of electricity, and unit prices. In Germany as a whole, many providers are now automatically enrolling people in green energy.[26] Field evidence—based not on experiments but on what is actually happening—shows that the nudge really works (in Germany, Switzerland, and elsewhere). In general, most people are not opting out. As a result, the air is a lot less dirty and greenhouse gas emissions are a lot lower.

Norms and Transparency

We have said that people often do not know how much energy they are using. They also do not know how their energy use compares with that of their neighbors. Opower, a company now owned by Oracle, created a vivid nudge in the form of the Home Energy Report, which gives customers a clear sense of how their utility bill compares with the norm in their neighborhood, and what they might do to save energy.[27] The Home Energy Report is now in widespread use, and we can ask how well it works. The best study comes from economist Hunt Allcott, who estimates that the effect of sending these reports is reduction of consumption by about 2 percent.[28] Is that a lot or a little? Two percent may not seem like a big deal, but as we have said, every bit helps, especially in the use of power, which represents a large portion of emissions (about 20 percent in the United States).[29] In addition, Allcott finds that this reduction is roughly the same as what would be achieved by a temporary price increase of 11 to 20 percent. The key thing about this is that it is achieved at virtually no cost, since the information is included in the regular bill received by the customer. More low-cost interventions like this, please.

Here's a related idea: voluntary participation programs designed to assist not individual consumers, but companies both large and small. With such programs, public officials do not require anyone to do anything. Instead, they ask companies whether they would be willing to follow certain standards that are expected to have desirable effects on the environment. The basic idea is that even in a free market, companies often fail to use the latest products, and sometimes government can help them to make money while also reducing pollution.

Among the problems discussed in this book, climate change is the most serious and also the hardest. We have given an account of why the world has not yet addressed it. For individuals, climate change is the mother of all free-rider problems, compounded by behavioral biases; the same is true for nations. Large-scale emissions reductions are going to be essential for poor nations as well as rich ones, and that creates real challenges for international negotiators. To get those reductions, we are going to need to change incentives, if for no other reason than to stimulate the kinds of technological innovation that will be necessary to make break-throughs. Incentives can come in many forms; for example, taxes, subsidies, target dates, and contests. But better choice architecture, and a lot of nudges, can also play an important role. In particular, we hope and believe that the world will increasingly become automatically green—and prevent a lot of tragedy in the process.

PART V

THE COMPLAINTS
DEPARTMENT

15

Much Ado About Nudging

When we were trying to find a publisher for the first edition of this book, there were not a lot of takers. Most people did not expect a book about libertarian paternalism to find a readership beyond the authors' immediate family members. Much to our surprise, and to that of our publishers, somehow the book did find an audience. The title *Nudge* certainly helped. (It was suggested by one of the publishers who politely turned us down.) Of course, with more readers come more skeptics. We have had our share of critics from many fields (including economics, psychology, philosophy, political science, and law). They span the political spectrum from right to left.

With respect to politics, it is tempting to conclude that angering both extremes means that we are doing something right, but that conclusion would reflect a self-serving bias. A more likely explanation for creating furor on both the right and the left is that our ideas are bad, evil, ill-advised, confused, or at least poorly written! We have tried to clear up some of the examples of imprecise writing in this version, but these clarifications will not answer the substantive objections that we explore in this chapter. We emphasize that we have learned a lot from our critics and that this book is better because of their questions and doubts.

A whole book could easily be written about conceptual, ethical, empirical, and other objections to nudging, but we will try to be brief.[1] One way to achieve that is to avoid getting bogged down in semantic arguments—for example, about whether libertarian paternalism is either libertarian or paternalistic. As we have said, we use the word *libertarian* to mean "choice-preserving." We have also said that, realistically, even opting out can be difficult, especially if there is some sludge involved, and that our ideal nudges impose as small a cost as possible on anyone who prefers to do something else. For a day or so back in 2007, we considered calling this book *One-Click Paternalism*, and while we rejected that terrible title, it will give you the idea of our goals. To us, the directions from a GPS device are perfect nudges. Even if the nice, polite voice suggests a right turn, the voice does not complain if we decide to continue going straight. Of course, not all nudges and nudge-inspired policies can meet that ideal, but if they don't, we consider it a form of sludge, to be included in any cost-benefit analysis of the policy.

We have used the term *paternalism* to include efforts to protect people against their own errors by guiding them to the choices they would make if they were fully informed and free from behavioral biases. This is a paternalism of means, not of ends; nudges are generally designed to help people find the right means to their own ends. We certainly do *not* intend to nudge people toward the choices we prefer. How could we when we do not agree? As you know by now, Thaler loves wine, and Sunstein prefers Diet Coke. Thaler loves long dinner parties; Sunstein dreads them. Sunstein enjoys philosophical arguments. Thaler avoids them at all costs. You get the idea. Our preferences have nothing to do with what makes a good policy.

Finally, to get this out of the way quickly, no, we do not think that choice architects, from either the public or the private sector, are always smart and knowledgeable. We certainly do not think they are always well motivated, or that they necessarily have the best interests of those they influence at heart. We do not deny the power of well-organized interest groups. We agree that experts err. Please! We have been paying some attention to what has been going on in the world in recent decades. We have noticed that not every head of state is a stable genius. We have also noticed a worrying rise in authoritarian governments. And in the private sector, there is a lot of self-interested nudging (as we have pointed out many times in this book). We were also paying attention during the financial crisis, when it was hard to find a sector of the financial services industry that was devoid of bad actors. During the COVID-19 pandemic, a lot of people blundered, and a lot of them had their own interests at heart. So, yes, we want to go on the record as saying that not everyone has the well-being of others as a first priority. All choice architects are fallible, and some are even malicious.

But what lesson should we take from these obvious facts? Recall that choice architecture and nudging are inevitable; you cannot wish them away. We know we have said this earlier, but this point is so widely ignored that we feel the need to repeat it. You can object to graphic cancer warnings on cigarette packages, prefer active choosing to default rules, reject the whole idea of calorie labels, seek to abolish GPS devices, or reject social-distancing guidelines. But objecting to nudges per se makes as much sense as objecting to air and water. You can't avoid them. And one reason for nudging, as opposed to prohibiting, is precisely the fallibility of choice architects of all kinds. So long as people can go their own way—and easily say no thanks!—the risks are greatly reduced. If you are worried about the mistakes and incentives of public officials, your first target should be coercion and mandates, not nudges.

Still, are we worried that bad people will read our book and go out and find new and more effective ways to nudge people? Absolutely! As we discussed in the chapter on sludge, we definitely worry about such things. But the existence of villains clearly predates the publication of our book, and while we acknowledge that a sophisticated understanding of behavioral biases can be put (and is being put) to self-interested use, we don't think that the risk of our book falling into the hands of bullies and crooks should be at the top of anyone's list of things to worry about. Maybe fret more about climate change?

With these preliminary issues out of the way, we turn to the most prominent critiques. Some of them come from critics on the right, mostly from those of the libertarian persuasion. They like freedom (as do we), and they think that nudging compromises it (as we don't). Some of their concerns are important, but we sometimes think that critiques from libertarians arise in part because they don't like the fact that we not only borrowed their word and used it without asking permission, but also paired it with another word that they hate. It would be a bit like a bunch of baseball-loving kids borrowing a cricket ball and using it to play baseball (or vice versa). Blasphemy. We admit that libertarian paternalism was a phrase that was intended to be jarring, but after all these years we would say to our libertarian friends: Maybe it is time to get over it?

A lot of people would say we must go further than nudging. They think that nudges are mere tweaks. They want large-scale change, and they don't think that nudges will get us there. They think that nudges are a distraction. Many of them are concerned with economic inequality, with the rights of working people, with monopolies, with police violence, with discrimination on the basis of race and sex, with much more. So are we. And if you've read this far, you know that in some cases, well-designed choice architecture can achieve a lot; it is much more than a collection of tweaks. All over the world, public officials, including those who work in so-called Nudge Units, have accomplished a great deal. Still, it is right to emphasize that mandates, bans, and economic incentives can sometimes make a lot of sense, even for those who generally love freedom of choice.

Slippery Slopes

It is well known that some people have some pretty silly fears, many of which have been given names. There is sciophobia, for example, which is the fear of shadows, and even arachibutyrophobia, which is the fear of peanut butter sticking to the roof of your mouth. There is a particularly obscure fear that oddly seems especially common among libertarian legal scholars: bathmophobia. This is the fear of falling down a slope or a flight of stairs. We suspect that this phobia produces an obsession with *slippery slopes*.

We should clarify that we do not mean it is foolish to be wary of *literal* slippery slopes, such as expert-only ski trails after an ice storm. By all means, please stay away from those. Indeed, any combination of slippery and steep slope is worthy of at least a warning sign nudge, and in extreme cases, even a ban (THIS TRAIL/STREET IS CLOSED UNTIL FURTHER NOTICE). The slippery slopes we think get too much attention are not physical in nature; they are metaphorical and are used in a particular type of argument.

The way a slippery slope argument goes is that if we do something, call it X, then there is a serious risk that it will start a trend, which will lead to other things such as Y and Z, and although X in and of itself is fine, maybe even a good idea, Y and Z are pretty scary. The conclusion is that you shouldn't do X unless you are willing to accept Z.

Slippery slope arguments are popular in the United States among those who are opposed to gun control. In this case, X is any restriction on an individual's right to own a gun (say, a ban on the ownership of assault weapons), and Z would be the government comes and confiscates all weapons, including steak knives and water pistols. Well, that is an exaggeration, but you get the idea.

The problem with most slippery slope arguments is that they do not provide any evidence of an actual slope: that is, a reason to believe that doing X makes it more likely, much less inevitable, that we will get Y and Z. This has not stopped people from making such arguments that on their face are rather dubious. For example, there was a Supreme Court argument about the Affordable Care Act in which the issue being discussed was whether the government could constitutionally require citizens to purchase health insurance. Justice Antonin Scalia famously argued that if this requirement were legal, nothing would stop some future government from requiring people to eat broccoli.[2] Talk about scare tactics!

The track record of slippery slope forecasts in the political domain is not exactly stellar. An opponent of women's suffrage once predicted that giving women the right to vote would create a "race of masculine women and effeminate men and the mating of these would result in the procreation of a race of degenerates."[3] Another opponent, noting that women represent more than half the population, predicted that allowing women to vote would mean that all our political leaders would soon be women.[4] For the record, in 2021, women held only 26 percent of the seats in Congress.[5] We only wish that slope had been a bit more slippery!

We bring up slippery slope arguments because critics have used them to criticize nudging and libertarian paternalism. "First it's nudge, then it's shove, then it's shoot," as they say. (But why? The whole point of nudging is to avoid shoving, let alone shooting.) It is interesting that in some of these arguments, a behavioral bias has been invoked as the theoretical underpinning. For example, one critic, Glen Whitman, makes his argument based on the research finding of *extremeness aversion*: people tend to prefer options in the middle.

> To take just one example, legally mandated enrollment in savings plans (with exit option) seems like the middle ground right now. But once it becomes standard, it will occupy the laissez-faire position. Then a "Save More Tomorrow" policy (with exit option) becomes the new middle-ground. And once that has been adopted, it too becomes the low-end, while automatic enrollment with freedom to choose your investments but *without* the option to exit entirely becomes the middle. By this route, a series of minor steps can eventually make even mandatory enrollment with specified minimums, highly restricted investments, and no opt-out seem like the "reasonable middle."[6]

Really?

For the record, in the twelve years since *Nudge* was first published, it is true that both automatic enrollment and Save More Tomorrow have become more commonly adopted around the world. But we are not aware of any trend toward removing the right to opt out. Surely it is at least as likely that if an option seems like a sensible middle ground, it will simply become more widely used, as opposed to morphing into something perceived to be extreme. Maybe that slope is not so steep after all?

Social trends are unpredictable. In the United States, we ratified a constitutional amendment (which is an extremely sludge-ridden process) in order to ban the sale of alcohol. Did this lead to bans on other activities such as smoking and overeating? No.

Rather, some years later, the country saw the error in its ways and repealed the prohibition. Now states are rapidly passing laws legalizing the sale of marijuana. These slopes seem hard to anticipate.

We specifically see no reason to worry about nudge creep. One more time: nudging as such is inevitable, and by definition, nudges maintain freedom of choice. If we accept those boundaries, there is no reason to think that we cannot hold the line against coercion, if that is what we want to do. You can have warnings that products contain shrimp (to help those who, like Sunstein, are allergic to shellfish) without banning products that contain shrimp. You can set printers to double-sided printing by default without banning people from switching to single-sided printing. If the accusation is that as a policy, nudges have appeal because they strike a kind of middle ground, then we plead guilty, but let's evaluate them on their merits, rather than on the basis of some hypothetical risk that could just be a symptom of bathmophobia.

Freedom and Active Choice

Some freedom-loving critics have another arrow in their quiver, one for which we have more sympathy. They are concerned about liberty and free choice rather than welfare (which they are skeptical we can measure or assess). For this reason, they strongly prefer active choosing to well-designed defaults. At most, they would like to provide people with the information necessary to make an informed choice, and then tell people to choose for themselves. This way of thinking was reflected in that campaign by the Swedish government to get citizens to choose their own investment portfolios, and as we have seen, it is a strategy that has some downsides.

Active choosing is a form of choice architecture, and people can be nudged to make active choices. We agree that sometimes that's an excellent idea. But should people be required to choose? Generally? Always? We think that *required* active choosing is most suitable when the choices are simple, such as whether to opt in or out. In more complex situations, such as choosing a portfolio from a menu of hundreds of mutual funds, forcing people to choose is a dubious strategy. It's also pretty paternalistic. Why not provide a well-designed default and then offer people the freedom to pick something else? Often people choose not to choose, and we should respect their choice. We have seen that Swedes who have entered the labor market in the past decade are overwhelmingly declining the option of becoming their own portfolio manager. We don't expect people to be their own physicians; why should we *require* them to make other complex decisions if there are trusted experts who can do it better, and on whom they freely choose to rely? And yes, we know (and have said) that neither *trusted* nor *expert* are adjectives that can be presumed when it comes to advice givers.

In the context of organ donations, we do advocate something close to the active choice model. We prefer prompted choice to required choice because people can react badly to being told they must answer some question, but we also find the notion of presuming someone's consent in this domain to be overreach.

In addition to being an intrusion on freedom, required choice is simply impractical in many environments. Do you want to choose all the ingredients in your restaurant meals? If you buy a new car, don't you want the manufacturer to set the default for the headlights to be on when it is dark and off when it is light? If instead you insist on turning the lights on and off manually (more freedom!), there is a very good chance you will leave the lights on (draining the battery) if you leave for work when it is still dark but arrive when it is light. There are hundreds of such settings. Is it better for buyers to spend the first hour in their new car choosing the best setting for the brightness of the display? We think well-chosen defaults work well in this setting, and they could be improved by a salient tutorial on how to adjust the seat and mirrors since, especially for those settings, one size certainly does not fit all.

Active choosing is often a good idea, but in many domains, curation and well-designed defaults are a blessing. We should not wish them away.

Don't Nudge, Boost

Some emphasize that in a free society, people have the right to be wrong. It can be helpful for us to make mistakes, since that is how we learn. On these points we heartily agree, which is why we generally favor opt-out rights, as long as people are not causing harm to others. If people really want to invest a chunk of their retirement portfolio in high-tech Romanian stocks, we are reluctant to prohibit it (so long as people are adequately informed). But for unsophisticated choosers, there is little harm in putting up some warning signs along the way. We approve of the signs at some ski areas warning novice and intermediate skiers: "Don't even think about going down this trail if you are not an expert."

Some critics have a strong preference for education instead of nudges. In their view, private and public institutions should be teaching people, or "boosting" their capacities, rather than enlisting choice architecture.[7] The least lovely version of this claim comes from a psychologist from Germany: "The interest in nudging as opposed to education should be understood against the specific political background in which it emerged. In the US, the public education system is largely considered a failure, and the government tries hard to find ways to steer large sections of the public who can barely read and write. Yet this situation does not apply everywhere."[8]

We will refrain from reacting to the nationalistic name-calling and instead address the more substantive question of whether we should refrain from nudging in favor of education, or "boosting," understood as an effort to target and improve competences. Our first reaction is to say: Why do we have to choose one over the other? The two of us can be accused of many things, but being anti-education is probably not one of them. We like boosting, and agree that in some cases, it can be effective. Both of us are teachers by profession. Many nudges do try to educate (and require literacy); disclosure of information, warnings, and reminders are designed to inform people. Nevertheless, we still appreciate being offered well-curated options from which to choose, and well-considered defaults that we can reject if we wish. By all means, let's try to create a citizenry that has the skills and knowledge necessary to thrive in the world; it is valuable and important to increase people's competence and to help them to exercise their own agency. Statistical literacy, emphasized by those who like boosting, is an especially good thing. But we also need to be realistic. We are pretty sure that even the best German high schools do not provide training that is equivalent to a Ph.D. in financial economics.

This criticism is based on a fundamental misunderstanding about our view of human nature. We do *not* think that people are dumb. Instead, we think that the world is hard! We know of few economists who are confident that they can choose the best mortgage from a list of those available or calculate with any precision how much they need to save for retirement. We know personally many who have made a poor choice of health care plan. Isn't life easier if we live in a world with personalized defaults, easy-to-compare options, Smart Disclosure, and well-functioning choice engines? It should not be a choice between nudging and educating. Do both! Because nudges preserve freedom of choice, it's especially valuable to help people to exercise their freedom in an informed way.

Many people are enthusiastic about training high school students to be more financially literate. We share that enthusiasm. If we were designing a high school curriculum, we would replace trigonometry with statistics and household finance. Surely, compound interest and net present value are more useful concepts than sine and cosine. Even more basic is to teach people how to manage a household budget and the perils of credit card debt. Education can help, sometimes a lot, but both common sense and empirical research suggest that we should not be overconfident about its beneficial effects. Your commonsense reaction should be based on how much you remember from your high school chemistry class. Or trigonometry, for that matter. Do we think an understanding of compound interest will be much stickier?

The empirical results support the intuition from that thought experiment. An important meta-analysis of the efficacy of financial literacy training provides three important results.[9] First, the longer the training period, the bigger the results. A course that provides twenty-four hours of training yields larger effects than one lasting just twelve hours. Second, the effects are modest. You cannot create financial wizards quickly. Third, and most important, whatever beneficial effects created are found to vanish over time, and completely disappear after just two years. The authors of the study conclude that the most effective form of training would be delivered on a "just in time" basis—that is, in anticipation of a pending decision. Give high school juniors and seniors information about the returns to various forms of post–high school education, how to apply for available financial aid and student loans, how to deal with credit cards, and so forth. They will be able to put this training to use right away.

But don't think that what you teach them about fixed versus variable rates will necessarily help them choose a better mortgage a decade later. When they are ready to buy a house, offer free classes on the potential pitfalls. (And maybe a few simple nudges.)

Is Nudging Sneaky?

Some people argue that mandates, bans, and taxes have a big advantage over nudges: people know where they stand, and no one is fooled. By contrast, they say, nudges are covert and in a sense manipulative, a form of trickery.[10] They affect people without their knowledge.

For most nudges, this objection is hard to understand. Labels, warnings, and reminders are not exactly hidden; if they are, they will not work. Default rules should be, and usually are, entirely transparent. If people are automatically enrolled in green energy, they should be, and typically are, told that they have been automatically enrolled in green energy. When an employer automatically enrolls employees in a savings plan, subject to opt-out, nothing is hidden. If it is, we have a sludge problem; the steps to take to opt out should be clear, and preferably require just one click.

It is true that some nudges work even if those who are affected by them do not focus on them or even think about them. An example would be a cafeteria that puts the healthy foods in more salient and accessible locations, which could influence choices even though diners might be unaware that they have been nudged.

In this situation the design itself is not hidden; it is in plain sight. But the *reason* for the design may not be apparent. This is true for many forms of influence. Beer commercials do not include a warning that the presence of scantily clad models is designed to attract the attention of viewers and make them more likely to buy the beer. When politicians give a speech, they do not disclose that the wording of their message has been created (via testing) to maximize the chance the viewer will support the candidate. But is there anyone so naive as not to realize that commercials are designed to sell products and political speeches are written to attract votes? True, a cafeteria is not a commercial, but it does have a design, which was of course chosen for reasons.

If a cafeteria has been designed to encourage healthy eating, or if people have been automatically enrolled in some program, private and (especially) public institutions should not hide that fact. All the better if the reasons for nudges are revealed as well. We will return to this point shortly.

A somewhat different claim is that nudges work only if the recipients of the nudge are unaware that they are being nudged. This claim has been investigated in several contexts and has repeatedly been shown to be false. Existing studies find that transparency about nudging does not reduce its impact.[11] In fact, it can easily have the opposite effect. Telling people that they have been automatically enrolled in the retirement plan because the employer thinks it is a wise choice to take advantage of the employer match and tax break is likely to *increase* the number who enroll. Drawing attention to the healthy design of a cafeteria can actually magnify the effect of that design, because it will convey valuable information.[12]

Are nudges manipulative? To answer that question, we need a definition of manipulation. To make a (very) long and complex story short, philosophers and others have generally converged on

the view that an action counts as manipulative if it does not adequately respect people's capacity for rational deliberation.[13] On
this criterion, most nudges are not manipulative.[14] If people are
reminded that they have a doctor's appointment next Thursday,
no one is manipulating them. The same is true if people are given
information about the caloric content of food or if they are warned
that certain foods contain shellfish or nuts, or that if they take
more than the recommended dosage of a medicine, something
bad might happen. To be sure, we might be able to categorize a
default rule as manipulative if people are not told about it, or if it
is hard for them to opt out. We call this sludge—and sludge can
be manipulative.

Drawing Lines and the Publicity Principle

A number of years ago Sunstein took his daughter to Lollapalooza,
the three-day rock festival held in midsummer in Chicago. On
Friday night, a huge sign with changing electronic messages often
showed the schedule of performances, but interspersed that information with a message saying, "Drink more water." The print was
large; the message was accompanied by another one: "You sweat
in the heat: You lose water."

What was the point of this announcement? Chicago had been
in the midst of a terrible heat wave, and those who ran Lollapalooza were clearly trying to prevent the various health problems
that are associated with dehydration. The sign was a nudge. No
one was forced to drink. But those who created the content for the
sign were sensitive to how people think. In particular, the choice
of the particular words *more water* was excellent. Those words
were likely to be far more effective than blander alternatives, such

as "Drink enough water" or "Drink water." The suggestion that we "lose water" invoked loss aversion on behalf of staying hydrated. (As it happens, Sunstein wished that he had seen the sign earlier; he became very thirsty during the performance, but the crowd was so densely packed that it was impossible to go out to find water.)

Now compare an imaginable alternative. Suppose that instead of having a visible "Drink more water" sign, the schedules for the day were briefly and invisibly interrupted by subliminal messaging, that is, stimuli that are not consciously noticed but nevertheless register enough to alter beliefs or behavior. The subliminal message might say, "Drink more water," "Aren't you thirsty???" "Don't drink and drive," "Drugs kill," "Support your president," "Abortion is murder," "Buy ten copies of *Nudge*." Can subliminal messages, including paid advertising, be seen as a form of libertarian paternalism? After all, they steer people's choices, but they do not make their decisions for them.

We do not embrace subliminal messaging, and we do not count it as libertarian paternalism, even if it is used in the service of desirable ends. A general objection to libertarian paternalism, and to certain kinds of nudges, might be that they are insidious—that they empower government to maneuver people in its preferred directions, and at the same time provide officials with excellent tools by which to accomplish that task. Compare subliminal advertising to something just as cunning: If you want people to lose weight, one effective strategy is to put mirrors in the cafeteria. When people see themselves in the mirror, they might eat less if they are chubby. Is this okay? And if mirrors are acceptable, what about those that are intentionally unflattering? (We seem to run into more of those every year.) Are such mirrors an acceptable strategy for our friend Carolyn in the cafeteria? If so, what should we think about flattering mirrors in a fast food restaurant?

These are large questions, and one of us might have written a book or two about them.[15] To approach them in this space, we return to one of our guiding principles: transparency. In this context we endorse what the philosopher John Rawls called the *publicity principle*.[16] In its simplest form, the publicity principle suggests that no choice architect in the public or private sector should adopt a policy that she would not be able or willing to defend publicly. We like this principle on two grounds. The first is practical. If a firm or government adopts a policy that it could not easily defend publicly, it stands to face considerable embarrassment, and perhaps much worse, if the policy and its grounds are disclosed. We urge our colleagues and students to adopt this policy for all important choices in their personal and professional lives. The second, more important ground involves the idea of respect. Organizations of all forms should respect people, and if they adopt policies that they could not and would not defend in public, they fail to show that respect. Instead, they treat citizens as tools for their own use or manipulation.

We think that the publicity principle is a good guideline for constraining and implementing nudges, in both the public and private sectors. In the U.S. government, regulations are generally proposed to the public for comment and review before they are finalized; this includes many in the category of nudges. Some examples include fuel economy labels, nutrition facts panels, and graphic warnings for cigarettes. The nudges are transparent, and so are the supporting reasons.

The same conclusion holds for legal default rules. If government alters such rules—to encourage organ donation or environmental protection, or to reduce age discrimination—it should not be secretive about what it is doing. It should disclose its action, and it should explain it (and preferably allow members of the public to comment in advance). The same can be said for educational campaigns that enlist behavioral findings in order to provide a helpful nudge. If government officials use cleverly worded signs to reduce litter, deter theft, or encourage people to register as organ donors, they should be happy to reveal both their methods and their motives. Consider an American advertisement from long ago showing an egg frying in a hot skillet with the voice-over, "This is your brain on drugs." The vivid image was designed to trigger fear of drug use. Whether or not the advertisement is deemed manipulative, it did not violate the publicity principle.

So, to be clear, we like the idea of a bill of rights for nudging, and it should forbid subliminal advertising.[17]

On Mandates and Bans: Beyond Nudging?

We have seen that libertarians are worried that we will start with a nudge and then move on to shoving. Some critics of a more progressive persuasion have the opposite worry, namely that we will stop at nudging when much stronger measures are required. Some people even think that if governments nudge, they won't do anything more, even if nudges are palpably inadequate. Instead of getting serious about climate change, maybe regulators will rest content with energy efficiency labels!

If we (or anyone, for that matter) thought that most of the world's problems could be fully addressed with light-touch interventions, then this would be a serious concern. Murder, rape, assault, and theft are criminal offenses, properly met with coercion. Some problems, such as pollution, arise because people are imposing harms on others. As we have emphasized, nudges are not an adequate approach to such problems. To be sure, they might help. You can impose taxes on gasoline and encourage people, through nudges, to buy fuel-efficient cars. There are plenty of externality-reducing nudges. But by themselves, nudges are not enough to control externalities.

Nudging might be thought of as a Swiss Army knife type of tool. These knives are designed to be versatile and can be highly effective in certain circumstances, such as when a can has to be opened or a screw tightened. In the right situation, nudges can also accomplish quite a lot at very low cost. But as we have repeatedly stressed, taxes, subsidies, mandates, and bans also have their place. Graphic warnings do not accomplish all that should be done to reduce cigarette smoking. Changing the default does not eliminate the shortage of organs for transplant. And when it comes to climate change, we have spent an entire chapter emphasizing why we will need jackhammers and bulldozers, with pocketknives helping where they can.

We very much doubt that the use of nudges is likely to discourage officials from taking stronger measures. (Sunstein worked in the U.S. government for four years, and he never saw that happen. Not once.) A nation might impose severe alcohol taxes, nudge people not to drink and drive, and top it off by giving offenders stiff fines if they get caught driving while intoxicated. Countries in Scandinavia do all three. A nation might nudge people to buy fuel-efficient cars, for example with fuel-economy labels—while also imposing high gasoline taxes or subsidizing electric cars. A nation might make it a crime to use certain drugs—while also nudging people not to use those drugs. It might seem clever to suggest that the availability of nudging will discourage the use of more aggressive instruments. In the history of the world, that might have happened—but realistically, we're talking about a debater's point. It's not a serious concern.

Still, reasonable people can certainly disagree about when we should move from nudges to bans and mandates (or vice versa). To give one example, our friend and colleague David Laibson was involved with Thaler on the design of the retirement savings plan at a foundation. The plan has a well-designed inexpensive default, and a small number of other curated investment options. The question on which they (mildly) disagreed was whether eager participants would be allowed to access what is called the "mutual fund window," in which a large number of other funds are available. They agreed that the employees who used this option were unlikely to make great investment decisions, and on average would probably do worse in the long run (as judged by themselves, of course) than if they stuck to the basic offerings. They also agreed (based on empirical evidence in other settings) that only a small percentage of employees would make use of this option, especially if there was a bit of sludge involved in accessing the window, such as a warning label. Laibson would have excluded the option, Thaler would have allowed it, but neither is sure he is right. (On this one, Sunstein agrees with Laibson. Majority rule?)

This is an illustration of a more general dilemma. Enthusiastic paternalists who are especially worried about the risk of poor choices might want to push for bans and mandates. If Humans really make errors, why not protect them by forbidding them from erring?

The truth, of course, is that there are no hard-and-fast stopping points. We have defined libertarian paternalism to include actions, rules, and other nudges that can be easily avoided by opting out. We do not have a clear definition of "easily avoided," but we hold up "one-click" paternalism or its equivalent to be as close as we can get with existing technology. (We can hope for "one-thought" or "one-blink" technology in the future.) In many domains, it's best to allow people to go their own way at the lowest possible cost. To be sure, some of the policies we have advocated impose higher costs than one click. To opt out of an automatic enrollment plan, an employee might have to fill out and return some form—not a big cost, but more than one click. It would be arbitrary and a bit ridiculous to offer an inflexible rule to specify when costs are high enough to disqualify a policy as libertarian, but the precise question of degree is not really important. Let us simply say that in general, we want those costs to be low. The real question is when we should be willing to impose some nontrivial costs, or even very high costs, in the interests of improving people's welfare.

Consider a class of regulations requiring "cooling-off periods." The rationale is that in the heat of the moment, consumers might make ill-considered or improvident decisions. Self-control problems are the underlying concern. A mandatory cooling-off period for door-to-door sales, of the sort imposed by the United States Federal Trade Commission in 1972, provides an illustration.[18] Under the commission's rule, any door-to-door sale must be accompanied by a written statement informing the buyer of his right to rescind the purchase within three days of the transaction. The law came about because of complaints about high-pressure sales techniques and contracts with fine print. Again, a cost-benefit test, looking at the benefits for those who are helped and the costs for those who are not, could be used to decide when such laws would be imposed. Using such a test, regulators would want to consider how big the imposition is on those who have to wait a few days to receive the product, and how often buyers would want to change their minds. When the costs are low (did anyone ever really need to complete the purchase of an encyclopedia right away, even before Wikipedia was online?) and there are frequent changes of heart, such a regulation makes sense to us.

For certain fundamental decisions, often made on impulse, a similar strategy might well be best. Some states impose a mandatory waiting period before a couple may get divorced.[19] Asking people to pause and think before making a decision of that magnitude seems like a sensible idea, and outside of very extreme situations, we are hard-pressed to think of why anyone would need to change their marital status immediately. (True, spouses sometimes really don't like each other, but is it so terrible to have to wait a short while before the deed is done?) We could easily imagine similar restrictions on the decision to marry, and some states have moved in this direction as well.[20] Aware that people might act in a way that they will regret, regulators do not block their choices but do ensure a period for sober reflection. Note in this regard that mandatory cooling-off periods make best sense, and tend to be imposed, when two conditions are met: (a) people make the relevant decisions infrequently and therefore lack a great deal of experience and (b) emotions are likely to be running high. These are the circumstances in which people are especially prone to making choices that they will regret.*

Cooling-off periods are a relatively mild intervention. When should society take the next step to imposing bans and mandates? Again, reasonable people can differ on where they would draw that line. Our lodestar is human well-being, recognizing that reasonable people also differ about how to understand that concept. For example, fellow behavioral scientists Nick Chater and George

---

* Of course, there will be situations in which people will disagree about the merits of a mandated cooling-off period. Abortion is one such example. In this case, the issue is so emotionally and politically laden that it would be hard to sort out the merits of the cooling-off period policy from the more basic underlying disputes. Pro-choice advocates view cooling-off requirements as sludge, and there is no doubt that the costs of such requirements can be high. For a woman who has to travel a long way to find a clinic that can perform the procedure, the costs of a three-night stay, both economically and as a possible invasion of privacy, can be substantial. In such circumstances we would oppose such a rule even if it were well intended. As always, the details will matter. We are going to firmly opt out of sticking our necks out any further on this issue.

Loewenstein have argued that the defined-contribution retirement plans we have discussed in this book allow too much opportunity for errors, and that they should be replaced by mandatory savings schemes at set saving rates.[21] They praise the system in Australia, which is compulsory and does not permit people to borrow against their savings.

Now, it is true that a mandatory system will, by definition, achieve 100 percent compliance, at least for those employed in the formal economy. The comparable UK NEST system uses automatic enrollment and achieves over 90 percent participation. Is it obvious that this is worse? An evaluation will necessarily depend on how highly to value freedom of choice and how much harm will come to those who decide to opt out. It is at least possible that when people opt out, they do so for good and sufficient reasons, and some evidence supports that speculation.[22] For example, people might opt out because they really do need the money now, or because they have their own, separate retirement plan— possibilities that help explain why it is often a good idea to let people go their own way.

Mandates and bans are certainly justified in some contexts. We have said that if people's choices result in harm to others, we might want a prohibition (consider laws against assault and theft) or a corrective tax (consider greenhouse gas emissions). But even in such contexts, nudges can have an important place.

If people are making stupid, myopic, or self-defeating decisions, we wouldn't put mandates off the table.[23] We do not object to social security programs, to bans on trans fats, to energy efficiency mandates, to laws that require motorcyclists to wear helmets or drivers to wear seatbelts, or to requiring people to wear masks in public during a pandemic. If people's choices impose serious harms on their future selves (consider smoking), we might want to go beyond nudges (we favor cigarette taxes and bans on smoking in restaurants). The only point is that taxes, mandates, and bans raise distinctive problems and concerns. So long as people are making informed decisions about how to live their own lives, we would favor an attitude of humility and respect—and hence a presumption in favor of freedom of choice. But that presumption certainly protects your right to disagree with us.

Epilogue

When we wrote the first edition of *Nudge*, the world was entering a global financial crisis. We have produced this final edition in the midst of a global pandemic. The intervening years have been tumultuous. We have seen extraordinary creativity from the private sector, leading to the growth of gigantic firms of unprecedented size and power (Google, Apple, Facebook, Amazon, and more). We have watched some countries handle the COVID-19 crisis with stunning success (including the use of some exceptionally smart nudges), while others have badly floundered. Some elections have cheered us and others have filled us with despair. Our favorite teams and players have won, but they have also lost. In fact, except for Rafael Nadal, they usually lose the big one. And the world has made far too little progress in fighting climate change, even as the ice is melting and the fires are burning. But we are optimists by nature. We tend to focus on how much is in the glass, rather than how much of it is gone. That may reflect our personalities or just be a behavioral bias. (The latter is the view held by our spouses.) Nevertheless, we want to end this book on a hopeful note, while striving to be realistic.

When it comes to the possibility of applying the tools of behavioral science to some of the world's biggest problems, there has been enormous progress. Examples can be found in nations all over the world, including (but by no means limited to) the United States, the United Kingdom, Ireland, Denmark, Australia, New Zealand, India, Qatar, the United Arab Emirates, the Netherlands, Japan, France, and Germany. A great deal of work is being done at the United Nations, the World Health Organization, and the European Commission. Whether the issue involves the COVID-19 pandemic, climate change, terrorism, smoking cessation, economic growth, sex equality, or occupational safety, behavioral science is being used regularly and even as a matter of course. An idea that once seemed radical has morphed over time from chic to trending to commonplace to possibly passé. In some situations that is desirable. Thaler has long said that he hopes a day will come when the field of behavioral economics no longer exists because economists will incorporate the existence of Humans in their analyses to whatever extent that is appropriate (or even optimal).

The idea of incorporating behavioral science into public policy or managerial practice is starting to become as routine as doing a standard cost-benefit analysis or business plan. We are pleased that such thinking is not being limited to specialized nudge units, as much as we love them. Often the most important work is being done by high-level departments and ministries, or by the office of the president or the prime minister. Leaders all over the world have knowledge of, and even expertise in, behavioral science and nudging. We have stressed that all policies require some choice architecture, just as all products require some kind of design. You don't have to be Steve Jobs to strive for excellence in design. That includes putting the user experience at the top of the list of things to care about. If one set of people is in charge of how things look and others are in charge of how they work, you end up with those door handles that you want to pull when they need to be pushed. You get built-in sludge.

There is a much greater chance of success if creating good choice architecture is at the heart of every policy analysis and corporate decision. The people who created the Swedish Premium Pension Plan did not set out to create a system with hundreds of funds from which to choose. That just happened. They simply chose to delegate the task of curating the fund offerings to others. Those curators turned out to be regulators at the European Union, who set the rules governing who can operate the appropriate type of mutual fund and the entry decisions of the funds themselves. When that process produced hundreds of funds to choose from, it was too late to say oops and rethink.

We are decidedly not saying that policy designers can or should be omniscient. But they do need to think at least one step ahead about what Humans can and will do, and more important, be willing to revise the system as they see how things work. Unfortunately, inertia is a powerful force.

We have both had more than a little experience trying to incorporate behavioral science into policy. On the basis of these experiences, and the growing literature in the field, we believe that the biggest opportunities for breakthroughs can come from incorporating choice architecture (and other components of behavioral science) at the very earliest stages in the policy creation process. An example from that other form of architecture provides a useful illustration.

When the University of Chicago Booth School of Business decided to erect a new building, it held a competition for concept proposals from several well-known architects. The winning entry came from the renowned firm led by Rafael Viñoly, who hails from Uruguay. After winning the contest, but before getting to work on the details of the building, Viñoly and his team spent several days visiting with the students, faculty, and staff, learning more about how they spent their time and what they were hoping for in a building. The result was a structure that was not only physically beautiful, paying appropriate homage to a house across the street designed by Frank Lloyd Wright; it "works" amazingly well.

For example, Viñoly learned that faculty cherish opportunities for random encounters with each other. Well, at least they relish that more than chance encounters with students. Or members of the dean's office. The faculty offices are located on the top three floors, which are connected by open stairwells that help induce those chance encounters. The deans and students are relegated to lower floors, and chance meetings with those groups are limited to the cafeteria, which, we are happy to say, is designed so that customers have to circumvent the salad bar in order to get to the burgers.

Something similar could happen in designing public policies. If the goal is to promote public safety, on the roads and at work, policymakers could work to ensure that the safest choice is also the easiest choice. If the goal is to reduce poverty, legislators could design programs that take account of how people really think and behave, and that nudge people toward education and employment (and eliminate sludge). If the goal is to allow students, teachers, inventors, entrepreneurs, and those deserving asylum to come to your country, and to stay for a while, you could make it simple for them to do so. If the goal is to combat a pandemic by encouraging precautions and vaccination, policymakers could think hard about the importance of convenience and well-designed warnings—and the power of social norms.

This may all sound like a pipe dream. It isn't. It has started to happen, especially among the people who control how policies are implemented in practice. It is no accident that those giant companies that have risen to such prominence are good at choice architecture (among other things). But much more can be done to improve the choice architecture that is embedded (often only implicitly) in the way laws and regulations are written. The quiet heroes of this effort are the staff members who do the background research and often end up drafting the final language. If you know such a person, maybe pass on your copy of this book, now that you have finished it. Inscribe it for us with our plea: "Nudge for good." That plea is gradually becoming a description of countless reforms being developed and implemented all over the globe.

Acknowledgments

The final edition of this book was a bit of a sprint, and we are grateful to the many people who ran with us for the last few months. Special thanks for a terrific team of research assistants, including Lia Cattaneo, Dustin Fire, Rohit Goyal, Eli Nachmany, and Lukas Roth. Special thanks to Lukas for extraordinary work of many different kinds, and to Lia for that and also for heroic work, on substance and procedure, during the final stages. To say that we couldn't have done it without you is true, but not nearly enough.

Several friends read and commented on early drafts, including Rob Gertner, David Halpern, Alex Imas, and Emmanual Roman. Such friends are treasures. On organ donations in particular, we are grateful to Alexandra Glazier and Eric Johnson for helpful discussions. Sarah Chalfant was a font of wisdom. John Siciliano was an excellent editor. Thanks above all to so many readers of the original edition, whose comments, enthusiasm, concerns, and objections made this book much better.

Notes

Preface to the Final Edition

1. Tara Golshan, "Donald Trump Has Supported Hillary Clinton for Longer Than He's Opposed Her," *Vox*, August 16, 2016, https://www.vox.com/2016/8/16/12452806/trump-praise-hillary-clinton-history.

Introduction

1. "Adult Obesity Facts," Centers for Disease Control and Prevention, https://www.cdc.gov/obesity/data/adult.html.
2. "Obesity and Overweight," Centers for Disease Control and Prevention, https://www.cdc.gov/nchs/fastats/obesity-overweight.htm.
3. See, e.g., OECD, "Obesity Update 2017" (2017), https://www.oecd.org/els/health-systems/Obesity-Update-2017.pdf; Ben Tracy, "Battling American Samoa's 75-percent Obesity Rate," *CBS News*, July 7, 2013, https://www.cbsnews.com/news/battling-american-samoas-75-percent-obesity-rate/.

1. Biases and Blunders

1. Roger Shepard, *Mind Sights: Original Visual Illusions, Ambiguities, and Other Anomalies, with a Commentary on the Play of Mind in Perception and Art* (New York: W. H. Freeman and Co., 1990).
2. Fritz Strack, Leonard L. Martin, and Norbert Schwarz, "Priming and Communication: Social Determinants of Information Use in Judgments of Life Satisfaction," *European Journal of Social Psychology* 18, no. 5 (1988): 429–42.
3. Kareem Haggag and Giovanni Paci, "Default Tips," *American Economic Journal: Applied Economics* 6, no. 3 (2014): 1–19.
4. Paul Slovic, Howard Kunreuther, and Gilbert White, "Decision Processes, Rationality and Adjustment to Natural Hazards," in *Natural Hazards: Local, National and Global*, ed. Gilbert White (New York: Oxford University Press, 1974), 187–205.

5. Howard Kunreuther et al., *Disaster Insurance Protection: Public Policy Lessons* (New York: John Wiley & Sons, 1978); see also Howard Kunreuther et al., "Flood Risk and the U.S. Housing Market" (working paper, Penn Institute for Urban Research and Wharton Risk Center, October 2018), https://riskcenter.wharton.upenn.edu/wp-content/uploads/2018/11/Flood_Risk_and_the_U.S_._Housing_Market_10-30_.pdf.

6. Amos Tversky and Daniel Kahneman, "Extensional Versus Intuitive Reasoning: The Conjunction Fallacy in Probability Judgment," *Psychological Review* 90, no. 4 (1983) 293–315.

7. Stephen Jay Gould, "The Streak of Streaks," *New York Review*, August 18, 1988, https://www.nybooks.com/articles/1988/08/18/the-streak-of-streaks.

8. Paul C. Price, "Are You as Good a Teacher as You Think?" *Thought & Action*, Fall 2006, http://ftp.arizonaea.org/assets/img/PubThoughtAndAction/TAA_06_02.pdf.

9. Heather Mahar, "Why Are There So Few Prenuptial Agreements?" (John M. Olin Center for Law, Economics, and Business discussion paper no. 436, September 2003), http://www.law.harvard.edu/programs/olin_center/papers/pdf/436.pdf.

10. Arnold C. Cooper, Carolyn Y. Woo, and William C. Dunkelberg, "Entrepreneurs' Perceived Chances for Success," *Journal of Business Venturing* 3, no. 2 (1988): 97–108.

11. For references for the central findings in this paragraph, see Cass R. Sunstein, Christine M. Jolls, and Richard H. Thaler, "A Behavioral Approach to Law and Economics," *Stanford Law Review* 50, no. 5 (1998): 1471–550.

12. Daniel Kahneman, Jack L. Knetsch, and Richard H. Thaler, "Anomalies: The Endowment Effect, Loss Aversion, and Status Quo Bias," *Journal of Economic Perspectives* 5, no. 1 (1991): 193–206.

13. Tatiana A. Homonoff, "Can Small Incentives Have Large Effects? The Impact of Taxes Versus Bonuses on Disposable Bag Use," *American Economic Journal: Economic Policy* 10, no. 4 (2018): 177–210.

14. William Samuelson and Richard Zeckhauser, "Status Quo Bias in Decision Making," *Journal of Risk and Uncertainty* 1, no. 1 (1988); 7–59.

15. Samuelson and Zeckhauser, "Status Quo Bias in Decision Making."

16. Amos Tversky and Daniel Kahneman, "The Framing of Decisions and the Psychology of Choice," *Science* 211, no. 4481 (1981): 453–8.

17. Daniel Kahneman, *Thinking, Fast and Slow* (New York: Farrar, Straus and Giroux, 2013).

18. Philip Lieberman, *Human Language and Our Reptilian Brain* (Cambridge, MA: Harvard University Press, 2002); Joseph LeDoux, "The Emotional Brain, Fear, and the Amygdala," *Cellular and Molecular Neurobiology* 23, no. 4–5 (2003): 727–38.

19. Drew Westen, *The Political Brain* (New York: PublicAffairs, 2007).

20. Alexander Todorov, Anesu N. Mandisodza, Amir Goren, and Crystal C. Hall, "Inferences of Competence from Faces Predict Election Outcomes," *Science* 308, no. 5728 (2005): 1623–6; Daniel Benjamin and Jesse Shapiro, "Thin-Slice Forecasts of Gubernatorial Elections," *Review of Economics and Statistics* 91, no. 3 (2009): 523–36.

21. Shane Frederick, "Cognitive Reflection and Decision Making," *Journal of Economic Perspectives* 19, no. 4 (2005): 25–42.

2. Resisting Temptation

1. See Colin F. Camerer, "Neuroeconomics: Using Neuroscience to Make Economic Predictions," *Economic Journal* 117, no. 519 (2007): 26; Samuel M. McClure et al., "Neural Correlates of Behavioral Preference for Culturally Familiar Drinks," *Neuron* 44, no. 2 (2004): 379–87.
2. Nina Semczuk, "Should You Open a Christmas Account?" SmartAsset, https://smartasset.com/checking-account/christmas-club-accounts.
3. The famous exchange can be found at http://www.youtube.com/watch ?v=t96LNX6tkoU.
4. Richard H. Thaler and Eric J. Johnson, "Gambling with the House Money and Trying to Break Even: The Effects of Prior Outcomes on Risky Choice," *Management Science* 36, no. 6 (1990): 643–60.

3. Following the Herd

1. Chad R. Mortensen et al., "Trending Norms: A Lever for Encouraging Behaviors Performed by the Minority," *Social Psychological and Personality Science* 10, no. 2 (2019): 201–10.
2. George A. Akerlof, Janet L. Yellen, and Michael L. Katz, "An Analysis of Out-of-Wedlock Childbearing in the United States," *Quarterly Journal of Economics* 111, no. 2 (1996): 277–317.
3. Harold H. Gardner, Nathan L. Kleinman, and Richard J. Butler, "Workers' Compensation and Family and Medical Leave Act Claim Contagion," *Journal of Risk and Uncertainty* 20, no. 1 (2000): 89–112.
4. Robert Kennedy, "Strategy Fads and Strategic Positioning: An Empirical Test for Herd Behavior in Prime-Time Television Programming," *Journal of Industrial Economics* 50 (2002): 57–84.
5. See, e.g., Bruce L. Sacerdote, "Peer Effects with Random Assignment: Results for Dartmouth Roommates," *Quarterly Journal of Economics* 116, no. 2 (2001): 681–704; David J. Zimmerman, "Peer Effects in Academic Outcomes: Evidence from a Natural Experiment," *Review of Economics and Statistics* 85, no. 1 (2003): 9–23; Nirav Mehta, Ralph Stinebrickner, and Todd Stinebrickner, "Time-Use and Academic Peer Effects in College," *Economic Inquiry* 57, no. 1 (2019): 162–71.
6. See Akerlof, Yellen, and Katz, "An Analysis of Out-of-Wedlock Childbearing in the United States" (teenage pregnancy); Nicholas A. Christakis and James H. Fowler, "The Spread of Obesity in a Large Social Network over 32 Years," *New England Journal of Medicine* 357, no. 4 (2007): 370–9 (obesity); Sacerdote, "Peer Effects with Random Assignment" (college roommate assignment); and Cass R. Sunstein et al., *Are Judges Political? An Empirical Analysis of the Federal Judiciary* (Washington, DC: Brookings Institution Press, 2006) (judicial voting patterns).
7. Solomon E. Asch, "Studies of Independence and Conformity: I. A Minority of One Against a Unanimous Majority," *Psychological Monographs: General and Applied* 70, no. 9 (1956): 1–70.
8. Rod Bond and Peter Smith, "Culture and Conformity: A Meta-Analysis of Studies Using Asch's Line Judgment Task," *Psychological Bulletin* 119 (1996):

111–37. For an emphasis on cultural differences in general, and with respect to conformity in particular, see Joseph Heinrich, *The Weirdest People in the World* (New York: Farrar, Straus & Giroux, 2020), 198–204.

9. Micah Edelson et al., "Following the Crowd: Brain Substrates of Long-Term Memory Conformity," *Science* 333, no. 6038 (2011): 108–11.

10. Cass R. Sunstein, *Conformity: The Power of Social Influences* (New York: New York University Press, 2019).

11. Muzafer Sherif, "An Experimental Approach to the Study of Attitudes," *Sociometry* 1, no. 1/2 (1937): 90–8.

12. Lee Ross and Richard E. Nisbett, *The Person and the Situation: Perspectives of Social Psychology* (New York: McGraw-Hill, 1991): 29–30.

13. Robert C. Jacobs and Donald T. Campbell, "The Perpetuation of an Arbitrary Tradition Through Several Generations of a Laboratory Microculture," *Journal of Abnormal and Social Psychology* 62 (1961): 649–58.

14. Lindsey C. Levitan and Brad Verhulst, "Conformity in Groups: The Effects of Others' Views on Expressed Attitudes and Attitude Change," *Political Behavior* 38, no. 2 (2015): 277–315; Jing Chen et al., "ERP Correlates of Social Conformity in a Line Judgment," *BMC Neuroscience* 13 (2012): 43; Charity Brown and Alexandre Schaefer, "The Effects of Conformity on Recognition Judgements for Emotional Stimuli," *Acta Psychologica* 133, no. 1 (2010): 38–44.

15. H. Wesley Perkins, "Sober Lemmings," *New Republic*, April 13, 2003, https://newrepublic.com/article/64811/sober-lemmings.

16. Matthew J. Salganik, Peter Sheridan Dodds, and Duncan J. Watts, "Experimental Study of Inequality and Unpredictability in an Artificial Cultural Market," *Science* 311, no. 5762 (2006): 854–6.

17. Michael Macy et al., "Opinion Cascades and the Unpredictability of Partisan Polarization," *Science Advances* 5, no. 8 (2019): eaax0754.

18. Linton Weeks, "The Windshield-Pitting Mystery of 1954," National Public Radio, May 28, 2015, https://www.npr.org/sections/npr-history-dept/2015/05/28/410085713/the-windshield-pitting-mystery-of-1954.

19. Clarissa Simas et al., "HPV Vaccine Confidence and Cases of Mass Psychogenic Illness Following Immunization in Carmen De Bolivar, Colombia," *Human Vaccines and Immunotherapeutics* 15, no. 1 (2019): 163–6.

20. Katie Nodjimbadem, "The Trashy Beginnings of 'Don't Mess with Texas,'" *Smithsonian Magazine*, March 10, 2017, https://www.smithsonianmag.com/history/trashy-beginnings-dont-mess-texas-180962490/.

21. Timur Kuran, "Ethnic Norms and Their Transformation Through Reputational Cascades," *Journal of Legal Studies* 27, no. S2 (1998): 623–59.

22. Leonardo Bursztyn, Alessandra L. González, and David Yanagizawa-Drott, "Misperceived Social Norms: Women Working Outside the Home in Saudi Arabia," *American Economic Review* 110, no 10 (2020): 2997–3029, https://www.aeaweb.org/articles?id=10.1257%2Faer.20180975.

23. Stephen Coleman, *The Minnesota Income Tax Compliance Experiment: State Tax Results* (Munich Personal RePEc Archive, paper 4827, 1996).

24. Michael Hallsworth et al., "The Behavioralist as Tax Collector: Using Natural Field Experiments to Enhance Tax Compliance," *Journal of Public Economics* 148 (2017): 14–31.

25. Noah J. Goldstein, Robert B. Cialdini, and Vladas Griskevicius, "A Room with a Viewpoint: Using Social Norms to Motivate Environmental Conservation in Hotels," *Journal of Consumer Research* 35, no. 3 (2008): 472–82.

26. Josh Earnest, "President Obama Supports Same-Sex Marriage," *The White House President Obama* (blog), May 10, 2012, https://obamawhitehouse.ar chives.gov/blog/2012/05/10/obama-supports-same-sex-marriage.

27. *Obergefell v. Hodges*, 135 S. Ct. 2071 (2015).

28. "Same-Sex Marriage Around the World," Pew Research Center, October 28, 2019, https://www.pewforum.org/fact-sheet/gay-marriage-around-the -world/.

29. Adam Liptak, "Exhibit A for a Major Shift: Justices' Gay Clerks," *New York Times*, June 8, 2013, https://www.nytimes.com/2013/06/09/us/exhibit-a-for -a-major-shift-justices-gay-clerks.html.

30. Mortensen et al., "Trending Norms."

4. When Do We Need a Nudge?

1. Colin F. Camerer, Samuel Issacharoff, George Loewenstein, Ted O'Donoghue, and Matthew Rabin, "Regulation for Conservatives: Behavioral Economics and the Case for 'Asymmetric Paternalism,'" *University of Pennsylvania Law Review* 151, no. 3 (2003): 1211–54.

2. Colin F. Camerer and Robin M. Hogarth, "The Effects of Financial Incentives in Experiments: A Review and Capital-Labor-Production Framework," *Journal of Risk and Uncertainty* 19, no. 1 (1999): 7–42.

5. Choice Architecture

1. J. Ridley Stroop, "Studies of Interference in Serial Verbal Relations," *Journal of Experimental Psychology* 18 (1935): 643–62.

2. Kurt Lewin, *Field Theory in Social Science: Selected Theoretical Papers*, ed. Dorwin Cartwright (New York: Harper and Brothers, 1951).

3. Howard Leventhal, Robert Singer, and Susan Jones, "Effects of Fear and Specificity of Recommendation upon Attitudes and Behavior," *Journal of Personality and Social Psychology* 2, no. 1 (1965): 20–9.

4. Joel Gunter, "The Greek Referendum Question Makes (Almost) No Sense," *BBC News*, June 29, 2015, https://www.bbc.com/news/world-europe-33311422.

5. Zachary Brown et al., "Testing the Effects of Defaults on the Thermostat Settings of OECD Employees," *Energy Economics* 39 (2013): 128–34.

6. Gabriel Carroll et al., "Optimal Defaults and Active Decisions," *Quarterly Journal of Economics* 124, no. 4 (2009): 1639–74.

7. Michael D. Byrne and Susan Bovair, "A Working Memory Model of a Common Procedural Error," *Cognitive Science* 21, no. 1 (1997): 31–61.

8. Jeffrey B. Cooper et al., "Preventable Anesthesia Mishaps: A Study of Human Factors," *Anesthesiology* 49, no. 6 (1978): 399–406.

9. Michael O. Schroeder, "Death by Prescription," *U.S. News & World Report*, September 27, 2016, https://health.usnews.com/health-news/patient-advice /articles/2016-09-27/the-danger-in-taking-prescribed-medications.

10. John M. Jachimowicz et al., "Making Medications Stick: Improving Medication Adherence by Highlighting the Personal Health Costs of Non-Compliance," *Behavioural Public Policy* (2019), 1–21.

11. "Gmail Will Now Remind You to Respond," Google Workspace Updates, May 14, 2018, https://gsuiteupdates.googleblog.com/2018/05/gmail-remind-respond.html.

12. Steven B. Zeliadt et al., "Why Do Men Choose One Treatment over Another? A Review of Patient Decision Making for Localized Prostate Cancer," *Cancer* 106, no. 9 (2006): 1865–74.

13. Samuli Reijula and Ralph Hertwig, "Self-Nudging and the Citizen Choice Architect," *Behavioural Public Policy* (2020), 1–31.

14. Raj Chetty et al., "Active vs. Passive Decisions and Crowd-Out in Retirement Savings Accounts: Evidence from Denmark," *Quarterly Journal of Economics* 129, no. 3 (2014): 1141–219.

15. Whitney Afonso, "The Challenge of Transparency in Taxation," Mercatus Center, https://www.mercatus.org/publications/government-spending/challenge-transparency-taxation.

16. "Governor Ronald Reagan Opposes Withholding of State Income Tax," Seth Kaller Inc., https://www.sethkaller.com/item/1567-24387-Governor-Ronald-Reagan-Opposes-Withholding-of-State-Income-Tax.

6. But Wait, There's More

1. Maria Yagoda, "Singapore Hawker Stands with Michelin Stars," *Food & Wine*, August 20, 2018, https://www.foodandwine.com/travel/singapore-hawker-stands-michelin-stars-where.

2. "Volunteer and Job Opportunities," Mark Twain Boyhood Home and Museum, https://marktwainmuseum.org/volunteer-employment/.

3. "Speed Reduction Measures—Carrot or Stick?" ITS International, https://www.itsinternational.com/its2/feature/speed-reduction-measures-carrot-or-stick.

4. Richard H. Thaler, "Making Good Citizenship Fun," *New York Times*, February 13, 2012, https://www.nytimes.com/2012/02/14/opinion/making-good-citizenship-fun.html.

5. Emily Haisley et al., "The Impact of Alternative Incentive Schemes on Completion of Health Risk Assessments," *American Journal of Health Promotion* 26, no. 3 (2012): 184–8.

6. Thaler, "Making Good Citizenship Fun."

7. Smart Disclosure

1. Edna Ullmann-Margalit, *Normal Rationality: Decisions and Social Order*, ed. Avishai Margalit and Cass R. Sunstein (Oxford: Oxford University Press, 2017).

2. Richard P. Larrick and Jack B. Soll, "The MPG Illusion," *Science* 320, no. 5883 (2008): 1593–4.

3. Memorandum from Cass R. Sunstein, Administrator, Office of Information and Regulatory Affairs, Office of Management and Budget, "Informing

Consumers Through Smart Disclosure," to Heads of Executive Departments and Agencies, September 8, 2011, https://obamawhitehouse.archives.gov/sites/default/files/omb/inforeg/for-agencies/informing-consumers-through-smart-disclosure.pdf.

4. Sebastien Bradley and Naomi E. Feldman, "Hidden Baggage: Behavioral Responses to Changes in Airline Ticket Tax Disclosure," *American Economic Journal: Economic Policy* 12, no. 4 (2020): 58–87.

5. "Food Allergies: What You Need to Know," FDA, https://www.fda.gov/food/buy-store-serve-safe-food/food-allergies-what-you-need-know.

8. #Sludge

1. *Oxford Dictionary*, s.v. "sludge," accessed November 12, 2020, https://en.oxforddictionaries.com/definition/sludge.

2. Cait Lamberton and Benjamin Castleman, "Nudging in a Sludge-Filled World," *Huffington Post*, September 30, 2016, https://www.huffpost.com/entry/nudging-in-a-sludgefilled_b_12087688?guccounter=1&guce_referrer=aHROcHM6Ly93d3cuZ29vZ2xlLmNvbS8&guce_referrer_sig=AQAAAMYs-ouJGASCdY_xY8PGX3Ni2BfUI9Zvr5dx8gDkgOleohBZ3HlhYnpX6-lbZvflXt8CucilXVeGpfLFNN9DakYYw6vHYrbwOVhte7AoFVZTbm42GbvPjHxZjS0-sVwARNkU9hpCe4dofptGvmevun9LW9OkloMdgFRZrRS-hpAe.

3. Cal. Bus. & Prof. Code § 17602(c); N.Y. Gen. Bus. Law § 527 (McKinney 2020).

4. Joshua Tasoff and Robert Letzler, "Everyone Believes in Redemption: Nudges and Overoptimism in Costly Task Completion," *Journal of Economic Behavior and Organization* 107 (2014): 107–22.

5. Xavier Gabaix and David Laibson, "Shrouded Attributes, Consumer Myopia, and Information Suppression in Competitive Markets," *Quarterly Journal of Economics* 121, no. 2 (2006): 505–40.

6. David M. Cutler and Dan P. Ly, "The (Paper) Work of Medicine: Understanding International Medical Costs," *Journal of Economic Perspectives* 25, no. 2 (2011): 3–25.

7. Reed Hastings and Erin Meyer, *No Rules Rules* (New York: Penguin Press, 2020).

8. Hastings and Meyer, *No Rules Rules*, 70.

9. Susan Dynarski et al., "Closing the Gap: The Effect of a Targeted, Tuition-Free Promise on College Choices of High-Achieving, Low-Income Students" (National Bureau of Economic Research working paper no. 25349, 2018).

10. "Admissions Decisions," University of Texas at Austin Office of Admissions, https://admissions.utexas.edu/apply/decisions.

11. Cass R. Sunstein, "Automatic Enrollment in College Helps Fight Inequality," *Bloomberg*, June 19, 2020, https://www.bloomberg.com/opinion/articles/2020-06-19/college-automatic-enrollment-addresses-inequality.

12. Bart Jansen, "TSA Gets Boost in Funding, Including Testing 3D Scanners, Without Fee Hike Trump Proposed," *USA Today*, March 21, 2018, https://www.usatoday.com/story/news/2018/03/21/tsa-spending-3-d-scanners/447410002/.

13. Christine Utz et al., "(Un)informed Consent: Studying GDPR Consent Notices in the Field," in 2019 ACM SIGSAC Conference on Computer and Communications Security (CCS '19), November 11–15, 2019, London, UK (2019), https://arxiv.org/pdf/1909.02638.pdf.

14. "1040 and 1040-SR Instructions: Tax Year 2019," Internal Revenue Service (2020), https://www.irs.gov/pub/irs-pdf/i1040gi.pdf; Demian Brady, "Tax Complexity 2016: The Increasing Compliance Burdens of the Tax Code," National Taxpayers Union Foundation, https://perma.cc/BT3X -VHFY.

15. Glenn Kessler, "Claims About the Cost and Time It Takes to File Taxes," *Washington Post*, April 15, 2013, https://perma.cc/C7FJ-L7LM; Brady, "Tax Complexity 2016." Note: Thirteen hours is for all taxpayers; for nonbusiness filers it's eight hours. These are IRS estimates that include record keeping, tax planning, and form filling.

16. T. R. Reid, *A Fine Mess* (New York: Penguin Press, 2017).

17. Austan Goolsbee, "The Simple Return: Reducing America's Tax Burden Through Return-Free Filing," Brookings Institution, https://www.brook ings.edu/research/the-simple-return-reducing-americas-tax-burden -through-return-free-filing/.

18. Scott Eastman, "How Many Taxpayers Itemize Under Current Law?" Tax Foundation, https://taxfoundation.org/standard-deduction-itemized-deduc tions-current-law-2019/.

19. John Paul Tasker, "Feds Promise Free, Automatic Tax Returns—A Change That Could Send Benefits to Thousands," CBC, September 27, 2020, https:// www.cbc.ca/news/politics/free-automatic-tax-returns-benefits-1.5739678.

20. "Earned Income Tax Credit Overview," National Conference of State Legislatures, https://www.ncsl.org/research/labor-and-employment/earned -income-tax-credits-for-working-families.aspx.

21. "Wealth Tax TL;DR," Warren Democrats, https://elizabethwarren.com /wealth-gap.

22. Elizabeth Aubrey, "The World's Last Remaining Blockbuster Store Still Open Despite Coronavirus Pandemic," *NME*, May 14, 2020, https://www .nme.com/news/the-worlds-last-remaining-blockbuster-store-still-open -despite-coronavirus-pandemic-2668617.

9. Save More Tomorrow

1. "Otto von Bismarck," Social Security, https://www.ssa.gov/history/ottob .html.

2. James Choi et al., "Defined Contribution Pensions: Plan Rules, Participant Choices, and the Path of Least Resistance," *Tax Policy and the Economy* 16, no. 1 (2002): 67.

3. Richard H. Thaler, "Psychology and Savings Policies," *American Economic Review* 84, no. 2 (1994): 186–92.

4. Sana Siwolop, "When Saving for Retirement Comes with the Job," *New York Times*, May 18, 1997, https://www.nytimes.com/1997/05/18/business /when-saving-for-retirement-comes-with-the-job.html.

5. See, e.g., IRS Revenue Ruling 98-30; IRS Revenue Ruling 2000-8; IRS Revenue Ruling 2000-35; IRS Revenue Ruling 2000-33; and IRS Announcement 2000-60.

6. Brigitte C. Madrian and Dennis F. Shea, "The Power of Suggestion: Inertia in 401(k) Participation and Savings Behavior," *Quarterly Journal of Economics* 116, no. 4 (2001): 1149–87.

7. Jeffrey W. Clark and Jean A. Young, *Automatic Enrollment: The Power of the Default* (Valley Forge, PA: Vanguard Research, 2018).

8. Richard H. Thaler and Shlomo Benartzi, "Save More Tomorrow™: Using Behavioral Economics to Increase Employee Saving," *Journal of Political Economy* 112, no. S1 (2004): S164.

9. U.S. Department of Labor Employee Benefits Security Administration, "Regulation Relating to Qualified Default Investment Alternatives in Participant-Directed Individual Account Plans," https://www.dol.gov/sites /dolgov/files/EBSA/about-ebsa/our-activities/resource-center/fact-sheets /final-rule-qdia-in-participant-directed-account-plans.pdf.

10. Raj Chetty et al., "Active vs. Passive Decisions and Crowd-Out in Retirement Savings Accounts: Evidence from Denmark," *Quarterly Journal of Economics* 129, no. 3 (2014): 1141–219.

11. John Beshears et al., "Borrowing to Save? The Impact of Automatic Enrollment on Debt," *Journal of Finance* (forthcoming), https://www.nber.org /papers/w25876.

12. See, e.g., "Americans Without a Retirement Plan, by State," AARP, https://www.aarp.org/politics-society/advocacy/financial-security/info -2014/americans-without-retirement-plan.html.

13. Chris Arnold, "Why Is It So Hard to Save? U.K. Shows It Doesn't Have to Be," NPR, October 23, 2015, https://www.npr.org/2015/10/23/445337261 /why-is-it-so-hard-to-save-u-k-shows-it-doesnt-have-to-be.

10. Do Nudges Last Forever? Perhaps in Sweden

1. For a discussion of required active choosing, see Gabriel Carroll et al., "Optimal Defaults and Active Decisions," *Quarterly Journal of Economics* 124, no. 4 (2009): 1639–74.

2. Kenneth R. French and James M. Poterba, "Investor Diversification and International Equity Markets," *American Economic Review* 81, no. 2 (1991): 222–6.

3. Shlomo Benartzi, Richard H. Thaler, Stephen P. Utkus, and Cass R. Sunstein, "The Law and Economics of Company Stock in 401(k) Plans," *Journal of Law and Economics* 50, no. 1 (2007): 45–79.

4. Henrik Cronqvist, "Advertising and Portfolio Choice" (Ph.D. diss., University of Chicago Graduate School of Business, 2006), https://citeseerx .ist.psu.edu/viewdoc/download?doi=10.1.1.423.3760&rep=rep1&type=pdf.

5. Hunt Allcott and Todd Rogers, "The Short-Run and Long-Run Effects of Behavioral Interventions: Experimental Evidence from Energy Conservation," *American Economic Review* 104, no. 10 (2014): 3003–37.

6. William Samuelson and Richard Zeckhauser, "Status Quo Bias in Decision Making," *Journal of Risk and Uncertainty* 1, no. 1 (1988): 7–59.

7. Henrik Cronqvist, Richard H. Thaler, and Frank Yu, "When Nudges Are Forever: Inertia in the Swedish Premium Pension Plan," *AEA Papers and Proceedings* 108 (2018): 153–8.

8. Anders Anderson and David T. Robinson, "Who Feels the Nudge? Knowledge, Self-Awareness and Retirement Savings Decisions" (National Bureau of Economic Research working paper no. 25061, 2018), https://ideas .repec.org/p/nbr/nberwo/25061.html.

11. Borrow More Today: Mortgages and Credit Cards

1. Kathleen Howley, "U.S. Mortgage Debt Hits a Record $15.8 Trillion," *Housing-Wire*, January 9, 2020, https://www.housingwire.com/articles/u-s-mortgage -debt-hits-a-record-15-8-trillion/.

2. Xavier Gabaix and David Laibson, "Shrouded Attributes, Consumer Myopia, and Information Suppression in Competitive Markets," *Quarterly Journal of Economics* 121, no. 2 (2006): 505–40.

3. Susan E. Woodward, *A Study of Closing Costs for FHA Mortgages* (Washington, DC: Urban Institute, 2008).

4. Hamilton Project, "An Opt-Out Home Mortgage System" (policy brief no. 2008-14, 2008), https://www.hamiltonproject.org/assets/legacy/files/down loads_and_links/An_Opt-Out_Home_Mortgage_System_Brief.pdf.

5. Fiona Scott Morton, Florian Zettelmeyer, and Jorge Silva-Risso, "Consumer Information and Discrimination: Does the Internet Affect the Pricing of New Cars to Women and Minorities?" *Quantitative Marketing and Economics* 1 (2003): 65–92.

6. Bureau of Consumer Financial Protection, *The Consumer Credit Card Market* (2019), https://files.consumerfinance.gov/f/documents/cfpb_consumer -credit-card-market-report_2019.pdf.

7. Drazen Prelec and Duncan Simester, "Always Leave Home Without It: A Further Investigation of the Credit-Card Effect on Willingness to Pay," *Marketing Letters* 12, no. 1 (2001): 5–12.

8. Sumit Agarwal et al., "Regulating Consumer Financial Products: Evidence from Credit Cards," *Quarterly Journal of Economics* 130, no. 1 (2015): 111–64.

9. Lauren E. Willis, "When Nudges Fail: Slippery Defaults," *University of Chicago Law Review* 80 (2013): 1155.

10. John Gathergood et al., "How Do Individuals Repay Their Debt? The Balance-Matching Heuristic," *American Economic Review* 109, no. 3 (2019): 844–75.

11. David B. Gross and Nicholas Souleles, "Do Liquidity Constraints and Interest Rates Matter for Consumer Behavior? Evidence from Credit Card Data," *Quarterly Journal of Economics* 117, no. 1 (2002): 149–85.

12. Bureau of Consumer Financial Protection, *The Consumer Credit Card Market*, 51.

13. Tally, http://www.meettally.com/.

14. Bureau of Consumer Financial Protection, *The Consumer Credit Card Market*, 68.

12. Insurance: Don't Sweat the Small Stuff

1. Solomon Huebner, "The Development and Present Status of Marine Insurance in the United States," *Annals of the American Academy of Political and Social Science* 26 (1905): 241–72.
2. James Read, "How the Great Fire of London Created Insurance," Museum of London, https://www.museumoflondon.org.uk/discover/how-great-fire -london-created-insurance.
3. Justin Sydnor, "(Over)insuring Modest Risks," *American Economic Journal: Applied Economics* 2, no. 4 (2010): 177–99.
4. Saurabh Bhargava, George Loewenstein, and Justin Sydnor, "Choose to Lose: Health Plan Choices from a Menu with Dominated Option," *Quarterly Journal of Economics* 132, no. 3 (2017): 1319–72.
5. Chenyuan Liu and Justin R. Sydnor, "Dominated Options in Health-Insurance Plans" (National Bureau of Economic Research working paper no. 24392, 2018), https://www.nber.org/papers/w24392.
6. "Health Insurance Deductible: How It Works," CZ, https://www.cz.nl/en /health-insurance/deductible.
7. Benjamin R. Handel et al., "The Social Determinants of Choice Quality: Evidence from Health Insurance in the Netherlands" (National Bureau of Economic Research working paper no. 27785, 2020), https://www.nber.org /papers/w27785.
8. Handel et al., "The Social Determinants of Choice Quality."
9. Katherine Baicker, Sendhil Mullainathan, and Joshua Schwartzstein, "Behavioral Hazard in Health Insurance" (National Bureau of Economic Research working paper no. 18468, 2012), https://www.nber.org/papers /w18468.
10. Niteesh K. Choudhry et al., "Full Coverage for Preventive Medications After Myocardial Infarction," *New England Journal of Medicine* 365 no. 22 (2011): 2088–97.
11. Amitabh Chandra, Evan Flack and Ziad Obermeyer, "The Health Costs of Cost-Sharing," (National Bureau of Economic Research working paper no. 28439), https://www.nber.org/papers/w28439.

13. Organ Donations: The Default Solution Illusion

1. Eric J. Johnson and Daniel G. Goldstein, "Defaults and Donation Decisions," *Transplantation* 78, no. 12 (2004): 1713–6.
2. "National Data: Transplants by Donor Type (January 1, 1988–July 31, 2020)," Organ Procurement and Transplantation Network, https://optn .transplant.hrsa.gov/data/view-data-reports/national-data/#.
3. "National Data: Overall by Organ, Current U.S. Waiting List," Organ Procurement and Transplantation Network, https://optn.transplant.hrsa.gov /data/view-data-reports/national-data/#.
4. "Organ Donation Statistics," Health Resources and Services Administration, https://www.organdonor.gov/statistics-stories/statistics.html.

5. Ali Seifi, John V. Lacci, and Daniel Godoy, "Incidence of Brain Death in the United States," *Clinical Neurology and Neurosurgery* 195 (2020): 105885.

6. Alvin E. Roth, Tayfun Sönmez, and M. Utku Ünverd, "Pairwise Kidney Exchange," *Journal of Economic Theory* 125, no. (2005): 151–88; see also Scott Simon, "Opinion: Kidney Transplant Chain Is a Touching Act of Kindness," National Public Radio, October 31, 2020, https://www.npr.org/2020/10/31/929802669/opinion-kidney-transplant-chain-is-a-touching-act-of-kindness.

7. Gary S. Becker and Julio Jorge Elías, "Introducing Incentives in the Market for Live and Cadaveric Organ Donations," *Journal of Economic Perspectives* 21, no. 3 (2007): 3–24.

8. Janet Radcliffe Richards, *The Ethics of Transplants* (New York: Oxford University Press, 2012).

9. Shashank Bengali and Ramin Mostaghim, "'Kidney for Sale': Iran Has a Legal Market for the Organs, but the System Doesn't Always Work," *Los Angeles Times*, October 15, 2017, https://www.latimes.com/world/middleeast/la-fg-iran-kidney-20171015-story.html.

10. Alvin E. Roth, "Repugnance as a Constraint on Markets," *Journal of Economic Perspectives* 21, no. 3 (2007): 37–58.

11. "Organ Donation Statistics," Health Resources and Services Administration, https://www.organdonor.gov/statistics-stories/statistics.html#:~:text=One%20Donor%20Can%20Save%20Eight,up%20to%208%20lifesaving%20organs.

12. James F. Childress and Catharyn T. Liverman, eds., *Organ Donation: Opportunities for Action* (Washington, DC: National Academies Press, 2006), 241.

13. Health Resources and Services Administration, *National Survey of Organ Donation Attitudes and Practices, 2019* (Rockville, MD: U.S. Department of Health and Human Services, 2020).

14. Donate Life America, "Stronger Together: 2020 Annual Update" (2020).

15. "Become an Organ Donor," New York State, https://www.ny.gov/services/become-organ-donor.

16. Daimy Van den Eede, "Gigantisch Succes: Meer Dan 26.000 Registraties voor Orgaandonatie in heel Vlaanderen" (Gigantic Success: More Than 26,000 Registrations for Organ Donation in Flanders), *Het Laatste Nieuws*, October 27, 2018, https://www.hln.be/nieuws/binnenland/gigantisch-succes-meer-dan-26-000-registraties-voor-orgaandonatie-in-heel-vlaanderen~af353bba/.

17. Section Belgian Transplant Coordinators, "Donor & Transplant Statistics 2018" (2018), https://www.transplant.be/assets/bts_-_donor_and_transplant_statistics_2018.

18. Gina Kolata, "Families Are Barriers to Many Organ Donations, Study Finds," *New York Times*, July 7, 1995, https://www.nytimes.com/1995/07/07/us/families-are-barriers-to-many-organ-donations-study-finds.html.

19. Ann C. Klassen and David K. Klassen, "Who Are the Donors in Organ Donation? The Family's Perspective in Mandated Choice," *Annals of Internal Medicine* 125, no. 1 (1996): 70–3.

20. Judd B. Kessler and Alvin E. Roth, "Don't Take 'No' for an Answer: An Experiment with Actual Organ Donor Registrations" (National Bureau of

Economic Research working paper no. w20378, 2014), https://ssrn.com /abstract=2482141.

21. "How We Help and Support Donors," Donor Care Network, https://www .donorcarenet.org/support-and-protections.

22. Jacob Lavee et al., "Preliminary Marked Increase in the National Organ Donation Rate in Israel Following Implementation of a New Organ Transplantation Law," *American Journal of Transplantation* 13, no. 3 (2012): 780–5.

23. "Donazione dopo la Morte" (Donation After Death), Ministero Della Salute (Ministry of Health), http://www.trapianti.salute.gov.it/trapianti /dettaglioContenutiCnt.jsp?lingua=italiano&area=cnt&menu=cittadini &sottomenu=diventare&id=245.

24. Alexandra K. Glazier, "Organ Donation and the Principles of Gift Law," *Clinical Journal of the American Society of Nephrology* 13, no. 8 (2018): 1283–4.

25. Rafael Matesanz and Beatriz Domínguez-Gil, "Opt-Out Legislations: The Mysterious Viability of the False," *Kidney International* 95, no. 6 (2019): 1301–3.

26. Rafael Matesanz et al., "Spanish Experience as a Leading Country: What Kind of Measures Were Taken?" *Transplant International* 24, no. 4 (2011): 333–43; Rafael Matesanz, "A Decade of Continuous Improvement in Cadaveric Organ Donation: The Spanish Model," *Nefrología* 21, no. S5 (2001): 59.

27. "Statistics About Organ Donation," NHS, https://www.organdonation .nhs.uk/helping-you-to-decide/about-organ-donation/statistics-about -organ-donation/.

28. Alexandra Glazier and Thomas Mone, "Success of Opt-in Organ Donation Policy in the United States," *JAMA* 322, no. 8 (2019): 719–20.

29. Health Resources and Services Administration, *National Survey of Organ Donation Attitudes and Practices, 2019*.

30. "Find Your Local Organ Procurement Organization," Health Resources and Services Administration, https://www.organdonor.gov/awareness/or ganizations/local-opo.html.

14. Saving the Planet

1. Michael Burger, Jessica Wentz, and Radley Horton, "The Law and Science of Climate Change Attribution," *Columbia Journal of Environmental Law* 45 (2020): 57; see also Rebecca Hersher, "Climate Change Was the Engine That Powered Hurricane Maria's Devastating Rains," National Public Radio, April 17, 2019, https://www.npr.org/2019/04/17/714098828/climate -change-was-the-engine-that-powered-hurricane-marias-devastating-rains.

2. Richard J. Lazarus, "Super Wicked Problems and Climate Change: Restraining the Present to Liberate the Future," *Cornell Law Review* 94, no. 5 (2009): 1153–234.

3. Edna Ullmann-Margalit, *The Emergence of Norms* (Oxford: Clarendon Press, 1977).

4. Garrett Hardin, "The Tragedy of the Commons," *Science* 162, no. 3859 (1968): 1243–8.

5. Paul A. Samuelson, "The Pure Theory of Public Expenditure," *Review of Economics and Statistics* 36, no. 4 (1954): 387–9.

6. Robyn M. Dawes, Jeanne McTavish, and Harriet Shaklee, "Behavior, Communication, and Assumptions About Other People's Behavior in a Commons Dilemma Situation," *Journal of Personality and Social Psychology* 35, no. 1 (1977): 1–11; R. Mark Isaac and James M. Walker, "Communication and Free-Riding Behavior: The Voluntary Contribution Mechanism," *Economic Inquiry* 26, no. 4 (1988): 585–608.

7. James Hansen et al., "Assessing 'Dangerous Climate Change': Required Reduction of Carbon Emissions to Protect Young People, Future Generations and Nature," *PloS One* 8, no. 12 (2013): e81648.

8. "China's Environmental Abuses Fact Sheet," U.S. Embassy and Consulates in Brazil, https://br.usembassy.gov/chinas-environmental-abuses-fact-sheet.

9. Linda Babcock and George Loewenstein, "Explaining Bargaining Impasse: The Role of Self-Serving Biases," *Journal of Economic Perspectives* 11, no. 1 (1997): 109–26.

10. Ernst Fehr and Simon Gächter, "Cooperation and Punishment in Public Goods Experiments," *American Economic Review* 90, no. 4 (2000): 980–94.

11. William Nordhaus, "Climate Clubs: Overcoming Free-Riding in International Climate Policy," *American Economic Review* 105, no. 4 (2015): 1339–70.

12. "Carbon Taxes II," Initiative on Global Markets, http://www.igmchicago.org/surveys/carbon-taxes-ii/.

13. "Carbon Taxation in Sweden," Government Offices of Sweden, Ministry of Finance (2020), https://www.government.se/government-policy/taxes-and-tariffs/swedens-carbon-tax/.

14. "Carbon Taxation in Sweden," Government Offices of Sweden.

15. Julius Andersson, "Cars, Carbon Taxes and CO2 Emissions" (Centre for Climate Change Economics and Policy working paper no. 238, Grantham Research Institute on Climate Change and the Environment working paper no. 212, 2017), https://www.cccep.ac.uk/wp-content/uploads/2017/03/Working-paper-212-Andersson_update_March2017.pdf.

16. Helga Fehr-Duda and Ernst Fehr, "Sustainability: Game Human Nature," *Nature* 530 (2016): 413–5.

17. Robert N. Stavins, "Assessing the Energy Paradox," *Environmental Forum* 32 (2015): 14, https://scholar.harvard.edu/files/stavins/files/column_67.pdf.

18. Hunt Allcott and Michael Greenstone, "Is There an Energy Efficiency Gap?" *Journal of Economic Perspectives* 26, no. 1 (2012): 3–28; Hunt Allcott and Cass R. Sunstein, "Regulating Internalities," *Journal of Policy Analysis and Management* 34, no. 3 (2015): 698–705; Renate Schubert and Marcel Stadelmann, "Energy-Using Durables—Why Consumers Refrain from Economically Optimal Choices," *Frontiers in Energy Research* 3 (2015), https://www.frontiersin.org/articles/10.3389/fenrg.2015.00007/full.

19. Congressional Budget Office, "Homeland Security and the Private Sector" (2004), https://www.cbo.gov/sites/default/files/108th-congress-2003-2004/reports/12-20-homelandsecurity.pdf.

20. "EPCRA Milestones Through the Years," United States Environmental Protection Agency, https://www.epa.gov/epcra/epcra-milestones-through-years.

21. Archon Fung and Dara O'Rourke, "Reinventing Environmental Regulation from the Grassroots Up: Explaining and Expanding the Success of the Toxics Release Inventory," *Environmental Management* 25 (2000): 115–27.

22. James T. Hamilton, *Regulation Through Revelation* (New York: Cambridge University Press, 2005).

23. "What We Do," CDP, https://www.cdp.net/en/info/about-us/what-we-do.

24. "With #Alpha, 2020 Atlantic Tropical Storm Names Go Greek," National Oceanic and Atmospheric Administration, https://www.noaa.gov/news/with-alpha-2020-atlantic-tropical-storm-names-go-greek#:~:text=Having%20reached%20the%20end%20of,by%20the%20World%20Meteorological%20Organization.

25. Felix Ebeling and Sebastian Lotz, "Domestic Uptake of Green Energy Promoted by Opt-Out Tariffs," *Nature Climate Change* 5 (2015): 868–71.

26. Micha Kaiser et al., "The Power of Green Defaults: The Impact of Regional Variation of Opt-Out Tariffs on Green Energy Demand in Germany," *Ecological Economics* 174 (2020): 106685.

27. Robert Walton, "Home Energy Reports: Still the 'Biggest, Baddest Way' to Drive Customer Behavior," *Utility Dive*, July 10, 2019, https://www.utilitydive.com/news/home-energy-reports-still-the-biggest-baddest-way-to-drive-customer-beh/558166/.

28. Hunt Allcott and Todd Rogers, "The Short-Run and Long-Run Effects of Behavioral Interventions: Experimental Evidence from Energy Conservation," *American Economic Review* 104, no. 10 (2014): 3003–37.

29. Benjamin Goldstein, Dimitrios Gounaridis, and Joshua P. Newell, "The Carbon Footprint of Household Energy Use in the United States," *Proceedings of the National Academy of Sciences* 117, no. 32 (2020): 19122–30.

15. Much Ado About Nudging

1. Some of the criticisms are also addressed in Richard H. Thaler, *Misbehaving* (2015); Cass R. Sunstein, *Why Nudge?* (2014); and Cass R. Sunstein, *How Change Happens* (2019).

2. James B. Stewart, "How Broccoli Landed on Supreme Court Menu," *New York Times*, June 13, 2012, https://www.nytimes.com/2012/06/14/business/how-broccoli-became-a-symbol-in-the-health-care-debate.html.

3. Richard H. Thaler, "Slippery-Slope Logic, Applied to Health Care," *New York Times*, May 12, 2012, https://www.nytimes.com/2012/05/13/business/economy/slippery-slope-logic-vs-health-care-law-economic-view.html; see also Henry L. Tischler, *Introduction to Sociology*, 11th ed. (Boston: Cengage Learning, 2013), 261.

4. Thaler, "Slippery-Slope Logic, Applied to Health Care."

5. "Women in the U.S. Congress 2020," Center for American Women and Politics, https://cawp.rutgers.edu/women-us-congress-2020.

6. Glen Whitman, "The Rise of the New Paternalism," Cato Unbound, https://www.cato-unbound.org/2010/04/05/glen-whitman/rise-new-paternalism.

7. Ralph Hertwig and Till Grüne-Yanoff, "Nudging and Boosting: Steering or Empowering Good Decisions," *Perspectives on Psychology Science* 12, no. 6 (2017): 973–86.

8. Gerd Gigerenzer, "On the Supposed Evidence for Libertarian Paternalism," *Review of Philosophy and Psychology* 6, no. 3 (2015): 361–83.

9. Daniel Fernandes, John G. Lynch, and Richard G. Netemeyer, "Financial Literacy, Financial Education, and Downstream Financial Behaviors," *Management Science* 60, no. 8 (2014): 1861.

10. Edward Glaeser, "Paternalism and Psychology" *University of Chicago Law Review* 73, no. 1 (2006): 133–56.

11. Hendrik Bruns et al., "Can Nudges Be Transparent and Yet Effective?" *Journal of Economic Psychology* 65 (2018): 41–59, https://papers.ssrn.com/sol3/papers.cfm?abstract_id=2816227; George Loewenstein et al., "Warning: You Are About to Be Nudged," *Behavioral Science and Policy Association* 1, no. 1 (2015): 35–42.

12. Craig R. M. McKenzie, Michael J. Liersch, and Stacey R. Finkelstein, "Recommendations Implicit in Policy Defaults," *Psychological Science* 17, no. 5 (2006): 414–20.

13. Anne Barnhill, "What Is Manipulation?" in *Manipulation: Theory and Practice*, ed. Christian Coons and Michael Weber (New York: Oxford University Press, 2014): 51–72. Barnhill's own account is more subtle.

14. Cass R. Sunstein, *The Ethics of Influence* (New York: Cambridge University Press, 2016).

15. See Cass R. Sunstein, *The Ethics of Influence*; and Cass R. Sunstein and Lucia Reisch, *Trusting Nudges* (New York: Routledge, 2019).

16. John Rawls, *A Theory of Justice* (Cambridge, MA: Harvard University Press, 1971).

17. See Sunstein and Reisch, *Trusting Nudges*.

18. Cooling-Off Period for Door-to-Door Sales, 37 Fed. Reg. 22934 (October 26, 1972; to be codified at 16 CFR 425).

19. See, e.g., Cal. Fam. Code §2339(a) (requiring a six-month waiting period before a divorce decree becomes final); Conn. Gen. Stat. §46b-67(a) (requiring a ninety-day waiting period before the court may proceed on a divorce complaint). For a general discussion, see Elizabeth S. Scott, "Rational Decision Making About Marriage and Divorce," *Virginia Law Review* 76 (1992): 9–94.

20. Camerer et al., "Regulation for Conservatives."

21. George Loewenstein and Nick Chater, "Putting Nudges in Perspective," *Behavioural Public Policy* 1, no. 1 (2017): 26–53.

22. John Chalmers, Olivia S. Mitchell, Jonathan Reuter, and Mingli Zhong, "Auto-Enrollment Retirement Plans for the People: Choices and Outcomes in OregonSaves" (National Bureau of Economic Research working paper no. w28469, 2021), https://www.nber.org/papers/w28469.

23. One of us discusses these issues in detail in Cass R. Sunstein, "Behavioral Welfare Economics," *Journal of Benefit-Cost Analysis* 11, no. 2 (2020): 196–220.

Index

Note: Page numbers in *italics* denote images and associated captions.